Fifty-Seven
Saints

Second Edition

By Eileen Heffernan, FSP
Illustrated by Jerry Rizzo

Pauline
St. Paul Books & Media

Library of Congress Cataloging-in-Publication Data

Heffernan, Anne Eileen.
    Fifty-seven saints / Anne Eileen Heffernan; illustrated by Jerry
Rizzo. — Rev. ed. / revised and edited by Theresa Frances Myers.
        p.   cm.
    Rev. ed. of: Fifty-seven saints for boys and girls.
    Includes index.
    ISBN 0-8198-2657-X — ISBN 0-8198-2656-1 (pbk.)
    1. Christian saints—Biography—Juvenile literature.
[1.Saints.] I. Rizzo, Jerry, ill. II. Myers, Theresa Frances.
III. Heffernan, Anne Eileen. Fifty-seven saints for boys and girls.
IV. Title. V. Title: 57 saints.
BX4658.H39 1994
282'.092'2—dc20
[B]   94-1866
                                         CIP
                                         AC

ISBN: 0-8198-2656-1 paper
ISBN: 0-8198-2657-X cloth
First edition by Eileen Heffernan, FSP
Second edition edited by Theresa F. Myers, FSP

Printed and published in the U.S.A. by St. Paul Books &
Media, 50 St. Paul's Avenue, Boston, MA 02130.

St. Paul Books & Media is the publishing house of the
Daughters of St. Paul, an international congregation of
women religious serving the Church with the
communications media.

1 2 3 4 5 6   99 98 97 96 95 94

CONTENTS

The Archangels 7
St. Joachim and St. Anne 10
St. Joseph 15
St. Peter 21
St. Paul 35
St. Thecla 49
St. Cecilia 57
St. Tarcisius 66
St. Sebastian 77
St. Lucy 83
St. Agnes 90
St. Helen 98
St. Martin of Tours 103
St. Monica and St. Augustine 109
St. Patrick 116
St. Brigid 124
St. Benedict 132
St. Kevin 139
St. Columban 145
St. Dymphna 158
St. Margaret of Scotland 169
St. Francis of Assisi 176
St. Clare 191
St. Anthony of Padua 200
St. Elizabeth of Hungary 208
St. Peregrine 217
St. Catherine of Siena 228
St. Bernardine of Siena 237

St. Joan of Arc 250

St. Francis Xavier 260

St. Stanislaus Kostka 284

St. Benedict the Moor 297

St. Aloysius Gonzaga 306

St. Philip Neri 316

St. Germaine 327

St. Camillus de Lellis 337

St. John Berchmans 347

St. Martin de Porres 357

St. Jane Frances de Chantal 373

St. Isaac Jogues and St. Rene Goupil 382

Bl. Kateri Tekakwitha 412

St. Margaret Mary Alacoque 428

St. Benedict Joseph Labre 434

St. Bartholomea 439

St. Elizabeth Ann Seton 449

St. Joseph Cottolengo 458

St. Dominic Savio 466

St. Bernadette Soubirous 471

St. John Bosco 482

St. Therese of Lisieux 488

St. Maria Goretti 495

St. Gemma Galgani 503

St. Frances Xavier Cabrini 514

Bl. Miguel Pro 523

Bl. Edith Stein 533

Index 541

The Archangels
St. Michael, St. Gabriel, St. Raphael

September 29

Angels were created by God just like you and I were, but they are much different than us! Angels have no bodies; they are pure spirits. They never get tired. They only have to think a thought to communicate—they don't have to speak out loud—and they never misunderstand one another.

The Bible mentions three angels by name: the archangels Michael, Gabriel and Raphael. These three angels brought special messages from God to his people. And in the book of Tobit (one of the books in the Old Testament), the Angel Raphael told Tobit that one of the things angels do best is present our prayers to God!

We can read about the Archangel Gabriel in the Gospel of St. Luke. Gabriel was the angel who brought the good news to Mary that she was going to be the mother of Jesus, God's own Son.

Michael is mentioned several times in the Bible. He is called the archangel because he led the angels who wished to remain faithful to God in a great

The Bible mentions three angels by name: Michael, Gabriel and Raphael. Angels are messengers of God, but they are also good at presenting our prayers to God.

battle against Satan. Satan and some other angels were rebelling against God. They did not love God and refused to do what God asked them to do. Satan and the other rebellious angels lost the battle and left heaven. They went to hell. Today we call them devils. After that big battle in heaven, Michael became a defender and protector of God's people on earth.

Boys named Michael and girls named Michelle may ask St. Michael to be their special helper, or "patron" in heaven. But Michael will help all who ask him. He is the leader of all the angels in heaven and a special protector of the Church today.

Jesus told us about another group of angels called the guardian angels. Each one of us has an angel in heaven to watch and guard us from dangers, especially from evil and the devil. We can pray to our guardian angels to help us in many ways. They can help us keep calm during times of stress or danger. They can help us think clearly and make good choices when life seems confusing. They can comfort us when we go through difficult times. The feast of the Guardian Angels is celebrated on October 2.

One way we can be like Michael is to listen carefully to God and try to understand what he wants us to do. We can listen to God by reading the Bible, paying attention to the homily at Mass and taking time every day to pray. We can pray to Michael when we are afraid of danger or tempted to do what is not right.

St. Joachim and St. Anne

(First Century)

July 26

Anne had been a young woman when she married Joachim. They were both prayerful people who tried to obey all the laws of their Jewish religion. At that time, all the Jewish people were praying that God would send the Messiah soon to save them. They were not a free nation; the rulers of Rome had conquered them and made them pay high taxes and work too hard. Every young Jewish woman hoped that she might be the mother of the Messiah. But Joachim and Anne had lived together many years already and still did not have any children.

Every day Anne took good care of their home while Joachim brought their flock of sheep out to the pastures. Anne would say many prayers as she carried water from the deep well, or as she spun the wool from the sheep into fine thread. She prayed that God would bless them with a child. At that time, people thought that children were a sign of God's blessing, and that a couple without children must have done something wrong. One day when Joachim went to the temple, the priests would not let him offer a sacrifice to God. They were afraid that God would not be pleased with him because he had no children.

But the priests were wrong. God was very pleased with both Joachim and Anne. He loved them very much. That day Joachim, feeling sad and confused, went out into the country by himself to pray. While he was there, an angel came to him and told him not to worry. Soon he and Anne would have a baby!

Joachim was gone a long time, and Anne had started to worry about him. Just as she was about to go to the temple and look for him, an angel appeared to her also! The angel told Anne, "Do not be sad anymore. God has heard your prayers, and soon you will have a child."

Anne was so excited! As she ran out of the house she saw Joachim running up the street yelling and clapping his hands. "Anne, Anne! We're going to have a baby!" he yelled.

At the same time, Anne was shouting, "Joachim! Something wonderful has happened. An angel came and told me...What? How do you know?"

"Anne, an angel came to me and told me, too. Surely we are the most blessed couple on earth today! And I know that our child will be blessed, too." He gave Anne a big hug.

"Yes, Joachim. We are blessed. And I think our

child must be very special to have an angel come and tell us the good news. We will consecrate our child to God." Anne wiped tears of joy from her eyes as they went to share their good news with their neighbors.

———————

Happily Anne prepared the house and made warm blankets and clothes for the baby. At last the day arrived. How happy they were to have a little girl! They decided to call their daughter Mary (or Miriam). Little did they realize that this beautiful little baby would grow up and become the mother of the Messiah!

Little Mary grew quickly. She slept, toddled about and soon began to walk and run and dance. Anne carefully taught her daughter the prayers of the Jewish people and told her the stories of how God had protected his people for many long years. But what Mary loved to hear about most was how God had promised to send a Messiah to save his people. She prayed often that this Messiah would come soon.

Seeing how much their daughter loved God and prayer, Joachim and Anne decided to let her go to the temple school in Jerusalem. They missed having Mary running about and singing in their home. But they knew that Mary was happy to go. There she would live with other young Jewish girls and learn more about God and about the Messiah to come.

Joachim and Anne were already old when Mary

Joachim and Anne were happy to do their daily work, loving God and loving their family and friends.

went off to the temple. We don't know when they died, but it was probably before Mary became the mother of Jesus. Certainly, while they were loving and caring for Mary, they did not know that they would be the grandparents of Jesus, the Messiah. But that did not matter. What they cared about most was doing their daily duties well, loving God and loving their family and friends. They knew that if they did those things well, God would be pleased and that his will would be done through them.

One of the best ways that we can imitate Joachim and Anne is to do our daily duties as well as we can, especially our "religious" duties of prayer and attending Mass on Sunday. We can pray that all people will come to know Jesus, the Messiah, the grandson of Joachim and Anne.

St. Joseph

(First Century)

March 19

"Joseph, don't be afraid to take your wife Mary into your house—the child who has been conceived in her is from the Holy Spirit. She will have a son and you shall name him Jesus. He is the Messiah and he'll save his people from their sins" (Mt. 1:20-21).

Joseph woke up, startled but happy. He had been upset and confused ever since Mary, his fiancée, had told him that she was going to have a baby. Now he knew that the baby was the Messiah—the one whom all of Israel was waiting for. Joseph realized that God wanted him to care for Mary and for this special child, whom he would name Jesus.

After Mary and Joseph were married, they lived in a small town called Nazareth, in Galilee. Joseph was a carpenter and spent his days making furniture and farm tools for the people of Nazareth. Mary took care of their house and got everything ready for the birth of her son. Then, just a few weeks before the baby was to be born, Caesar Augustus (the Roman emperor, who ruled all the land of Palestine at the time) announced that he wanted to count all the people in his kingdom. He ordered all the people to go to their home towns to be registered in a census.

At first Joseph and Mary were worried because they knew that it would soon be time for the baby to be born. But then they remembered that a long time ago one of the prophets had said that the Messiah would be born in the town of Bethlehem, in Judea. That was Joseph's home town! They realized that this trip was all part of God's plan. They packed some food and extra clothes onto their donkey and set out.

It was almost eighty-five miles to Bethlehem and the weather was cold. As they got closer to the city they were joined by many other travelers. Joseph told Mary, "I hope that some of our cousins will have room for us. It looks like all the inns will be full!"

Mary knew Joseph was worried about her and the baby. She reached out and put her hand on his shoulder. "Don't worry, Joseph. No matter where we end up tonight, this child belongs to God. He will take care of us."

But the conditions in Bethlehem were even worse than they had imagined. There was no room anywhere. At last they met an innkeeper who felt sorry for them and brought them to a stable, where the animals slept. It was a small cave in a hillside, but at least they would not have to sleep outside in the cold wind.

As they went into the cave a large ox moved over, as if to make room for Mary and Joseph. And a little donkey snorted, as if to greet them. Joseph found a pile of fresh, clean straw and spread his cloak over it. Mary rested while Joseph quickly lit a fire to heat their dinner. How safe Mary felt with Joseph there to help her!

A little later, after Joseph thought Mary had gone to sleep, he went out into the cool night. He began to think about the wonderful things he had read about the Messiah and wondered how he fit into God's plans. The stars were soon shining bright and had filled the sky when Joseph heard a wonderful sound—a baby's cry!

Joseph dashed into the cave and knelt at Mary's side. The newborn baby was soon wrapped in the warm blankets they had brought and was sleeping soundly in Mary's arms. Later that night, shepherds from the nearby fields came in to adore the infant. Angels had told them that the Messiah was there in that small little cave. How proud Joseph was of Mary and of the child as the shepherds crowded around.

After eight days Mary and Joseph brought the baby to the local synagogue. There he was circumcised according to Jewish law and given the name Jesus, which means "the one who saves."

———

Eventually Mary and Joseph returned to their

home in Nazareth. Jesus grew quickly, and everyone was happy that Joseph had such a fine son to help him in the carpenter's shop. The Holy Family loved each other very much. Mary and Joseph both taught Jesus his prayers, and Joseph made sure he learned all the skills of a carpenter. In the synagogue at Nazareth Jesus learned to read the Torah and listened to the explanations of the Jewish law given by the wise rabbi. No one in the town knew yet that Jesus was the Messiah!

When Jesus was twelve, Joseph decided that it was time for the family to make a pilgrimage to the holy city of Jerusalem. It was near the time of the Passover Feast and many of their neighbors were also going. They traveled with people from other small cities of Galilee. The festival was glorious, and the little family spent hours in the huge temple. They also visited with the many friends and relatives they had there.

At last it was time to return home and they started out early in the morning. Mary traveled with the women and Joseph with the men, as was the custom in those days. At night Mary went to find Joseph and say good-night to Jesus. How surprised and upset she was to discover that Jesus was not with Joseph! And Joseph had thought all day that Jesus was traveling with Mary! They were both very worried and decided to go back to Jerusalem. They had to find their son!

After three days of looking in that big city, they went to the temple. And there was Jesus, in the midst of a circle of rabbis and Jewish teachers. These important men were discussing the prophe-

Joseph was a carpenter and spent his days making furniture and farm tools for the people of Nazareth.

cies about the Messiah with Jesus. They were all amazed at the boy's wisdom and learning, but they did not dream that the Messiah was right there with them.

Mary hurried over to Jesus. "Son, why have you done this to us? Your father and I have looked all over for you and have been so worried about you!"

Joseph did not say anything, but his face shone with pride as he took the boy's slim hand into his big rough one. He didn't mind that Jesus had been there in the temple. He knew that Jesus had been busy with his Heavenly Father's business!

They went home to Nazareth, and Jesus obeyed Mary and Joseph. The days and years of hard work and study passed, with Joseph and Jesus working side by side in the carpenter's shop. While Jesus was still a young man, Joseph died peacefully in the arms of Mary and Jesus.

What a humble and holy man was Joseph, the man whom God had chosen to be his own foster father. He did few things that anyone would think extraordinary. But he did everything with a great love for God and for his family. Today, we pray to St. Joseph to be with us and with people we love at the moment of death. We pray that he will watch over and protect the Church, the "family" of Jesus, as he watched over and protected his own family. St. Joseph was a quiet man. He knew what God wanted him to do, and he was happy to do it. He is the special friend of all fathers who work hard to care for their families.

St. Peter

(d. 64)

June 29

Simon was strong and tan, with a curly brown beard and sparkling eyes which took in everything around him. For a moment his gaze rested on his treasured fishing boat and the large, mended fishing nets. Then he looked out across the Sea of Galilee—that unpredictable lake where he fished every day—and breathed in the clean, fresh air. Simon had been born a fisherman, and he planned to die a fisherman.

One day his older brother, Andrew, rushed up to him. "We have found the Messiah!" That day Simon's life changed forever.

Andrew brought Simon to Jesus, who gazed long and hard at the sturdy fisherman. At last Jesus said to him, "From now on you shall be called Peter." (In Greek, the word was Cephas, and means "rock.")

Simon Peter did not understand why Jesus had given him that name, but he didn't care. He was convinced that there was something wonderful about this new teacher. He decided right then to spend as much time as possible with Jesus and learn all that he could from him.

Jesus had other followers, too. They were John, Philip and Nathanael. One day the little group hiked up the high Galilean hills to the town of Cana. There a young couple was getting married. Jesus, his friends and his mother had all been invited. The wedding was quite large and the party was going well until an unexpected thing happened—they ran out of wine!

Mary, the mother of Jesus, realized what had happened. She did not want the young couple to be embarrassed, so she went to Jesus and told him. But Jesus had not planned to do anything extraordinary yet; the people only knew that he was a teacher. But Mary told the waiters, "Do whatever Jesus tells you to do."

The waiters laughed when Jesus told them to fill up their large stone jars with water, but they did it. How amazed everyone was when they saw that the water had been changed into the best wine! Peter was convinced that day that Jesus was the Messiah, the long-awaited King of Israel.

Many months later Peter was discouraged. He had spent the whole night fishing, but had caught nothing. Now the hot morning sun beat down on him and Andrew as they bent over the nets, scraping away barnacles and muck. Nearby, John and James and their father

Zebedee, were doing the same thing.

Suddenly they heard the noise of a large crowd coming over the hill. Looking up, they saw Jesus. There were so many people with him that Peter was afraid someone would get hurt, or that Jesus would be pushed into the water. He started to run toward Jesus when the Master turned and looked at him.

"Peter," called Jesus, "row your boat out into the deep water and lower the nets for a catch."

A catch! But night was the best time to catch fish. Surely Jesus knew that! Besides, Peter was tired from the long night. He said, "Master, the whole night we have worked hard and caught nothing. But if you say so, I will go out again."

Peter and his crew rowed their boat out on the lake and lowered their nets. Within minutes the nets were full of fish! They even had to call James and John to come out and help haul all the fish in. "We almost sank," gasped Andrew when they reached the shore.

But Peter was not thinking of the fish. He was thinking about how many times he had been impatient, even with Jesus. How many times he had been rude and had not listened when others had offered him suggestions.... Who was he that such a wonderful thing could have happened? He looked at Jesus and thought, this is really a holy man. Then he knelt at Jesus' feet and told him, "Jesus, go away from me. I am only a sinful man."

But Jesus told him, "Do not be afraid, Simon. From now on, you will catch men."

That day Simon, John and James left their boats

and nets. They had decided to give up everything to follow Jesus.

_____

The group of disciples grew and grew. People heard about Jesus' miracles and teachings and came from all over to see and hear him. One night Jesus went up on a hill by himself to pray. The disciples and the crowd of people camped at the bottom of the hill. The next morning, Jesus came down and chose twelve of the disciples to be his closest followers. "Peter!" Jesus called out. Peter's tanned face broke into a broad grin. He was thrilled to be chosen, along with John, James and Andrew. Jesus continued to call out names "Philip. Bartholomew. Matthew. Thomas. James. Simon. Jude. Judas."

The group of twelve was complete. These twelve, the apostles, followed Jesus from village to village. They witnessed many miracles and heard many of the stories and sermons which Jesus told. Some of the stories they didn't understand right away, but Jesus would explain things to them when they were alone with him.

_____

One evening, after spending several days with crowds of people, Jesus told the disciples, "Take the boat and go over to Capernaum. I'm going to stay here for a while, but I will join you later." So Peter and his companions set sail for Capernaum.

As darkness fell, the wind grew stronger and

the men had to pull hard on the oars to keep the boat steady. But the small boat tossed and pitched, going nowhere. They had been fighting the wind for hours, and the waves were growing bigger and bigger, when suddenly they saw a tall, pale form gliding across the water toward them. "A ghost!" someone gasped. Frantically, the disciples strained harder at the oars.

"Be brave," a gentle voice called. "It is I; don't be afraid."

"Master!?" cried Peter. "Lord, if it's really you," he yelled, "tell me to come to you across the water!"

"Come," said Jesus.

Immediately Peter was over the side of the boat, hurrying across the waves toward Jesus. Suddenly, Peter looked away from Jesus and realized what he was doing. How could he be walking on water? Peter looked down in terror. Sure enough, the black water was surging up around his feet. Another second and he would go under.... "Master!" he cried. "Save me!"

And then he felt the grip of Jesus' strong hand, and Peter rose to the top of the water once again.

"Oh you of little faith," said Jesus. "Why did you doubt?"

Standing there with the Master on top of the wild waves, Peter wondered: Would he ever doubt again?

———

The Master had said once, to a very large crowd, that anyone who would eat his Flesh and drink his Blood would have everlasting life. Many people had stopped listening to Jesus that day; Peter had not understood what Jesus had said either. Now, almost three years after Peter had left everything to follow Jesus, he witnessed a very remarkable thing. It was the Feast of Passover, and Jesus and the apostles were celebrating together in an upstairs room which they had rented for the occasion.

When it came time for the traditional Jewish blessing of the meal, Jesus took the bread. He passed it around to them saying, "This is my Body which is being given for you; do this in remembrance of me." Next, Jesus took the cup of wine and passed it around. He said, "This cup is the new covenant in my Blood, which shall be shed for you."

Peter was thinking about these strange words when the Master began to speak again. Jesus told them to serve each other, that the most important person among them should act as the least important. Just before supper Jesus had washed their feet as an example of the service they should give one another. Now he turned to Peter and added, "Simon, Simon, Satan has desired to have you so that he may sift you as wheat. But I have prayed for you that your faith may not fail. Someday, you will strengthen your brothers."

"Lord," said Peter, hardly understanding what Jesus was saying, "I am ready to go to prison with you. I will die for you!"

But Jesus said, "I tell you, Peter, before a rooster

crows twice, you will deny that you even know me."

Later that night, Jesus and the disciples went to the Garden of Olives. Jesus took Peter, John and James farther into the garden, and then he went by himself into a private area to pray. The three men grew very sleepy as they waited for Jesus, and soon they were sound asleep.

Suddenly, Peter felt a hand on his shoulder, shaking him awake. "It's time," Jesus was saying. "The Son of Man has been betrayed into the hands of sinners. Come on, the person who did this is here."

The disciples staggered to their feet. Noise and flickering lights came closer and closer, casting strange shadows in the night. A large group of men was marching through the trees, carrying clubs and swords. Leading them was Judas, one of the apostles.

"Hello, Master," Judas said. Then he bent forward and kissed Jesus in greeting. Jesus looked into his face and asked, "Do you betray the Son of Man with a kiss?"

The men rushed forward and grabbed Jesus, who did not resist them. Peter was frightened and angry. He grabbed a sword from someone's hand and lunged at the high priest's servant, cutting off his ear.

"Put back the sword," Jesus told him. "Those who use the sword will perish by it. Do you not know that my Father would send thousands of angels if I asked him? How else can the Scriptures be fulfilled that say this must take place?" Reaching out, Jesus touched the servant's head and the ear was healed immediately.

The mob was pushing all around him. Jesus was speaking to them, asking why they had come at night, with weapons, as if he were a criminal. Peter slipped into the shadows. From where he hid, he watched them lead his Master away. Then he followed.

———

Peter followed them to the palace of the high priest. There were guards all around and he hesitated before entering the courtyard. Seeing John already inside, Peter started through the gate. He was stopped by a maid who asked him, "Are you also one of this man's disciples?"

"I don't know who you are talking about," replied Peter as he pushed his way into the courtyard and joined the servants, who were warming themselves around a fire. Meanwhile, he tried to listen for any news about Jesus. Suddenly he heard loud, angry cries of, "Death! Death!" and a lot of yelling and swearing. He shuddered, and his fear showed in his face.

"This is one of them," someone exclaimed, pointing at Peter.

"No," he replied. "Not I!"

But a relative of the man whose ear had been cut off was looking at him. "Weren't you there in the garden with him?"

This time Peter made his point loudly. He swore with an oath, "I do not know this man you are talking about!"

Just then, above the noise all around him, Peter heard a rooster crow. Then soldiers came out of the palace, leading Jesus through the courtyard. For an agonizing moment, the Master turned and looked straight at him. And Peter realized what he had done.

He turned and fled outside the courtyard into the night, losing himself in the darkness. Stumbling as he ran, Peter felt the tears pouring down his face.

No one knows where Peter went or what he did during the next two days. Perhaps he stayed at the edge of the crowd gathered at Jesus' trial before Pilate. He must have heard the crowd screaming, "Crucify him! Crucify him!" And maybe he followed the painful procession to Calvary and watched from a distance as Jesus suffered and died on the cross. But Peter did not dare approach the cross, even though Mary and John were there.

The following Sunday, Mary Magdalene, a good friend of the Master, came rushing into the room where the apostles were staying. She told them that Jesus' body had disappeared from the tomb! Peter and the disciples ran to the tomb and found it empty, but they were not sure what all of this meant.

In Galilee a few weeks later, Peter and some of his companions were fishing on the lake, when

Jesus called to them from the beach. Peter recognized him and jumped into the water, swimming to the shore. The others brought the boat in, and they ate breakfast there with Jesus.

After they had eaten, Jesus turned to Peter and asked him, "Simon, son of John, do you love me more than these?"

"Yes, Lord, you know that I love you!"

"Feed my lambs," said Jesus. Then he said again to Peter, "Simon, son of John, do you love me?"

"Yes, Lord, you know that I love you!"

"Feed my lambs."

A third time Jesus asked Peter, "Simon, son of John, do you love me?"

"Lord," said the big fisherman, "You know all things; you know that I love you!"

"Feed my sheep."

Just as Peter had denied knowing Jesus three times, he now declared his love for him three times. At the same time, Peter received the command from Jesus to take care of the entire Church.

Forty days after his resurrection, Jesus ascended into heaven. His mother, Peter and the other apostles and disciples stood on the top of Mount Olivet watching their Master rise steadily into the sky. Finally a small cloud hid him from view. They were alone, but Jesus had said, "I shall not leave you orphans; I will send you another Advocate." The little group made their way back to Jerusalem to wait for what would happen next.

For nine days they prayed together in the

Just as Peter had denied knowing Jesus three times, he now declared his love for him three times. At the same time, Peter received the command from Jesus to take care of the entire Church.

same large room where they had celebrated the Passover with Jesus. On the morning of the tenth day they heard a loud roaring sound, like a strong wind blowing. Tongues of fire came above their heads. And all at once, all those things which they had found so difficult to understand about Jesus and his teachings became clear in their minds! They finally understood his mission—and their own.

Peter and his companions hurried out into the street, where they found a growing crowd of Jewish people who had come from almost every part of the known world to celebrate the annual harvest feast of Pentecost. They had heard the rushing wind and had come to see what was happening. Peter and the disciples began to tell them about Jesus—how he had fulfilled the prophecies, how he had been crucified, how he had risen from the dead and ascended into heaven. They told the people that Jesus is God!

The listeners understood, too, for God's Spirit had been poured out in abundance upon the people. "What shall we do now?" they asked the disciples.

"Repent of your sins and be baptized in the name of Jesus Christ."

By nightfall three thousand people had been baptized.

The sacrifice of the cross, renewed as Jesus had taught at the Last Supper, became the center of their lives. They found themselves being transformed by the Eucharist and by the Spirit, until they found themselves living more and more as Jesus had lived—with great love for all people, with humility and patience, spending time to pray to their Heavenly Father as Jesus had taught them. The Acts of the Apostles, which tells us how these first Christians lived, says, "The many believers were of one heart and one soul."

From this community of believers the Church began to grow. It grew in spite of being persecuted and misunderstood by many people. People who were not Jewish also began to believe in Jesus and were baptized. Soon Peter went to live in the city of Antioch, which was much larger than Jerusalem. It was there that members of this new Church were first called "Christians." Later, Peter went to Rome, the center of the Roman Empire.

From Rome, Peter encouraged and comforted and taught Christians from all over, especially those who were being mistreated because they were Christian. He urged Christians to be humble and kind and to be good examples to all who saw them.

When Nero became the emperor of Rome, a fierce persecution of the Christians started. Nero did not understand why the Christians did not worship him as the Romans did, or why they did not pray to the Roman gods as the other citizens did. Peter was taken prisoner and put on trial. He was sentenced to death. It was almost the same time that another great disciple, Paul, was sentenced to death in Rome. Paul was a Roman citizen and would be beheaded. But Peter was not a citizen and so he would be crucified.

While the soldiers were leading Peter to a hill called the Vatican, he remembered the day that Jesus had been led up another hill, called Golgotha, and to another cross. I am not worthy to die in the same way as Jesus, he thought.

"Please," Peter asked the soldiers. "Crucify me upside down."

They placed him upside down on the cross, and the agony began. Pain seemed to tear at every limb and organ until his blood-filled eyes could see no more and numbness overcame him. And then he saw Paradise and gazed once again into the gentle face of his Master.

One of Peter's most beautiful attitudes was his humility. He often spoke at the wrong time, or said things before thinking. But he always admitted when he had made a mistake, and he let Jesus correct him and teach him. We can be like Peter by admitting our mistakes and apologizing when we have hurt another person.

St. Paul

(d. 67)

June 29

While Jesus was preaching in the towns near Jerusalem in the Galilean foothills, a young Jewish boy named Saul was growing up in a seaport city called Tarsus. Many Jewish people lived in Tarsus, and Saul's father was a well known and wealthy Pharisee. Saul was hoping to be a rabbi when he grew up, so he went to Jerusalem to study the laws and rituals of his Jewish faith.

At that time the Romans ruled all of the lands around Palestine, and the Jewish people were often persecuted for their faith. Some of them found it easier to pray to the Roman gods. Saul wanted to convince all the people of his faith to be fervent; he tried especially hard to convince a new group, called the Christians, to go back to their original Jewish faith.

One day when Saul was in Jerusalem he saw a crowd of angry Jews screaming at a man named Stephen. Saul recognized Stephen from his school days. He knew that Stephen had been baptized a Christian and was teaching other Jews about Jesus. This made Saul furious. He helped the angry men to gather up stones and he watched over their cloaks as they threw the stones at Stephen. After that day, Saul became known among all the Christians as a fierce and violent persecutor of the new faith. He would go from city to city, killing all the Christians he could find.

One afternoon Saul was on his way to Damascus with some friends. They were going to kill the Christians who lived there. All of a sudden Saul's horse began to tremble and Saul fell to the ground. The very air about him seemed to explode with light and he heard a voice saying to him, "Saul, Saul, why do you persecute me?"

"Lord," he cried out, "who are you?"

Terrified, Saul heard the reply: "I am Jesus, whom you persecute."

Jesus! The one who had been crucified and whom the Christians claimed had risen and was alive! And not only that, now this Jesus was identifying himself with those whom Saul was persecuting! Saul felt sick. What terrible mistake had he made?

"It is hard for you to accept this," added the voice.

Yes, Saul thought, this was very hard indeed. But humbly he asked, "Lord, what do you want me to do?"

Jesus told Saul to go into the city to the house of a man named Jude. Jude took care of Saul, who had been blinded by the brilliant light.

One day, as Saul was still resting at Jude's house, an old Christian named Ananias came to him. Jesus had come to Ananias in a dream and told him to go and tell Saul all about Jesus and the new faith. "Saul, my brother," said Ananias, "the Lord Jesus has sent me to you so that you may see and be filled with the Holy Spirit." When Saul heard Ananias speak and felt his touch, peace filled his heart and his eyes opened—he could see again!

Soon Ananias baptized Saul, making him a member of the same Church he had been so violently persecuting. Now he promised to do everything he could to spread the Good News about Jesus. Saul sat down that evening for a meal with his new friends. These Christians had seen his transformation and conversion. They forgave him for all the terrible things he had done to them and accepted him as a new disciple of Jesus.

Saul went right out to preach the Good News to others. But many of the Christians recognized him as the man who used to kill them. They were afraid of Saul and did not believe that he had truly accepted Jesus. Some of the Christians even wanted to kill Saul! But others persuaded them to wait. They told Saul that he was in danger and he sadly left the city. Disguised as an Arab, Saul went out alone into the desert. Saul stayed in the desert for many months.

While he was there Jesus instructed him through inspirations and revelations. Saul prayed and fasted and thought about all the things he was learning about Jesus. Finally he returned to Damascus and began to preach again. But the people still did not trust him. This time some friends had to lower him out of the city walls in a basket! He ran through the night and headed for Jerusalem.

In Jerusalem, Saul met with some of the apostles, who now led the new Church with St. Peter as their leader. They were not convinced of Saul's conversion, however, and were not friendly to him. At last one of the disciples, Barnabas, believed Saul and was able to convince the others. Saul spent fifteen days in Jerusalem, talking with Peter and walking with him through the same streets in which Jesus had walked.

"I persecuted him," cried Saul with great sadness.

"I denied him," recalled Peter gently. Together they thanked God for the mercy and love he had shown both of them. Together they continued to preach about Jesus to the Jewish people living in Jerusalem. But many of the people still would not listen to Saul. One night, in a dream, the Lord told him, "Do not be discouraged. Hurry and leave this city. I shall send you to the people of distant nations."

Saul obeyed. He went to his home in Tarsus and gathered a community of Christians there while he waited to learn what Jesus wanted him to do next.

A few years had gone by when Barnabas arrived in Tarsus, looking for Saul. "Come with me to Antioch," he said. "We need you there."

Saul and Barnabas set out. Antioch was the third largest city in the Roman Empire, and there were already many Christians living there. Saul found that his days were busy and full as he preached the Gospel. Many people there came to believe in Jesus.

One day there was bad news from Jerusalem. A famine had struck the land and many people were in danger of starvation. The Christians of Antioch decided they could help. Quickly they collected money for the Christians of Jerusalem and asked Saul and Barnabas to deliver it for them.

How much Jerusalem had changed! The city and its buildings were the same, but its people were angry and hostile. James, one of the apostles who had been closest to Jesus, had been arrested and killed. Peter was in prison awaiting trial. An anxious community of Christians had gathered in the home of Mary, the mother of a young disciple named Mark, to pray.

Peter was to be executed the next day. What would happen to the little community of Christians without Peter's guidance? No one wanted to think about it; they fervently prayed that he would be released and returned to them.

Late that night they heard someone knocking on the door. Who could it be? More soldiers? Perhaps they would all be arrested now. They stared at each other in terror. At last one of the servant girls went to investigate. "Peter!" she exclaimed. "It's you!"

"An angel of the Lord delivered me," said Peter simply. "Let us rejoice and give thanks to God."

———————

Soon Saul and Barnabas, joined by young Mark, set out on their first missionary journey together. Their hearts beat with excitement as they set sail for the Mediterranean island of Cyprus. They would be the first to go there and proclaim the Gospel of Jesus.

They had been preaching there for several days and had baptized many of the people when they received a summons to appear before Sergius Paulus, the governor of Cyprus. The disciples felt honored to be called before the governor. They thought that he, too, wanted to learn about Jesus. They began to tell him about the new faith as soon as they arrived. But Sergius Paulus had a crafty magician named Elymas, who urged Paulus not to listen to Saul and Barnabas. "They are speaking a lot of nonsense," he said scornfully.

"Son of the devil!" said Saul. He suddenly felt himself full of the power of the Holy Spirit. "Here! As punishment you shall be blind for a while!" Elymas cried out and began to grope about. He was blind!

Governor Paulus was amazed. These men, he thought, must be representatives of the true God to have such power. "Saul, will you baptize me into

your faith?" he asked. And so Sergius Paulus became a Christian.

It was after this that Saul (who was now called
Paul) and Barnabas set off for Asia Minor. Mark
returned home to Jerusalem. Together they established Christian communities in Antioch, then
Iconium, then Lystra. Because the Christians were
not understood, they were persecuted almost everywhere. Often Paul and Barnabas had to leave a town
in order not to be killed.

It was while they were in Lystra that they met a
cripple, who listened to them intently. Paul looked
at the man, and knew that he had faith. "Get up,"
said Paul, "and walk." The man stood up, healed!

"It's Zeus himself," whispered one of the Romans to a companion. "It's Zeus and Hermes!" said
another. The people began shouting, convinced
that Barnabas and Paul were two of their pagan
gods. "To the temple!" they cried. "Cover them
with flowers! Call the priests!"

When Paul and Barnabas realized what was
happening, they began to protest. But by then a
new rumor had started. The people began to shout,
"They have tricked us! Stone them! Stone them!"
Instead of being surrounded by flowers, Paul and
Barnabas had to run for their lives. But the crowd
and the stones caught them and the two fell to the
ground. The people, thinking they were dead,
picked them up and threw them over the city walls.

Fortunately, Paul and Barnabas had made a few
friends in the city. When some of these recent

converts heard what had happened, they went out to find the two men. Paul and Barnabas opened their eyes to see a circle of anxious and compassionate faces. They were tenderly cared for and soon recovered enough to move along to the next city, still limping a bit.

Four years later the two friends returned to Antioch. They also went to Jerusalem, where they spent time with Peter, telling him of the many new Christian communities in Asia Minor. And Peter happily sent them back again to evangelize other parts of Asia Minor. They passed through the towns and cities of their previous trip, giving encouragement to the Christian communities in each one and telling them news of the Christian communities in Palestine. In Lystra a young man named Timothy joined them.

While the three men were in Troas, a city near the sea, Paul heard a voice one night in a dream. The voice was saying, "Come over to Macedonia and help us!" In his dream, Paul saw an angel dressed as a Macedonian, begging him to bring the knowledge of Christ to the peoples across the sea. Paul awoke, excited as always to bring the Gospel to all who had not yet heard the Good News.

In Philippi, the first European city they visited, a woman named Lydia was baptized. She opened her home to the three apostles, and many of the new Christians often gathered there to pray. It was in

Philippi that a doctor named Luke joined them. Luke would one day write down all he knew about Jesus and the early Christian communities. The books he wrote would be called the "Gospel of Luke" and the "Acts of the Apostles."

The small group of men traveled to every city they could, making converts and establishing new Christian communities as they went. Unlike the new Christians in Palestine, who were most often converts from Judaism, Paul and Barnabas made many converts among the non-Jewish peoples.

After spending a year and a half in the busy port city of Corinth, Paul and Barnabas returned again to Jerusalem. On their way, they stopped at all the Christian communities which they had started during their two missionary journeys. How happy the Christians were to have these two great teachers with them for even a little while. Paul also wrote letters to the different communities, reminding them to help one another and to remain confident in their faith in Jesus.

Returning soon to Asia, Paul stopped in the city of Ephesus, which had a large Christian community. He stayed there for almost three years, preaching and working miracles. So great were the gifts of healing which God had given Paul that sick people only had to touch his clothes or objects that belonged to him to be cured.

Once the people brought to Paul all the books in the city that taught magic or superstitious things. He made a huge pile of them in the city square and burned them. These books had confused and harmed many people. Seeing the bright light from the fire, they were reminded of the light of faith they now possessed in their belief in Jesus Christ.

After traveling to the various communities of Asia, Paul knew that it was time again to return to Jerusalem. As he boarded the ship in Ephesus, the people hugged him and begged him to write often and to return to them as soon as he could. Through his tears, Paul said good-bye, knowing that he might never see his dear friends again. "Be true to the faith," he urged them.

The boat docked at a port in Palestine, and Paul set out on the overland journey to Jerusalem. On the way, he met an old prophet named Agabus, who was enlightened by the Holy Spirit. He came up to Paul, took his belt and tied his own hands and feet together with it. "The man who owns this belt shall be bound just this way in Jerusalem," he said. There was no doubt that he was talking about Paul!

"Paul, turn back," his friends urged him. "You're risking your life to go to Jerusalem now!" Luke himself was in tears, thinking of what might be ahead for Paul.

"Why do you cry and break my heart?" Paul asked them. "I am ready to be chained and even killed in Jerusalem. It will be for the honor and glory of Jesus, my Lord."

Luke listened, then said, "You are right, Paul. May God's will be done."

Tense and anxious, the little group entered Jerusalem. They found the place where the

As he boarded the ship in Ephesus, the people hugged Paul and begged him to write to them often. Paul said good-bye through his tears, knowing that he might never see his dear friends again.

Christians met for prayer and were greeted joyfully by their old friends. How many new Christians there were! And how eagerly the Jerusalem Christians listened to Paul's stories about the new Christians in Asia. But soon the non-Christians heard that Paul had been converting non-Jews to this new faith and they became very upset. It was bad enough to have the Jewish people among them not worshiping the Roman gods, but to convert even their own people was too much. They decided to stone Paul.

A Roman soldier caught up to Paul just as the angry crowd was ready to kill him. Thinking that Paul must be a criminal, he took him into custody and threw him in jail. Because people were plotting to kill him even while he was in jail, the Roman officers sent him out of Jerusalem to the palace of the governor, Felix, where he would be safe until his trial.

For two years Paul remained in the dungeon of Felix's palace. It was not until a new governor, Festus, took office that the Apostle was brought forward and questioned. Festus did not find Paul guilty of anything, but decided to keep him in prison because he knew the people would be angry if Paul was released.

"I appeal to Caesar," Paul said at last. That was the right of every Roman citizen, and Paul had inherited Roman citizenship from his father, who had purchased it at a great price. When a man appealed to Caesar, he had to go to Rome for his trial.

Two good friends, Luke and Aristarchus,

started out for Rome with Paul. Of course, the Apostle was still a prisoner, so a Roman centurion named Julius was sent along as a guard. He was a very kind and considerate man who came to like and respect Paul during the long and dangerous sea voyage.

After many adventures, including a shipwreck on the island of Malta, Paul, Luke, Aristarchus and the guard took the overland route to Rome. Christians living near Rome came out to meet Paul and give him encouragement along the way. In Rome, while Paul was waiting for his trial, he met often with the Christian community. Even though he was under arrest, he was allowed to live in a rented room and have visitors. From that little room Paul wrote many letters to his friends in the communities of Asia Minor. At last his trial came to court and he was found innocent of any major crime and set free!

The Apostle sailed next to Spain, then returned to Greece and Macedonia for the last time. It was while he was visiting the Christians in Corinth that he probably met Peter, and the two returned together to Rome. The Christians were now being persecuted by the cruel Emperor Nero. Nero was mentally ill. He had lit a great fire to destroy part of the city which was very old. To calm the angry people, he blamed the fire on the Christians and began to kill them.

Soon Peter and Paul were taken prisoner and sentenced to death. Paul found time to write a few last letters to his friends. In a letter to Timothy, he said: "I have fought the good fight; I have finished the course; I have kept the faith." Now he was looking forward to meeting Jesus again face to face—only this time it would be for eternity.

On June 29, in the year 67, Paul was led outside the city walls and whipped, then blindfolded. The executioner lifted a sharp sword over his head and brought it down with all his strength. Tradition tells us that Paul's head bounced three times, and in each place a spring of water bubbled up from the ground. We can believe that Paul was welcomed into heaven by St. Stephen, the first martyr, who had prayed for him ever since the day of his own stoning so many years before.

From heaven, St. Peter, the first Pope, and St. Paul have watched over the Church down through the centuries. They were responsible for many of the early Christian communities, and their spirit lives on in the work of missionaries even today. Their letters to various Christian communities are part of our New Testament, and they are often included in the readings at Mass.

St. Paul's letters speak to us today just as they spoke to the people to whom they were first written. In reading and studying them, we can become filled with faith and love for the Lord Jesus just as Paul was. We can pray to St. Paul for the strength to live and spread our faith in Jesus as he did.

St. Thecla

(First Century)

September 23

Tradition tells us that Thecla was born in A.D. 30 in the city of Iconium, Asia Minor. She is reported to have been the daughter of an important citizen, whose house was noted for its wealth and the wonderful parties that were given there. Thecla's family believed very strongly in the pagan gods and magical superstitions which were popular at the time.

Like all Greek girls who were born into wealthy families, Thecla spent her time studying great works of art and literature. But the more she learned, especially about philosophy, the more unhappy she felt. It seemed that none of the many books she read, or the many teachers that she had, could answer her deepest questions about life.

Often, after long hours of study, she would go out on the balcony and gaze at the sunset, wondering silently: If my soul is to die out like that setting sun, why was it created? If it is to go on living

49

after death, what will happen to it? Will some God take it to live with him? If so, who will he be? In her heart, Thecla would speak to that unknown God, saying, O mysterious Being, if you exist, if you love me as I believe, make yourself known to me!

Thecla was eighteen when her parents began to think of finding a husband for her. She seemed to have no interest in marriage, but her father at last chose a rich and powerful young man named Tamiridus to be her fiancé.

Tamiridus was extremely happy to be the fiancé of Thecla and everyone envied him. Thecla was not only rich, but she also had a reputation for being mature, intelligent and gracious. Her sense of modesty set off her natural beauty like a white background sets off a brilliant bouquet of flowers.

But while her parents and fiancé were busily preparing for the wedding, something happened that would change the whole course of Thecla's life. The apostles Paul and Barnabas arrived in Iconium.

Coming home one night, Thecla passed by the temple of Castor and Pollux. She heard the voices of two speakers who were teaching the people.

"Who are those philosophers?" Thecla asked, ordering her servants to stop.

"Two preachers who come from Antioch," she was told.

"What are they talking about?"

"They are teaching about the true God, Creator of heaven and earth, who is our Father."

Thecla was excited. Could this be the God whom she had sought for such a long time? Could it be him whom she loved? She continued on her way home with her heart beating rapidly.

Thecla couldn't sleep all night. The two speakers filled her imagination, and she felt sorry that she had not spoken to them.

At daybreak, she knew what she would do. Calling one of the servants to accompany her, Thecla hurried to the temple of Castor and Pollux. A man directed her to where Paul and Barnabas knelt in prayer in a dark corner.

"Speak to me," she begged them. "Speak to me about your God. I need to know all about him."

Paul stood up, thanking God in his heart, for he could see Thecla's sincere desire to know God. He greeted her kindly and immediately began to teach her about the life of Jesus. When he taught her about the mystery of the Eucharist, Thecla was astonished at the infinite love this God had for his creatures—it was so unlike any god she had learned of before. Warm and tender tears flowed down her cheeks. She asked to be baptized immediately, and asked Paul to complete her religious instruction as soon as possible.

Together with her servant, who had also become a Christian, Thecla assisted often at the Eucharistic Celebration. When she received the Body of Jesus, she was filled with a love which made her completely forget the world.

Thecla's family and Tamiridus were very angry when she told them that she was a Christian. She also told them that she would not marry Tamiridus because she was now consecrated to God. First with kindness and then with threats they tried to change her mind, but it was no use. Thecla refused to give up her Christian faith.

Finally Thecla was charged with being a Christian and taken before the governor, who tired to make her give up her belief. "For your own good, young lady, leave this new religion to the miserable and to the poor for whom it seems to have been made. Sacrifice to the gods of Greece with me!"

"No, I cannot obey you.... It is not right to disobey God in order to obey a human person."

"You will not even obey your governor?"

"No, for God is much greater than you."

"You are a proud and superstitious girl," he retorted. "I'm sure that the devil has taken possession of you so that you can no longer listen to reason. Stubborn girl! Guards, take her to the prison!"

Thecla was put in chains and shut up in a dark, filthy cell. Anyone else may have been overwhelmed by hunger, fear, loneliness and the awful smell of the prison. But not Thecla, who placed all her hope in the Lord. It is said that angels came from heaven to comfort her in the silence of that dark prison.

Eight days later, she was taken before the governor in the arena, appearing more beautiful, more joyful, more radiant than ever before. She still refused to give up her faith, so the governor ordered a tall stake to be placed in a corner of the forum. The trumpets sounded, announcing a death sentence.

The soldiers tied Thecla to the stake, piled the wood around her and lit a fire. Soon, thick smoke filled the air. The flames sent out long, writhing tongues, which licked about Thecla's delicate body.

A shiver of horror went through the crowd. Some screamed. Others called for silence. Some hoped that she would change her mind. Others wished that they could save this noble and beautiful girl. But all in vain!

Yet, what was happening? Thecla stood calmly in the flames, her face shining with heavenly beauty. Her gaze was fixed on the sky, for she was deep in prayer.

A miracle! God had saved his faithful servant. The fire did not burn Thecla.

The governor could not watch any more. He ordered that Thecla be heavily guarded and sent to the city of Antioch. There she was to be taken to the arena to be fed to the lions.

A large crowd came to see a Christian girl being fed to the lions. They murmured excitedly as her slender form appeared at the edge of the arena. They grew silent as she walked out into the center, knelt down and prayed. Even some of the most heartless and cruel people felt sorry for the girl. Mothers embraced their daughters, as they thought with horror of what would soon happen to Thecla in that arena. Even the governor was touched—and that had never happened to him

Although the lion's breath was hot on her face, Thecla stood peacefully looking up toward the sky. The lion lowered his large head and lay down beside her.

before! Someone suggested that Thecla be freed, but then superstition won out again, and the crowd began to yell, "The Christian to the lions! The Christian to the lions!"

The attendants opened the cage door. A huge, fiery-eyed lion leaped out. He stretched himself and roared, showing two rows of fierce teeth and a mouth which made even the governor shiver.

The lion pawed the ground and shook his long mane. After running around a while he stopped and looked at Thecla. He switched his sides with his tail, then let out a great roar and crept toward her. The people held their breath.

Only Thecla seemed unworried. Although the lion's breath was now hot on her face, she stood peacefully, looking up toward the sky. The lion lowered his large head and lay down beside her. He began to lick her feet!

A murmur of astonishment arose from all sides.

"Another lion!" the governor shouted angrily.

A short-furred lioness leaped out of the cage. She also ran around the arena, roared fiercely and pawed the ground. Then, attracted by the peaceful woman, she rubbed up against Thecla's hands like a little kitten!

At this sight, the wonder and anger of the spectators grew. The governor was furious. Two more unsuccessful attempts on her life convinced a few important citizens that she should be freed. Thecla went to live by herself in a small cave in the country, where people from all the cities around came to hear her talk about Jesus and his redemption of humankind. Many became Christians. Thecla had been so generous and trusting of God, that he used her as his instrument to bring others to believe in him.

When early Christians wished to praise a woman for her courage, they would say, "She's like Thecla!" Even though Thecla survived the attempts to put her to death, she is revered as the first woman martyr because of her bravery in facing death for her belief in Jesus Christ.

Thecla was brave in the face of death because she knew that she had already found the greatest treasure in her faith in Jesus. If she were to die, she knew she would be with her Lord in heaven. If she were to live, she wanted only to tell others about the love of the true God, the Creator and Father of all people.

St. Cecilia

(230-250)

November 22

Cecilia was born in the city of Rome some time during the third or fourth century. Her father was a Roman senator and her family was very rich. Although her father was not a Christian, he allowed his Christian wife to baptize Cecilia when she was still a young child. Dressed in her tiny tunic and sandals, Cecilia would go around the large family estate singing, dancing and amusing everyone. Her mother taught her the prayers of the Christians and told her many stories about Jesus. Together they would often pray for an end to the persecution of the Christians.

Although she was young, Cecilia understood what the persecutions meant. "Mother, won't they ever stop killing Christians? Every day so many die in the arena while the people laugh at them. I feel so sorry for them."

Cecilia's mother told her, "It is good to feel sorry for them, but we should be happy for them, too. The martyrs are killed because they love

Jesus and believe he is God. They go straight to heaven to live forever with Jesus."

Cecilia asked, "Can only the poor people who are Christians become martyrs?"

"Oh no, Cecilia! We must all be ready to die for our faith."

With eyes shining, Cecilia exclaimed, "I want to be a martyr, too!"

Cecilia could not hide her great desire for martyrdom and often talked about it with her mother. If her mother was busy, Cecilia would talk with Lyda, one of the family's servants, whom she loved like a sister.

The years passed and finally it was Cecilia's fourteenth birthday. In the family's large courtyard, many of Cecilia's friends had gathered for her party. It was already time for the party to begin, but Cecilia had still not come down from her room. Her mother went up and found Cecilia crying.

"Why are you crying, Cecilia? You should be happy. Today you are a young lady! All your friends are waiting downstairs for you."

Smiling through her tears, Cecilia stood up and straightened her dress. Yes, today she was a young lady—a special young lady. How could she not cry? She answered her mother, "I'll go down now, Mother. Thanks for coming to get me."

Cecilia ran downstairs to the party. For the rest of the afternoon she and her friends had a good time. They played many games and ate all the good food which had been prepared for them. In the late evening the young people began to leave. Soon, Cecilia was gone, too. Her mother looked all over for her and finally found her in the kitchen, washing the dishes.

"Cecilia, what are you doing?" Cecilia's mother was shocked to see her daughter working like a servant. "You know Lyda and the other servants will clean all this up tomorrow!"

Cecilia calmly answered, "I am no better than Lyda, Mother. I must work, too. Besides, I don't mind helping wash all these dishes."

"Never mind, Cecilia. Let's go up to your room. I want to talk with you. Why were you crying this afternoon? Did someone hurt you?"

Cecilia looked down as they climbed up the marble stairs. Quietly, she answered, "No, Mother. No one has hurt me."

"Then why were you crying? Are you unhappy? Or do you want something that you didn't get for your birthday? You know you can have anything you ask for."

Cecilia shook her head as she and her mother entered her room. "No, Mother. I am very happy with what I have. I don't want anything else. If I did, I would ask for it and I'm sure that you and Father would give it to me. I was crying today because I am so happy to be a Christian. But I want to be more. I want to love and please Jesus Christ by doing something special for him. I have talked with our bishop, and I have decided to consecrate myself to God. I want to be a virgin forever."

Cecilia's mother was silent for a few moments. Finally, she said, "Cecilia, you are young yet.

Why not wait a few more years before you make such a decision? Besides, I'm afraid that your father will not understand this...."

Cecilia's mother began to cry then, for she knew that her husband had already begun to look for a suitable husband for their daughter. Leaving her daughter's room, she went to her husband and told him, "I must talk to you about Cecilia. She told me that she never wants to marry. She wants to remain a virgin all her life. She is in love only with God."

Her husband was angry. "In love with God? What foolishness! Of course she will marry. She will marry a wealthy Roman senator, and I'll see to that."

Cecilia's father went angrily up to her room and knocked on the door, calming himself as he heard his daughter unlatch the hook to let him in. "Cecilia, my daughter, tell me it isn't true. You don't want to hurt me by remaining a virgin all your life, do you?" He tried to act kindly, hoping to change her mind.

"I don't intend to hurt you, Father. You have always told me that you would let me do what I wanted. This is what I want. Won't you let me do it?"

At once her father grew angry. "Never speak of this nonsense again, Cecilia. I will not listen to you now, because you don't know what you are saying. You are tired—go to bed!"

Obediently, Cecilia turned and closed the curtain. In a soft voice she said, "Good-night, Father."

Cecilia did not sleep all night. She kept thinking of what her father had said. She never spoke of it again, but prayed that God would guide her in the years ahead.

———————

Three years passed with nothing more said about marriage for Cecilia. But one day her father brought a handsome young man home to meet Cecilia. He wanted to marry her and her father had already began to arrange for the wedding. Cecilia had no choice because in those days marriages were arranged by the parents.

Soon, there was great excitement in Cecilia's home. A large room was decorated and tables were spread with all kinds of food and drink. When it was time for the ceremony to begin, Cecilia's mother ran upstairs and called out, "Cecilia, are you ready? Valerian is waiting downstairs."

Cecilia opened the door and stepped back. Her mother smiled and kissed her. "Cecilia, you look beautiful! Your hair is so shiny, and your dress is lovely." Then she reached up and fixed the white roses that crowned Cecilia's head. "Now, let's go down together and greet the guests."

All through the wedding ceremony, Cecilia thought about her desire to remain a virgin. She did her best to be a good hostess and make sure that her guests enjoyed themselves. The party lasted all day and part of the night. Finally, she took Valerian aside and told him of her vow. She told him that she was the bride of Jesus Christ. Valerian was not a Christian, but he wanted to know more about her "Bridegroom." As she explained, he understood more and more.

Finally, Cecilia took Valerian aside and told him of her vow. She told him that she was the bride of Jesus Christ. Valerian was not a Christian, but he wanted to know more about her "Bridegroom."

After some months of instruction about Jesus Christ and the Church, Valerian was baptized. His brother Tiburtius was also baptized. Together, the three young Christians worked among the poor people of the city and buried the martyrs. But one day the emperor found out that Valerian and Tiburtius were Christians. Since it was against the Roman law, he had both men arrested and ordered them to be killed in the arena. They were happy to die for Jesus, because they wanted to go to heaven. But poor Cecilia! She was left by herself now. Although she was sad, she was happy for her husband and his brother.

After their deaths, she waited until everyone had left the arena. Then, with the help of friends, she took their bodies to the catacombs. The catacombs were extensive underground tunnels where the Christians buried their dead. They also met secretly in the catacombs to pray together and celebrate the Eucharist.

Each day Cecilia prayed that God would grant her the joy of dying as a martyr for him. She did not have long to wait, for soon two Roman soldiers came to take her to the emperor, who condemned her to death. She was to be martyred in a large room which would be heated until she suffocated.

Cecilia entered the deathroom, knelt down and said, "Oh, Jesus. I thank you for having given me the grace to die a martyr. I believe and hope in you, O Lord. I love you with all my heart! I go now to my death, a day for which I have waited so very long. I die for you, dear Jesus. Take me to

Paradise quickly. Have mercy on all these people who don't know you yet. Bless and protect all the Christians, that they may worship you in peace. Amen."

The soldiers turned their backs when they saw her continue to pray silently. They closed and locked the door. For about three hours they left her alone, expecting to find her dead when they returned. Instead, they heard music coming from the room. The soldiers jumped up and rushed in. There was Cecilia, standing up with her arms outstretched, singing and praising God.

The captain of the soldiers was startled. After a few moments he ordered a soldier, "Go tell the emperor of this!"

Within fifteen minutes the royal carriage arrived. The emperor, in all his glory and majesty, walked into the house. He had never been so angry. "So, she did not die?" he roared. "Then we will kill her in another way! You fools didn't heat the room enough, that's why she didn't die. But now she will suffer more. Take your sword and cut off her head!"

Two soldiers stepped forward to bring Cecilia to a wooden platform. Before they reached her, she had already put her head down, letting her long hair fall to one side. The captain of the soldiers let his sword fall once swiftly, then again. Cecilia's head would not come off!

Fearfully, the captain turned to the emperor and said, "Her head won't come off. What shall I do?"

The cruel emperor smiled. "Let her suffer," he

commanded. "Let her die in misery." Then he turned and left the room.

Cecilia's friends gathered around her, crying. Her eyes opened and she gazed upon them all. She was silently blessing them and praying for them. Then her eyes closed and remained that way. At the end of the second day, Cecilia again opened her eyes. She looked at her friends, and then toward heaven. Her friends gathered closer, hoping that she would say something. But, no, she was looking at Someone whom they could not see. In her heart, she was talking with God. The hours passed slowly, while Cecilia remained in the same position. At the beginning of the third day, she moved a little. Her eyes opened once again, and she looked up. Her friend Lyda went close to her and watched her for a few moments. Then she turned to the others and whispered, "Jesus Christ came to take Cecilia just now. Let us pray for our beloved sister, who is now a saint in heaven."

All her friends knelt down to pray to and for their beloved sister. They prayed, asking her to intercede for all the Christians. They asked her to pray for each of them, too, for they knew that she was now very close to Jesus and Mary.

St. Cecilia loved everyone sincerely, whether they were rich or poor. She tried to help anyone in need and knew that all people were children of the same God. We can imitate Cecilia by showing respect for each person we meet.

St. Tarcisius

(Third Century)

August 15

For a few years, while an emperor named Valerian ruled the Roman Empire, the Christians lived in peace. But in A.D. 258, Macrian, the prefect of Rome, was thinking, Who cares if the common people follow the teachings of that poor Hebrew, Jesus Christ! But when the rich noblemen and soldiers join in, that's too much!

Macrian went to the emperor and told him what he had been thinking.

"You are right, Macrian," said Valerian. "I will order a persecution of the Christians, beginning today. Rome cannot bow to the teachings of Jesus."

And so Valerian ordered that all who declared themselves to be Christian should be punished with death. Only those who denied that Jesus was God and honored the gods of Rome would be set free.

That very night, the elderly Pope Sixtus II called the Christians together in the catacombs.

"My brothers and sisters and beloved children in our Lord Jesus Christ," he began. "As you already know, the persecution has begun once again. Some of the faithful have already been taken to prison. Let us pray for them!"

The hunt for the Christians grew more and more cruel with each passing day and the persecution raged in all its fury. Into the homes of the Christians went the emperor's soldiers, dragging them away until the city's prisons were full. Every evening when the sun was setting, the condemned Christians sang hymns to God. The beautiful sound of their singing floated up from the damp, dark underground cells.

Late one afternoon, a young boy was walking near the horrible prisons. His name was Tarcisius and he was the son of a wealthy Christian, Senator Tarsente. With his heart full of pity, Tarcisius was listening to the singing of the prisoners. He knelt down by the barred windows and stayed there, listening.

When Tarcisius returned home later that evening, his governess was waiting for him in the doorway. "Why are you so late, Tarcisius? I was worried about you! Especially since your father is not at home. He had to go into hiding. They are trying to find him to question him."

"He went into hiding?"

"Yes, Tarcisius. For your sake."

"But if they find him, he won't deny Christ, will he?" the boy asked.

"No. Your father is a brave man and he loves

Jesus more than life itself. He won't betray his faith. Now come and eat. Supper is ready."

Tarcisius ate slowly. It was a sad supper without his father. Suddenly he asked, "I have heard people say that my mother was a martyr. Is that true?"

"Yes," replied the governess. "She was killed when Decian was emperor. Your father was going to tell you when you were older."

"But I'm already old!" exclaimed Tarcisius. Then he pleaded, "Please tell me more about my mother."

"Yes, yes, I will tell you tonight, Tarcisius. Your mother told me that she would be waiting for you in heaven. She loved you very much."

Tarcisius' eyes glowed at the words of his governess. "Tell me more," he begged.

"Your mother was young and a very kind woman, Tarcisius. Although she loved you very much, she was faithful to Christ." The governess went on with her story. Then, very late that evening, she and Tarcisius went down into the catacombs to meet with the other Christians.

The Pope was facing them, seated on a stone chair, the chair of Peter. His face was pale and marked with suffering, but his bright eyes shone with piety and tender affection.

"My brothers and sisters, many Christians will be judged tomorrow," he said. "Their fate is certain—they will all be killed!" Sighs and moans were heard in the crowd. Quadratus, a tall, strong young man stepped forward. He was a Roman soldier who had become a follower of

Christ. He said, "Holy Father, I have seen them! Today I was on guard at the prison. They made me promise to ask you to send them the Bread of Heaven."

"How can we get the Holy Eucharist to them?" sighed Pope Sixtus. "Who will dare to go into the prison? Can you, Quadratus?"

"No," he answered. "Tomorrow I am assigned to guard the Appian Way. I cannot go to the prison."

"Who dares to undertake this dangerous mission?" asked the Pope. "Who will take the risk?"

There was a chorus of "I!" "I!" "No, I!"

Tarcisius made his way forward through the crowd of people until he was standing in front of Pope Sixtus.

"Holy Father, send me!" he cried.

"You Tarcisius—so young?" exclaimed the Pope in surprise. "Why, you're just a boy!"

"Because I am just a boy, perhaps no one will pay any attention to me," he answered hopefully.

Pope Sixtus looked at him intently. In Tarcisius' eyes he saw a strong desire to carry the Eucharist to the prisoners.

"All right," he decided, "you shall be the one. I'll entrust the Eucharistic Jesus to you, in this little case."

"I'll carry It on my heart," promised Tarcisius joyfully. "I'll hold it tight like this! I am ready to die rather than expose It to unbelievers."

The next day, along the Appian Way, some schoolmates of Tarcisius were sitting on a pile of

Tarcisius made his way forward through the crowd of people until he was standing in front of Pope Sixtus. "Holy Father, send me!" he exclaimed.

stones. With them was Fabian, a good friend of Tarcisius.

"Fabian, where's Tarcisius?" asked one of the boys. "Why isn't he here today?"

"Oh, he'll come. He always comes to play."

"Yes, and we'll have a stone-throwing contest," said Mark. "I've been practicing, and I'm sure I will beat him this time!" he boasted.

The other boys laughed loudly with him. Mark was a bully, and the others were afraid of him when Tarcisius was not around to keep him in line.

Mark grew impatient as the minutes slipped by with no sign of Tarcisius. He was anxious to begin the contest and prove himself the best of the group for once.

"Tarcisius is taking his time," said Fabritius. "Let's start without him."

"He'll come, and he'll win the contest," stated Fabian. "He's the best stone-thrower and the best student, too."

"He was," said Mark. "Lately, he's always sleepy. His head rolls from side to side...like this!" The boys laughed as he imitated Tarcisius.

Fabritius said, "The teacher has begun to notice it, too."

"Maybe Tarcisius doesn't feel well," Fabian defended. "Anyway, he'll beat you just the same—he's a born winner!"

"And what were you born for? To defend him?" retorted Mark.

"I like him a lot, that's all," replied Fabian. "He treats me like a brother."

He was interrupted by Fabritius, who had

caught sight of Tarcisius coming along the road. "Here he comes!"

Tarcisius was coming toward them silently and cautiously, his arms pressed firmly to his chest.

"Come and play!" called Mark. The other boys took up the cry, "Come on, Tarcisius! Mark has challenged you!"

But Tarcisius answered, "I can't. I have an errand to do."

"My, how important you think you are!" sneered Mark. "Cut it out! Come on, let's play."

"I really can't," Tarcisius said firmly. "Let me go. We can play tomorrow."

"No," said Fabritius, "we'll play today. Right now. Choose your stones."

Again, Tarcisius said, "I can't, I tell you! I can't."

"Oh," sighed Mark in disgust. "You're whining like a baby! Hey, why do you have your arms like that? What are you hiding?"

"I don't have to tell you," protested Tarcisius. "I can't tell you."

"Smarty!" scowled Fabritius.

Mark kept up his questioning. "Tell us, Tarcisius. What can you have that is so important?"

In his heart, Tarcisius prayed, Please, Jesus, make my arms as strong as steel! I'll press you close to me! I'll defend you!

Tarcisius was afraid as the boys closed in around him. His heart was pounding, and his eyes were nearly blinded with tears. The circle of boys grew tighter.

"We've had enough, Tarcisius," warned Mark. "I'll give you time to tell us. I'll count to three. One..."

Tarcisius prayed silently, Oh, Lord, Lord, help me!

"Two!" said Mark.

"Mark, stop it!" cried Tarcisius. "Let me go, Mark. I'll give you my bow and arrows, all of them. I'll give you anything you want, but please let me continue on my errand!"

"It's no use, Tarcisius!" yelled Mark. "You're hiding something and we're going to find out what it is! I'll start counting just once more." Glaring at Tarcisius, he began, "One, two..."

"No!" cried Tarcisius.

"I'll repeat it!" Mark's eyes were flashing angrily. "Two..."

"Just a second, Mark," interrupted Fabritius. "Listen to me, I just had an idea."

"I know!" shouted Mark, in a wicked voice. "I had the same idea myself. Tarcisius must be a Christian. And maybe he's carrying around his neck the mysteries!" By that word Mark meant the Holy Eucharist. "Yeah, the mysteries! The mysteries!" shouted the other boys, none of whom were Christian.

Mark glanced at Tarcisius and demanded, "Did you make up your mind, Tarcisius? I said two and— and—"

"I said no, and I mean it!" said Tarcisius firmly.

"Leave him alone!" pleaded Fabian.

"No, no, Mark, go ahead!" yelled Fabritius.

Tarcisius prayed earnestly. King of martyrs, I beg you, don't let me be separated from you. I would rather die.

"Three!" shouted Mark.

There was a scramble, and several voices shouting, "Let him have it! Hit him! Hit him!"

Tarcisius fell to the ground and, like wild animals, the boys jumped on top of him. Yet his arms remained crossed over the Eucharist on his chest like two iron bands.

With a terrific effort, he struggled to his feet and managed to run a few steps.

"Grab some stones!" yelled Fabritius. "Let him have it!"

One after another, stones struck him from all sides, until there was not a part of his body that was not bleeding.

Yet he managed to stumble on, until one struck his forehead. Then Tarcisius fell.

"Tarcisius! Tarcisius!" sobbed Fabian in terror. "Leave him alone, you bullies!"

But Mark urged them on. "Come on, let's get him and have a look at those 'mysteries.'"

Just then Fabritius yelled, "Look out! A soldier is coming!"

"He's coming right this way," said another. "Let's get out of here!" In an instant the boys were gone.

Only Fabian did not run away. He stayed close beside his friend, who was in terrible pain.

"Jesus," murmured Tarcisius. "I am dying, but I defended you. Forgive my friends, forgive them!"

Meanwhile, the soldier had drawn near. It was Quadratus, the Christian. As soon as he saw Tarcisius lying on the ground, he exclaimed, "Poor boy! What have they done to you?" Then noticing Fabian, he demanded sharply, "What are you doing here?"

"I'm Tarcisius' friend. I love him," wept Fabian. "I didn't throw stones at him. Let me stay here, near him."

"Tarcisius, open your arms," Quadratus urged tenderly, bending over the boy.

"No," whispered Tarcisius. "I won't open my arms. Bring me to Pope Sixtus. I will give my treasure—Jesus—only to him."

"Are you in great pain?" asked Quadratus, gently raising the boy's head.

"Yes, I hurt very much," gasped Tarcisius. "But that doesn't matter. Nobody touched Jesus. He is here, right here with me." He was breathing hard, struggling to talk. Suddenly he said, "I already see the angels. Take me to the Pope!"

"Don't die, Tarcisius! Don't die!" It was Fabian pleading tearfully. "You have been like a brother to me."

"I see the angels," Tarcisius repeated. "My faith is true. And you,"—he gasped for breath—"you, Fabian, do you believe?"

"Yes," declared Fabian. "I believe, Tarcisius. I want to become a Christian, too. Then we can be together again some day."

Quadratus picked up the dying boy in his arms and carried him to the catacombs.

"Tarcisius," Pope Sixtus whispered gently, shocked at seeing the boy in such a condition. "Tarcisius, Jesus is safe because of your loving sacrifice."

Pressing Jesus in the Eucharist close to his heart, Tarcisius died. Only then did his arms fall away from his chest.

This was the way in which St. Tarcisius, the boy martyr of the Holy Eucharist, died—with his beloved Jesus resting on his heart.

A strong, sweet odor of lilies filled the air at that moment. And Tarcisius' soul ascended joyfully to the throne of God, to the throne of the King who is waiting for all of us in eternal glory.

Although we may never have to defend the Eucharist with our life, we can show our love for Jesus in the Blessed Sacrament by receiving Holy Communion reverently and with love. We can make visits to the Blessed Sacrament when we pass by a church. And we can show love for the Eucharistic presence of Jesus in the tabernacle by always dressing and acting respectfully when we are in the church.

St. Sebastian

(d. 288)

January 20

Sebastian, a young officer in the Roman army, had just found out that two Christians had been put in prison and sentenced to death because they believed in Jesus Christ. Sebastian was a Christian, too, although the other soldiers didn't know it. In fact, he had become a soldier in Rome hoping that he would be able to secretly comfort and assist the Christian prisoners. With deep concern he thought of the twin brothers, Mark and Marcellinus, who were newly baptized and the only Christians in their family.

Lord Jesus, prayed Sebastian silently as he hurried toward the prison, let me die, if need be, but please give Mark and Marcellinus the courage to remain faithful to their Baptism!

As he entered the cell, Sebastian found the two brothers surrounded by a group of their friends. Their father was there, too. All of them were urging the twins to give up their Christian faith and save their lives. Mark and Marcellinus were obviously torn between love for their Heavenly Father and love for their earthly father.

At that point, Sebastian's clear voice rang out. "My brothers in Christ!" All heads turned in his direction as he continued. "You who have always shown yourselves so brave and courageous, will you now turn your backs on the Lord Jesus, the Heavenly King who has prepared for you a place of eternal glory?"

All were silent. Sebastian's face glowed with supernatural light as he continued. "What has this poor world to offer, in the end, but death? Will you exchange an eternity of joy for a few years of passing pleasure?"

The brothers looked at one another silently and bowed their heads. They chose God! Even their father and friends were impressed. They crowded around Sebastian, asking him questions about Jesus. And Sebastian, with the fervor of an apostle, spoke on and on.

"I wish to be baptized," said one of the men.

"And I!" cried another.

"And I!"

Only one man remained unconvinced. "I need more proof than your words," he told Sebastian. This man was Chancellor Nicostratus, and he was known to be a stubborn man. But Sebastian saw Nicostratus' wife beside him, her eyes full of belief. "You believe, don't you, Zoe?" he asked. "Why don't you speak to your husband? A word from you might convince him, too."

Sebastian's face glowed with supernatural light as he continued: "What has this poor world to offer in the end but death? Will you exchange an eternity of joy for a few years of passing pleasure?"

To Sebastian's surprise, tears began to stream down Zoe's cheeks. What had he said? Why should she start to cry like this?

Nicostratus stepped forward. "Sebastian, don't you know that she has been unable to say a word for over six years?"

No wonder she had not spoken, Sebastian thought. Lifting his eyes, the young soldier prayed silently for a moment. Then he turned to the woman.

"Zoe, look at me."

She turned her sweet, sad eyes toward him. Sebastian made the sign of the cross on her lips and asked, in a voice that trembled with emotion, "Zoe, do you believe in our Lord Jesus Christ?"

The woman opened her lips and said clearly, "I do believe in Jesus, our Lord!"

Hardly had she finished speaking when her husband had thrown himself in a heap at Sebastian's feet. He, too, had been won to Christ!

Shortly afterward, the privilege of martyrdom came to Mark and Marcellinus. They suffered bravely for twenty-four hours with their feet nailed to a post. Then they were shot to death with arrows. Surely they were received with great joy in heaven!

Sebastian continued his work of preaching and of comforting the Christians who had been captured and sentenced to death. The persecution was worse than ever, and the prisons were full. Then, in a vision, Sebastian was warned that his own death was near.

"That's the man! Seize him!"

The soldiers closed in on Sebastian and quickly bound him in chains. How had his faith been discovered? Sebastian wondered. Then he saw the face of one of the newly baptized smirking at him from the shadows—the man had betrayed Sebastian.

They brought Sebastian to Emperor Diocletian, who had always considered Sebastian to be one of his best soldiers. Now that Diocletian knew the truth about him, he was angry. "Death!" he yelled. "Death by arrows!"

Sebastian was tied securely to a sturdy tree and the guards stepped back to let the archers do their work.

Twang! Twang! Thud! Thud! Arrow followed arrow, sinking deep into Sebastian's body. He writhed in pain, but did not cry out. He was willing to suffer this, and even more, for the Lord Jesus. The archers left the field, satisfied that he would die after several hours' torment. They had deliberately avoided shooting him in the heart, for that would have brought death too quickly!

But had he been abandoned? There was a rustle in the bushes, and someone came to his side. Sebastian blinked the blood out of his eyes, and gazed dimly on the face of Irene, a pious old woman whom he had seen among the Christians in the catacombs.

"I had come to give you a decent burial, my son," she murmured, "but I see there's still hope for you. Let us take you to shelter!"

In the security of Irene's home, Sebastian slowly regained his strength. Perhaps God has spared me for a reason, he thought. Perhaps I may be able to try to convert Diocletian from his cruel ways. He pondered and prayed over the question.

At last, a little unsteady on his feet, but with the old fire in his eyes, Sebastian put on his soldier's uniform and went to stand guard where he knew the emperor would pass by. "The hour of justice has come!" he called out as Diocletian came near. "Repent. Ask God's forgiveness for the sins you have committed!"

Diocletian stood, shocked for a moment at seeing Sebastian alive. But then he screamed in rage. "Take that man! Beat him until he is dead!" At once the soldiers fell upon Sebastian. He felt blow after blow, then...nothing.

The soldiers then took Sebastian's body and threw it into the sewer. The Christians rescued it later and erected a splendid church above it, but Sebastian's soul was already happy with God, where it will be for all eternity.

St. Sebastian always had one thought before him: heaven. That goal was so precious that he would never do anything that might make him lose it. We all can work for heaven by doing what is right and avoiding what we know is wrong.

St. Lucy
(d. 304)

December 13

During the time when Diocletian was emperor of Rome, a daughter was born to a wealthy family on the island of Sicily. The little girl's eyes sparkled so brightly that she was named "Lucy," which means "light." Lucy's father died when she was about six-years-old, but the family had enough money to live comfortably in their home in the city of Syracuse.

Lucy and her mother were both Christians. They often met other Christians, in caves near the city, to pray and to celebrate Mass. At that time, the Christians were being persecuted and put to death for their faith in Jesus Christ.

As Lucy grew older, her love for Jesus grew stronger. She saw the great difference between the way of life which Jesus had taught to his followers and the way in which the non-Christian Romans lived. The world was full of violence, injustice and immorality, but Lucy refused to be drawn into the sinful lifestyles of many of her friends. For Lucy, God's love was infinitely more precious than anything else in the whole world.

In those days, every young girl was expected to marry and have children. Not to marry was considered a social disgrace. Lucy had often dreamed of the day she would have her own family, but after praying about it she believed that Jesus was asking her to remain single. In that way, she could give all her time and energy to prayer and to serving people in need. Her only "husband" would be Jesus and his people.

Of course, Lucy accepted the "proposal." She would remain a virgin forever for Jesus. She didn't mind when a small voice inside her said that she would suffer because of this choice. She loved Jesus, and she already knew that suffering often came with love.

Having made her decision, Lucy felt great peace for several days. Then her mother announced that a young man had asked to marry Lucy, and her mother had agreed. The engagement would soon be announced! Lucy was surprised and upset, but she didn't say anything to her mother—not yet, anyway!

Lucy's mother had been ill for years, and the girl decided to ask St. Agatha to cure her. So the two set out for the neighboring city of Catania, where they visited the tomb of the virgin martyr, Agatha. After assisting at Mass, they remained before the tomb in prayer. Suddenly, in a vision, Lucy saw the saint coming toward her. She was dressed in radiant garments and sparkling jewels and was surrounded by angels.

"Dear sister," said the Vision, "why do you ask *me* to obtain your mother's cure? Your mother is now well, because you have great faith. And the Lord is pleased with your promise to be his alone."

The glorious Vision continued. "Soon you will become the splendor of Syracuse, just as Jesus has made me the glory of Catania."

The saint disappeared. Lucy got up and went over to her mother. She had been cured!

This seemed to be Lucy's chance to ask her mother two favors. One was not to go through with the marriage engagement. The other was to give the family wealth to the poor. Her mother agreed to both, but was afraid to tell the young man, who was not a Christian.

It came as a shock to the young man when he heard that the poor were swarming to Lucy's home to divide among themselves the wealth he had expected to be his one day. At first, he couldn't believe it, but then he saw for himself and decided to take action. In the early morning of December 11, 304, he arrived on Lucy's doorstep. He was ushered inside, and waited nervously in the entrance hall. As soon as Lucy appeared, he said, "Your mother has promised you to me!"

The dreaded moment had come. Steadily, Lucy replied, "I have already been pledged to Another. Please leave, and permit me to remain true to him."

Like a flash of light, the young man saw the

truth. Lucy was a Christian! He was furious. Storm-
ing out of the house, he rushed to the palace of
Governor Paschasius.

Very soon, the soldiers were at Lucy's door.
Grimly they marched her through the streets, to
appear before the governor. She was calm.
Paschasius was stern.

"You must offer a sacrifice to the gods of
Rome!" he told her.

"I have sacrificed my riches to help the poor,
as my Heavenly Bridegroom wished," replied the
girl. "The only other possession I have is my
body, which I have also given to God."

"Don't tell me such nonsense!" retorted the
governor. "It is my duty to carry out the commands of the Roman emperor, and his command
is that you worship the gods of Rome."

"Just as you respect the emperors and their
laws, so I respect God and his laws," Lucy explained. "In fact, nothing will stop me from obeying his laws and worshiping him alone."

Paschasius stiffened. "You are bold enough
now, but the torturers will change you."

"The words of God are changeless," replied
Lucy. "Jesus said that when his disciples would
be brought before a judge, the Holy Spirit would
speak through us."

"Oh, so you think this Holy Spirit is speaking
through you now?"

"He is in everyone who lives in chastity and
purity, because such a person is a temple of God."

With fire in his eyes, the governor retorted,

"Just as you respect the emperors and their laws, so I respect God and his laws," Lucy explained. *"In fact, nothing will stop me from obeying his laws and worshiping him alone."*

"Unless you worship our gods, I'll have you taken to a place where you will lose your purity. Then the Holy Spirit will leave you!"

At that threat, Lucy was frightened, for she had heard of other young Christian girls being forced into houses of prostitution in order to violate their purity. But she hid her feelings and said firmly, "The body does not sin if the will does not consent. Even if you took my hands by force and made me offer incense to idols with them, God would know that I did not want to do so. It would be the same if you made me a prostitute by force; because it would be against my will, I would not have done wrong in God's sight."

Nevertheless, Paschasius commanded that Lucy be taken away as he had already announced. Four soldiers stepped forward to drag her away as the calm young woman prayed fervently. The combined strength of all four could not move her!

Others sprang forward, but their help was of no use. At last Paschasius ordered that Lucy be dragged away by a team of oxen, but even those strong animals could not budge the girl.

Nor could pagan magicians move her. "What is the secret of your magic?" the governor asked Lucy in a fury.

"It is not magic," replied the girl. "It is God's goodness toward those who are true to him."

Curious spectators were crowding around on every side. Paschasius' anger mounted, for he was being made a fool in front of everyone. He shouted for wood, for pitch, for oil! "Light a fire and burn the Christian girl!" he roared.

Materials were brought and the fire was lit. As the flames blazed up, sweeping through the pitch and oil and licking hungrily at the wood, Lucy remained unharmed. She knelt in prayer, now and then speaking to the crowd. "I have asked God to spare me from the fire," she explained, "so that the faithful may gain courage from my tortures, and so that unbelievers may see the beauty and glory of the Christian religion."

But now Lucy's mission had been accomplished. God would delay her flight to heaven no longer. An executioner came forward with a sharp-bladed dagger, which he plunged into Lucy's throat. As blood spurted out and soaked into the ground, the young martyr's soul flew to the waiting arms of Jesus!

St. Lucy had a deep love for God. Such a love comes from prayer. The more we pray and speak to our Lord, the stronger will be our love for him and our desire to stay close to him always.

St. Agnes
(d. 304)

January 21

Almost three-hundred years after Jesus died for us on the cross, a family named Clodius lived in the beautiful city of Rome. They were a noble and wealthy family, and lived in a magnificent palace with many servants. But the most precious treasure of the Clodius family was their daughter, Agnes.

The name "Agnes" means "lamb," and it suited the young girl well. Her cheeks were pink, like roses; her eyes, which were a soft blue like the sky, shone with a beautiful light. She was warm-hearted and kind to everyone, always doing good to those around her.

By the time Agnes was thirteen, she was already tall and graceful. She often wore a snow-white dress with no ornaments or jewels, which made her look very much like a bride. And she always seemed to look as happy as a bride, as if she was always thinking of someone very special to her.

As she walked to school each morning, returning the same way in the evening, the people whom she passed talked about her gracefulness and charm. Her outward behavior reflected her noble mind, her generous disposition and her high moral standards.

One day a boy named Procop, who was the son of the prefect of Rome, met her and said, "Stop, Agnes. I want to talk to you."

"What do you want?" she replied.

"Agnes, I love you because you are beautiful and good. Will you promise me that someday you will marry me?"

"I am already engaged!"

"What?" Procop had heard no news of this. "To whom are you engaged?" he demanded. "Who is richer or more honorable than I? Who has more gold or more servants?"

"He who has angels for servants and owns heaven and earth," Agnes replied. "He who has put a necklace of precious gems about my neck and has dressed me in white linen woven with pearls. He who loves the pure and sweet scent of lilies. He will be my Husband and he alone!"

Procop went away sad. Because he did not understand what Agnes had said, he thought that she had been teasing him, or else that she was making up daydreams.

Sorrowful and forlorn, he no longer cared for games. He did not even read or study any more, although he was supposed to be preparing to become the next governor.

One night, an old servant of the family said to Procop's father, "I know why Agnes refused your son! She must be a Christian. There are many young women who are...and many refuse to marry because they say they love someone named Jesus Christ!"

The prefect was startled. He was not a Christian. And, like most of the Romans, he hated the Christians because they refused to worship the Roman gods.

When the Romans discovered that someone was a Christian, they usually killed that person in a horrible way. Procop's father decided to make Agnes marry his son by threatening to kill her if she didn't do so.

The prefect went to talk to Agnes' parents. "Either Agnes will marry my son, or I will call her to court," he said. "And if she confesses to being a Christian I will have her killed. You know of the law of Rome. It is severe, and it commands enemies of the gods to be condemned without pity."

Agnes' parents were terrified, for they knew that their daughter was a fervent Christian. They also were Christians—as had been their parents before them.

Because the Christians were hated so much, they met in secret to assist at Mass. They often gathered in tunnels and caves called *catacombs* which were underneath the city. Sometimes they even met in the palace of Agnes' family.

Her parents tried to remain calm until the prefect left. Then they called Agnes and told her what he had threatened.

"I fear nothing for Jesus' sake," declared Agnes. *"There is an angel always guarding me and he will not permit Christ's handmaid to suffer any harm!"*

"Mother! Dad! Have courage," she replied. "I will not betray the faith you have given me. I will not be a traitor to my faith even if it means suffering and death! Do not cry for me. Jesus will protect me."

A few days later, the palace of Agnes and her parents was surrounded by armed guards. Agnes was taken to the court where the prefect came forward to accuse her.

"Do you know why you are here?" he asked.

"I can guess. It is because I am a Christian."

"Foolish girl! You say something so serious and dangerous and you smile? You should be trembling. Do you know what is going to happen to you?"

"I know," Agnes answered. "But Jesus told his disciples, 'You will be persecuted and tortured because I was. Remember that you were made for my kingdom and not for this world.' I would give up my life a thousand times rather than give up my faith in Jesus Christ."

"Enough! My son is suffering on your account. If you promise to marry him, I shall free you!"

"I am the bride of Jesus, and his alone. I'm not afraid of you or your soldiers!" she added. "I fear nothing for Jesus' sake. There is an angel always guarding me and he will not permit Christ's handmaid to suffer any harm!"

"You are so bold!" shouted the prefect. "Guards, take this rebel to the arena!"

The prefect, his son Procop, the nobles and crowds of people were waiting at the arena when

Agnes arrived. She was led out to the center of the arena, but remained firm and refused to sacrifice to the pagan idols. She made the Sign of the Cross instead.

Full of anger, the prefect told Agnes that she would be taken to a horrible place where she would lose her innocence and purity. But she replied, "You may stain your sword with my blood, but you will never be able to profane my body, which is consecrated to Christ."

At that, Aspasian ordered the soldiers to bring Agnes to the stake to be burned to death.

The brave young girl walked up to the pile of burning wood. And the flames divided right in half, leaving Agnes untouched at the stake.

There she stood, a witness to the great King of heaven. In a loud voice, she cried, "O Jesus, if you wish, give me martyrdom. I want it. I want to come to you and never leave you."

The sight of her standing there so strong, so calm and so firm made others want to imitate her and learn more about Jesus, for whom she was willing to suffer so much. They, too, wanted to embrace her religion.

Aspasian looked around him. The crowds of people who had come to see Agnes die were frightened and restless. Many fell to their knees, shouting, "I want to be a Christian!" "I'm a Christian, too!"

They had never before seen anyone as brave as Agnes, nor anyone who had such a great faith. They knew that her religion must be truly wonderful.

Aspasian was terribly angry at what was happening. He ordered one of his soldiers to cut off Agnes' head. As Agnes knelt down, a soldier stepped forward with a gleaming blade. Many people began to cry.

Calmly, Agnes pulled back the golden wave of hair from her white neck. She bowed her head, and awaited the death blow. As the soldier lifted his blade, the crowd grew still. "Take me, O Lord," Agnes prayed. "Death is really life, the sweet life of eternity. Take me, O Lord."

The executioner was trembling; for a moment he could not even move. Then the blow fell. Agnes' head was cut off. Blood spurted forth, dyeing her dress a deep red and staining the sands of the arena. Many Christians who had come in secret now sprang forward and began to wipe up the blood with sponges and linen cloths. Savagely the guards turned upon them and many of them, too, were killed or wounded.

The body of Agnes was taken to a spot near the Nomentana Road, not far from Rome. Later on, during the reign of Emperor Constantine, a church would be built over the place where the martyr was buried.

A very old legend tells us that on the twenty-eighth of January, Agnes' father and mother were praying at her grave when Agnes appeared to them! She was in the midst of a group of holy virgins, and in her arms she held a little lamb.

"Do not cry for me, my dear ones," she said, "I am ever so happy with all the saints in heaven. And there will be as many saints as there are stars in the sky—and I will be waiting for them here with the God of the pure and the strong!"

From then on, on the twenty-first of January, after Holy Mass is celebrated in the catacombs of the Via Nomentana in Rome, lambs are blessed and then brought to the Pope. The Holy Father gives them to sisters to raise.

On Wednesday in Holy Week, these lambs are sheared and their wool is used to make the sacred pallia, which are part of the vestments given to new archbishops and patriarchs.

All this is done in memory of Agnes, to honor the little lamb of Jesus, who is waiting for us all in the eternal joys of heaven.

St. Agnes knew that purity is a virtue very precious to God. One way we can follow her example is always to dress modestly, refuse to listen to dirty jokes and watch programs or movies which are disrespectful of the human person.

St. Helen

(d. 330)

August 18

In the late third century in a small province of the western part of the Roman Empire known as Bithynia, a daughter was born to an innkeeper and his wife. The little girl was named Helen, and as she grew up she learned to help her parents care for the travelers who stopped at the inn. Like most of their neighbors, the family was not Christian; they were pagans who worshiped the gods of the Roman Empire.

One day there was tremendous excitement in the little town. A great general named Constantius Chlorus was coming with his troops. They would stay for several days at the inn. Helen helped her parents serve the soldiers their meals and made sure they were comfortable. She must have been a very gracious hostess, for General Constantius fell in love with her and asked for her hand in marriage. Her parents were sorry to lose their daughter's help, but they were happy for Helen. As the general's wife, she would be well cared for financially and would travel throughout the western part of the empire with him.

Constantius was a brilliant soldier, and won many victories. He became more and more important in the army. Then he was appointed Caesar of the western empire. That was when the blow fell. Constantius was persuaded to divorce Helen and marry the step-daughter of Emperor Maximian—for political reasons! This type of marriage was not uncommon at the time, and Helen had no choice but to agree with the divorce.

Poor Helen! She loved her husband and it was hard to leave him and their young son, Constantine. But she accepted the situation as best she could and began to live the life of an exile. Perhaps it was during this period that Helen became interested in Christianity and began to learn all she could about it.

We don't know very much about Helen's life over the next twenty years. But at last her ex-husband, Constantius, died and their son Constantine became emperor. Helen was now almost sixty-five. One of the first things that he did was to call his mother from exile. He gave her the title of empress and had coins made in her honor.

At the same time, Helen finished her instruction in the Christian faith and received Baptism. With Constantine's permission she spent great sums of money to provide food and clothing for the poor and to free many people from prison. She invited the men and women who were living as consecrated religious to dine at the palace, and she herself served them. She also had many churches built and decorated them with beautiful art work and gold. She even went to Jerusalem to oversee the building of a church on Mount Calvary.

Jerusalem had long been governed by the Romans, who had built a temple to Venus, a pagan goddess, on Mount Calvary. This was torn down at Helen's orders, and a basilica was built over the Holy Sepulchre, the place where Jesus had been buried. Helen had another basilica built on the Mount of Olives.

At Calvary, Helen began a search for the cross upon which Jesus had been crucified. Although it had been preserved by the first Christians, it had been lost when the Romans had taken over the city. Workmen began to dig, and soon three wooden crosses were discovered! In the earth nearby they found long, sharp nails.

Helen rejoiced—but which cross was the cross of Christ? She turned for help to the holy Bishop Macarius. "Your Excellency, how are we to distinguish the true cross?"

"Your Highness," he replied, "let us ask God's help in this matter."

So the bishop and the empress, together with several distinguished people, took the three crosses to the home of a lady who was ill. They said a prayer, and then touched the sick woman with the crosses. At the touch of the true cross, the lady was miraculously cured!

Helen had a beautiful church built, in which the

With Constantine's permission, Helen spent great sums of money to provide food and clothing for the poor and to free many people from prison.

relic of the true cross was kept thereafter. News of what she had done spread throughout the empire. Everywhere people learned the central fact of our faith—that Christ died on his cross to redeem us. Thousands and thousands of people were baptized in the following years. Many of these made a pilgrimage to Jerusalem, to see the holy cross for themselves.

Having been God's instrument in reawakening the Christian world, Helen died peacefully at the age of eighty. She was a woman of remarkable character who was able to accept and grow from difficult circumstances. After Helen accepted Jesus as her Lord and Savior, she spent all her energy and resources on teaching the Gospel to all.

Sometimes, even when we are young, we think it is too late to make a new start in life. Sometimes things happen to us or to our families which are beyond our control. St. Helen's life shows us that it is never too late to start over, and that there is no situation so bad that we cannot face it, finding peace and courage in our Catholic faith.

St. Martin of Tours

(317-397)

November 11

"Take me with you, Father! I'm not afraid of the long journey." Young Martin's eyes were wide with excitement as he pleaded with his father, a strong Roman officer.

"Yes," agreed Martin's father. "You will come now to live in Italy with your mother and me. You will be living in a land very dear to the gods."

"Do you still believe in the gods, Father?" Martin asked. "Don't you realize that there is only one God?"

Martin's father did not reply. He became thoughtful, wondering—as he had wondered before—who could have told his son such strange things.

The truth was that Martin, born in the Roman province of Hungary, had learned about the Christian faith from the woman who had cared for him during his early childhood. She had told him of Jesus, who had died and then rose from the tomb, and of the martyrs who had been killed because they believed that Jesus was God.

Now Martin's father was going to take him to Italy. The boy was very excited, for he knew that soon he would see Rome, which was the capital of the entire world.

It was a long journey. Mounted on a single horse, father and son rode through green valleys and up rocky mountain passes. At night they would roll up in their blankets beneath the stars. Sometimes Martin would dream of Jesus. The boy was only ten, but already he felt a strong desire to become a Christian.

Life in Rome was exciting for Martin, and soon he was celebrating his fourteenth birthday. Martin's father told him, "I have always wanted you to become a soldier like me. It is time now for you to begin your training."

Martin felt uneasy. He was not sure that he wanted to be a soldier. Yet he did not know exactly what it was that he wanted, so he entered the Roman army as his father wished. Soon he became an officer and was stationed in a Gallic city, in the country we now call France.

During his off-duty hours, Martin prayed, helped the poor and the sick and told everyone he could about Jesus of Nazareth. He was an unusual soldier indeed! Although he had begun to take instructions in the Christian faith, he was not yet baptized.

One cold night Martin was riding near the city gates when he noticed a ragged, shivering beggar standing beneath a tree. Everyone was passing right by the poor man without doing a thing to help him.

"Jesus must have intended that I should help him," thought Martin. But what could he give? He had no money with him. All that he had was his cloak. Martin drew out his sword, cut the cloak in half and gave one piece to the beggar, while he wrapped the other piece about himself. Some passers-by laughed, but others felt ashamed because they had not helped the poor beggar.

That night Martin had a dream. Jesus appeared to him surrounded by a dazzling light and wearing the half of the cloak he had given to the beggar!

Soon after that, Martin was baptized.

One day, the general ordered his army into battle. Martin approached him and said, "Until today I have served you; from now on I wish to serve only the Lord Jesus."

"You're a coward," retorted the general angrily. "You want to run out on us. Until now I thought you were the bravest of my men, but I see that you are really a coward!" And he ordered that Martin be thrown into prison.

Of course, Martin did not change his mind. After a while he was released from prison and discharged from the army. He became a pilgrim, then a hermit. He founded a community of monks and his holiness became well known. Soon the people of the city of Tours were demanding to have him for their bishop.

Martin wanted none of it. He felt that honors might keep him from being united with God. But

Martin drew out his sword, cut the cloak in half, and gave one piece to the beggar. He wrapped the other piece around himself.

the people tricked him into entering the city, and took him to the church, where he was consecrated bishop.

The honor of being a bishop did not change him at all. He lived just as plainly as before and treated himself just as sternly. He was always very kind to the poor and unfortunate. One day he saw some people mistreating a leper, and thought, Charity does not only mean giving people food and clothing; it also means giving them a smile and a good word. He went up to the leper and hugged him, saying, "Jesus is suffering in you, my brother."

One day Martin saw a group of men and women, all in chains, in the public square of a village. They were waiting to be beheaded the next day because they could not pay taxes to the powerful Count Avitius. Moved by pity, Martin hurried to the count's palace. But it was night, and every gate was shut. Kneeling before the main entrance, he began to pray: "O Lord, send an angel to bid him listen to me. O Lord, save those innocent people from such a painful death."

While Count Avitius slumbered in his huge bed and his armed guards slept peacefully nearby, an angel of the Lord, surrounded by a halo of golden light, appeared to the Count in a dream and said, "Arise, Avitius! A servant of our Lord is waiting for you outside the palace."

Avitius arose and put on his cloak. Trembling, he went out through the main gate. Martin opened his arms and embraced the fiery and powerful warrior, saying, "Come to free the poor people you have sentenced to such a cruel death. Forgive them their trespasses, and God will forgive you yours!"

Near the end of his life, Martin stopped on one of his journeys to see some monks who had come to him for guidance. He found them arguing. "If the shepherds are not united," Martin scolded, "what will become of the flock? Be at peace, brothers; be at peace."

Truly sorry, the brothers fell on their knees, and Bishop Martin blessed them. Then he said, "My sons, gladden my last days with your good deeds. I am now over eighty-years-old, and my ears hear the music of heaven. Serve God in joy!"

It was the month of November. The leaves were falling from the trees and the sun was hidden by clouds. Martin was dying, and the monks who attended him wept, for they knew how much they would miss his encouragement and guidance.

A strange and wonderful thing happend when Martin died. All the coldness and gloominess of autumn disappeared, and for three days everything was as bright and beautiful as if it had been summer. Of course, no one really needed to see that miracle in order to know that Martin had been a saint; the holiness of his whole life had been proof of that!

When St. Martin was faced with the choice of being called brave and forsaking Christ, or being called a coward and following Christ, he chose Christ. It is what we are that is important, not what people call us.

St. Monica (332-387)
August 27

St. Augustine (354-430)
August 28

Although St. Monica lived many years ago, we know a lot about her life because of the writings of her famous son, St. Augustine. In fact, St. Monica is well known for the prayers she offered for her son's conversion.

Monica was born in Tagaste, North Africa, in 332. Her parents were devout Christians and were careful to teach their children their prayers and the commandments.

When Monica was twenty-two, she married Patricius, who was much older than she. Her friends were worried about the marriage, for Monica was gentle and kind, while Patricius was hot-tempered and not Christian.

"How do you manage to get along so well with such a sharp-tempered husband?" she was asked a few years later. Monica replied that she never argued with Patricius, but was always gentle and kind with him. When he was angry, she waited until he was calm before talking to him.

She was a great peacemaker among her friends, too. Monica always told people the good things that people said about them, never the bad. Her patience and kindness even won over her mother-in-law, who had not liked her at first.

Soon, Monica and Patricius had two young sons and a daughter—Augustine, Navigius and Perpetua. Like their parents, the children had the dark skin and handsome features of the Nubians. Monica taught her children to love Jesus. She told them about the Christian martyrs and encouraged them to think often about heaven. In those days, many people waited until they were grown up before being baptized. So Monica carefully taught her children their prayers, hoping that Augustine would be baptized first, since he was the oldest.

Even though Augustine was very smart, he did not like to study. But both Patricius and Monica were determined that he should learn Latin and Greek, which all educated people knew in those days.

By now Augustine was attending school in another city, where many of his friends drank and cheated at their studies. By the time he was seventeen he had also begun to drink, cheat and steal.

Meanwhile Monica's twenty years of prayer and patience with Patricius had changed him into a new person. He became a catechumen and received Baptism. A year later, at peace with God and with his family, he died.

Even though Augustine was very smart, he did not like to study. But both Patricius and Monica, his parents, were determined that he should learn both Latin and Greek.

Augustine was now studying in Carthage. Here he learned the teaching of a religious group called the Manichaeans and soon joined them. Monica felt as if he had died. She stormed heaven with her prayers and tried to convince her son that the Manichaeans were not true Christians. But nothing that she said would convince him.

One night she had a dream in which an angel told her, "Your son is with you."

When she told Augustine about the dream, he said, "Ah, so you are going to join us!"

At once Monica replied, "No. I was not told that *I* was with you but that *you* were with me!" In spite of himself, Augustine was impressed by his mother's quick answer and remembered it often in the years which followed.

At times, Monica asked bishops and priests to speak with her son. They told her that one day he would discover for himself that the teachings of the Manichaens did not make sense. When she continued to beg one bishop to speak to Augustine, he said, "It is impossible that the child of so many prayers should perish."

When Augustine was twenty-nine, he told his mother that he was moving to Rome to teach public speaking. Monica was determined that he should not go. How could she help him if he was so far away? Finally, Augustine promised her that he would wait a few days before leaving.

But that very night he slipped away and boarded a ship for Rome! Sad and silent with grief, Monica stood on the shore and watched the billowing sails grow small in the clear morning light. She had discovered his plan too late!

From Rome, Augustine went to Milan where he often listened to St. Ambrose preach. He wasn't interested in what the bishop was saying, but Ambrose was famous for his style as a speaker. But at the same time, Augustine was learning that some teachings of the Catholic Church which he had never understood did make sense, after all. He thought more seriously about the Manichaean teachings and decided to abandon them.

Meanwhile, his faithful mother made the dangerous trip to Milan to join him. Monica was convinced that her son would become a Christian before she died. When she learned of St. Ambrose's good influence on him, she prayed even harder.

Slowly, slowly, Augustine, aided by St. Ambrose, struggled to understand the Catholic teachings. At last his mind bowed to the truth. But his will still remained in chains, for to be a Christian means to keep the commandments—and Augustine felt that it was more than he could do.

One summer day, in his garden, he fought it out within himself. One minute he wanted to give up his sinful habits, but the next minute he didn't think he could. Yet he did not want to lose God, whom he had found after so much searching. Augustine burst into tears of sorrow and begged God to help him. He heard a child's voice saying, "Take up and read."

He had left a book of St. Paul's epistles lying

nearby. He opened it and read: "put on the Lord Jesus Christ, and make no provision for the flesh, to gratify its desires" (Rm. 13:14 NRSV). At last, light and peace flooded his soul. Augustine went into the house and told his mother that at last he belonged to God.

Augustine was baptized on Easter Sunday, 387, together with some of his friends. Not long afterward the group traveled to the coast in order to sail for Africa. In the seaport of Ostia, Monica said to her son, "Now I find no joy in anything of this life. All my hopes have been accomplished."

Five days later she became sick with a fever. To her sons, Augustine and Navigius, she said, "You will bury your mother here."

"Not here, Mother," protested Navigius. "Not here in a foreign land!"

But Monica, who had often said that she wished to be buried beside Patricius, said, "Put the body anywhere; don't worry about it. I ask only this: that wherever you are, you remember me at Mass."

Nine days later Monica died.

Augustine did not cry at the funeral, for his mother had died such a holy death. But when he was alone and remembered her loving care for him and her other children, he broke down and cried for her.

"If I am your child, O my God," he wrote, "it is because you gave me such a mother!"

For the next three years, Augustine lived in Carthage with some of his friends. They lived very simply, prayed every day and worked to help the poor. In 390, Augustine was ordained a priest, and in 395, he was made the bishop of Milan. Augustine never forgot how difficult it had been for him to give up his sinful habits. He preached the Gospel every day, and helped many others learn to love Jesus.

St. Monica is a model for all mothers. No matter what Augustine did, she never stopped loving him and praying for him. Augustine is a great saint who especially helps people who find it difficult to be good.

St. Patrick
(389-461)
March 17

In the fourth century, about a hundred years after the Roman emperor Constantine had declared that Christianity could be practiced freely throughout the empire, many of the people in Britain had been Christian for several years already. Most of the Christian families were farmers and lived out in the country.

Patrick belonged to one of these Christian families. He was born around the year 389, and grew up in the fields and forests. Even though Patrick had been baptized a Christian, he had not had very much instruction in the faith. But he loved God and often said the prayers his mother had taught him while he worked out in the fields.

One day a fleet of strange warships raided the British coast. The fierce men who attacked the peaceful villages, burning and killing and carrying off prisoners, were raiders of the Irish king, "Niall of the Nine Hostages." They robbed and destroyed the farmers' homes. And they took away everyone they could capture who was young and strong. Patrick was one of the prisoners.

The hold of the raider ship was dark and crowded. Patrick lay still, cramped, hungry and aching from his bruises. He listened to the swish and thump of the waves against the ship's hull, and felt the surge and roll of the vessel as it plowed through them. Would he ever see his family again? he wondered. Were his parents alive or dead? Where were these men taking him? Perhaps he was going to Ireland, to be sold into slavery!

"Dear God, be with me, strengthen me, protect me," Patrick prayed.

The slave market was crowded and noisy. The new prisoners stood silently while their captors haggled over prices with the Irish lords and their agents. Their Gaelic phrases sounded strange to Patrick, who spoke Latin. At last a bargain was struck, and Patrick was sold into the service of a lord named Milcho. He set out with his new master toward the northern province.

They journeyed through a land of hills and bogs, where wolves howled in the forests at night. This was a much wilder land than Britain, but its ruggedness appealed to Patrick. He dreamed of escaping and getting lost in the mountains, until he could find a ship that would take him home.

The estate of Milcho was in the wildest part of the country and was very well fortified against wolves and thieves. Patrick, however, did not sleep

within its walls. He tended the sheep in the mead-
ows and the pigs in the forest, keeping them safe
from wolves and making sure that they did not
wander into the cultivated fields and destroy the
crops. Trained dogs helped him. His home at
night was a small hut, with a roaring fire blazing at
the doorway to keep away the wild animals.

That was how Patrick spent the next six years.
He became used to all kinds of weather—bronzed
by the sun and hardened against the cold. Whenever he met one of the Irish, he tried to learn more
of their language. After a while, he knew it well.

Patrick grew to love the Irish people. In some
ways they seemed very rough, but sometimes
they were gentler and kinder than any Roman
he had known. They worshiped many things in
nature, especially the sun. Their priests, called
druids, were more like magicians than the
Christian priests of Britain.

"My Lord Jesus," Patrick would pray. "Please
give them the grace to see that there are not gods
in things, but rather that there is one God who
made everything. Give me the chance to study
about you so that I can someday explain you, the
Creator of all, to these people. Please give me a
chance to escape!"

Patrick prayed often while he was alone on
the slopes of Mount Slemish, in the pastures by day
and in his hut beneath the stars at night. Before
dawn, he would leave the warmth of his fire and
go out to pray in the snow, frost or rain. Looking
back on this period of his life a few years later, he

would write, "I could feel the Spirit of God acting within me!"

One night as he slept, he heard a voice say, "Your ship is ready!" Patrick thought it must be his guardian angel. He got up and set out at once for the coast.

How excited he was to see a ship lying at anchor, preparing to sail! Patrick went up to the captain and asked if he could be taken on as a member of the crew. "No way!" retorted the captain. Perhaps he could tell that this young man was a runaway slave!

Patrick turned away sad, but began at once to pray. As he walked slowly down the beach, he heard a sudden shout, "Come back! The sailors are calling you!"

God had touched their hearts. The captain and crew welcomed Patrick aboard their ship and they set sail.

After a long and dangerous journey, Patrick finally made his way to Britain and rejoined the members of his family who were still living. How glad they were to have him home! They had thought he was dead! He stayed with them a few years, until the burning desire to bring Christ to Ireland became too much for him. He decided to go to France, then called Gaul, to learn more about the Catholic faith from St. Martin, the bishop of Tours.

Sadly, Patrick had only spent a few months with this holy man when the elderly bishop died. Patrick went on to Auxerre and became a monk, joining

St. Martin's friend, St. Germanus. He studied diligently, and eventually was ordained a priest. But his guardian angel, speaking for the Irish people, told him in a dream that Ireland was calling him. Patrick heard the voices telling him: "We beg you, holy Patrick, return and walk among us!"

Patrick was no longer young when the sign from God came to him. But sixty years of preaching lay ahead of him. Most men couldn't have done it, but Patrick still had his youthful enthusiasm.

Germanus gave Patrick a blessing, and so did Pope Celestine. The Pope had already sent a missionary named Palladius to Ireland, but that mission had been unsuccessful. Now Patrick was to take his place. Before he went, he was consecrated first bishop of Ireland. They both knew that he might never return to Rome.

Patrick built the first Christian church in Ireland at a place called Saul—the same spot where he would be buried sixty years later.

He pushed on toward Tara, the palace of the Irish kings. He was in sight of it on Easter Eve, 433, when he and his companions stopped on the hill of Slane to celebrate the Easter vigil. Patrick lit the Paschal fire. It cut the darkness like a knife—the only light that could be seen in the dim, silent night.

Then, from the direction of Tara, angry cries split the darkness. A few moments later, the galloping of hooves and the rumble of chariots could be heard. What was happening? Patrick and his comrades turned to face the horsemen.

Patrick listened to the swish and thump of the waves beating against the ship's hull as it plowed through them. Would he ever see his family again?

What had happened was this: Ireland's pagan lords had been celebrating their biggest feast—the Feis of Tara. The druid priests had proclaimed that on that night no fire should be lit in all of Ireland before the fire of Tara. Without knowing it, Patrick had disobeyed their law.

And so King Laeghaire and his nobles came thundering up to Patrick. The bishop faced them calmly.

"Who are you? How dare you break the law?"

In a ringing voice Patrick began to explain. He told of his purpose in coming to Ireland. He told the great mysteries of the Christian religion, using the three-leafed shamrock to describe the Holy Trinity.

Naturally the druids challenged Patrick, and a terrible struggle followed between the magical powers of the druids and the miracles of the saint. In the end, Patrick won. Laeghaire was not converted, but he gave the bishop permission to preach about Jesus Christ in all of Ireland.

There are many stories about St. Patrick's journeys through Ireland and the many conversions that he made. Wherever he went, he built chapels and put up crosses as a reminder of our Lord's passion. It is said that he remembered the location of every roadside cross and paid a visit to each one whenever he had to pass near it—in order to make an act of love for the crucified Savior.

One year, at the beginning of Lent, Patrick was traveling along the western coast of Ireland.

Following an inspiration, he climbed the slopes of a rocky crag to spend some time in prayer. For forty days, between the desolate moorland and the wild sea, Patrick fasted and prayed. He begged God that all the people of Ireland would come to believe in his divine son, Jesus Christ, and be baptized. He prayed for all the people alive then, and for all the Irish people not yet born. Was it too much to ask for? Not for Patrick. He had always had a way of "taking heaven by storm." He prayed with such faith and love that God never refused him—and so it was this time, too. After many years of preaching and teaching, all of Ireland had become Christian.

On a cold March day in 461, Patrick died. He had converted an entire nation to Christ. That nation has remained Christian for over 1,500 years.

The course of history was changed because Patrick wanted to do good to his enemies. Let us, too, see the image of Christ in those who dislike us. Let us pray for their good.

St. Brigid
(d. 525)

February 1

Brigid was born during St. Patrick's lifetime—when Ireland was half-pagan and half-Christian. Her father was Duffy, a pagan chieftain, and her mother was Brocessa, a Christian slave. Shortly before Brigid's birth, Duffy sold Brocessa, with the understanding that the child would be returned to him in a few years. Brocessa had the child baptized at the first opportunity and taught her about Jesus and Mary.

When Brigid returned to be a slave in her father's household, she acted differently than the other slaves. If a hungry dog came whining to her while she was cooking, he got a piece of meat; if a poor person came by while she was tending the sheep, Brigid would often give away one of the woolly little lambs. She seemed to forget that she was Duffy's slave, and acted like she was his daughter.

One day Duffy called her: "Come here with me in the chariot."

Brigid scrambled in happily and sat next to her stern-faced master. A flick of the whip and off they went.

"I'm not doing this to make you happy," Duffy said abruptly.

Brigid gazed up at him wide-eyed.

"I'm going to sell you to the king. You've been too generous with things that don't belong to you."

Brigid said nothing. How could she explain that it was impossible for her to refuse someone who needed help?

They stopped before a grim fortress. "Wait here," growled Duffy, and he went in to speak with the king. Brigid sat quietly in the chariot, watching the horses' tails brushing away the flies. Then she saw a poor leper walking down the road. He came up to the chariot and Brigid looked down at him. His face was all eaten away by the horrible disease. His sad eyes seemed to be pleading.

"I have nothing to give him," she thought.

But there on the seat beside her was Duffy's sword—a beautiful jeweled sword with a sharp blade. She took it and handed it to the leper. He thanked her and hurried off with the splendid gift.

When Duffy returned to the chariot, he noticed the sword was gone right away.

"What have you done with it?" he asked, trying to remain calm.

"A leper came by..."

Duffy let out a roar like an angry lion. "A leper! You gave my jeweled sword to a *leper*! That sword was worth a fortune!"

"I know," replied Brigid calmly. "That's why I

gave it to God."

All her life Brigid saw God in people who were in need. That was why she felt she had to be generous to everyone.

Duffy pulled Brigid down from the chariot and rushed her into the fortress. "There," he sputtered angrily to the king. "There! She's done it again! She's given my famous jeweled sword to a leper. You see now why I will not keep her!"

The king was a Christian. He looked gravely down at Brigid, who stared back with big, round eyes. Suddenly, the king smiled. "She is a Christian," he said, "and a good one. You should be proud of her, Duffy. Take her back home with you, but give her her freedom. After all, she is your daughter."

Duffy gulped in dismay. If Brigid were freed, she might give away everything he owned!

As Duffy was driving home with the little girl beside him, he had an idea. Yes, he would free Brigid, for she was as fiery and independent as he. And he was proud of her in a way. Hadn't the king himself praised her? Nevertheless, he would have Brigid marry as soon as possible. That way she would no longer be able to give away his wealth!

"Father," said Brigid one day, "I wish to see my mother, Brocessa. May I visit her?"

"No," replied Duffy.

But Brigid went anyway, with Duffy-like stubbornness. Her mother, she knew, was sick and overworked. Brigid took her mother's place grinding corn, churning butter and tending cows.

Of course, Brigid's generosity went with her.

Duffy pulled Brigid down from the chariot and rushed her into the castle. "There!" he sputtered angrily to the king. "She's done it again! She's given my famous jeweled sword to a leper. This is why I will not keep her!"

Even though the butter and milk and cream were not hers, she could not help giving them "to God"—to the poor people who came daily. And God rewarded her by miraculously keeping the dairy stocked with butter and milk! The master of Brigid's mother was so amazed at this that he looked on Brigid as a saint (although he himself was still a pagan), and he offered to give her the whole dairy and all the cows.

"No, give my mother her freedom," begged Brigid. And this the good man did. Later, he became a Christian.

Brigid brought her mother to live with relatives and then returned to Duffy. She was now in her late teens. She was tall and strong with rosy cheeks and peaceful eyes. Duffy thought she would make someone a fine wife.

He decided on a poet, for poets in those days were educated, wealthy and highly respected. Brigid would have a high position if she married a poet.

Naturally, Brigid had other ideas. As soon as she met the poet of her father's choice, she told him where he could find a wonderful girl who would make him a fine wife. She told him she would pray for that intention. And the poet went on his way.

Duffy was furious, but Brigid was stubborn. "I'm going to be a virgin of Christ," she told him, and what could the irate father do but give in? After all, it was his own hardheadedness she had.

When Patrick had come to Ireland a few years before, he had started to form monasteries for men right away. But there were not yet any convents for women. Many young women wanted to consecrate their virginity to Christ, and did so. But they continued to live with their parents and brothers and sisters. They prayed, helped the poor and did needlework for the new churches Patrick had built. But their own families did not understand them. Patrick once wrote, "They do this without their fathers' consent, and suffer persecution and misunderstanding from their relatives."

Brigid had seven good friends who also wanted to consecrate their lives to God. "Let us live together in community as the monks do," she proposed to them. "Let us go to Bishop Mel. He will receive our vows in Christ's name." And the bishop gladly did so.

By this time, the fiery Duffy had changed his mind. He gave Brigid the financial support and political backing she needed to begin several convents all over Ireland. Whether or not he himself became a Christian, we do not know, but in view of all the other triumphs in Brigid's life, we can assume that he did.

Brigid also had acquired the friendship and support of the Irish bishops. Patrick had died a few years before and they saw in her much of his spirit. They encouraged her missionary labors. From these first Irish bishops, Brigid learned how Patrick had thought and felt about various situations that came up and she tried to do what Patrick would have done.

Those early convents were little groups of huts, made of clay, poles and branches, which the young women built themselves. Around the group of huts they would put up a large stone or earthen wall or a hedge of thick bushes. As soon as Brigid had one community set up, she would leave a sister in charge and, taking one or two others with her, she would go to a new spot and build another convent. Like Patrick, she traveled all over Ireland.

Brigid traveled in a little chariot, drawn by two horses. It was a dangerous way to travel on the bumpy roads, and at least twice she was thrown out of the chariot. Once the horse ran away and stopped at the edge of a cliff!

Brigid certainly had courage, but she was best known for her cheerfulness and generosity. Now that she was a religious sister, she gave even more generously to the poor than she had as a child. On one occasion the sisters were expecting company, and they had carefully put aside milk and butter, bread and meat for their dinner. But who should appear at the convent gates but a group of beggars! Brigid could not resist and gave them all the food she had prepared for the guests.

Once a wealthy lady brought Brigid a basket of apples. Brigid was delighted. She took all the apples and distributed them to some lepers who were standing hopefully near the convent gate.

"I brought them for you, not for those lepers!" the lady exclaimed.

"What is mine is theirs," said Brigid calmly.

Everyone got a royal welcome in Brigid's convents. Bishops, monks, young girls from the neighboring farms, all were fed with whatever provisions the sisters had on hand. And somehow they never ran out of food. Brigid was always giving "to God" and God always seemed to match her generosity.

Brigid loved to pray and to meditate on the lives of Jesus and Mary. Indeed, she loved our Lady so much and imitated her so well that people began to call her "the Mary of the Gael." Often Brigid prayed and meditated while she milked the convent's cows, churned the butter or tended the sheep.

Yet Brigid also loved and encouraged studies. In Kildare, the most famous of the convents she founded, women scholars continually studied books of religion and science. Kildare became famous for the beautiful workmanship of its decorated manuscripts, bells and chalices, which went to churches all over Ireland.

But Brigid was not only known for her hard work and prayers. She also liked to play jokes and listen to music. She loved to see people having a good time. And like other Irish saints, she was fond of animals. She saw God in everything around her and was forever thanking him for the beauties of creation.

When Brigid was born, Ireland was half-pagan and half-Christian. At the time of her death, around the year 525, Ireland was completely Christian and had begun to send out missionaries to other lands. They went with the spirit of Brigid—with enthusiasm, courage and a love that embraced the world.

Someone once said that a sad saint is no saint at all. Like St. Brigid, we should see God's beauty in everything around us and thank him joyfully, always.

St. Benedict
(d. 547)

March 21

At the age of fourteen, the young Roman noble Benedict had already become disgusted with the lawlessness and corruption of sixth-century Rome. It seemed that whoever had the biggest weapons or fought the hardest ruled the land. He asked his parents' permission to live at their country villa, where he could pray and study in peace. The fresh air and calm was a welcome change from the corrupt city of Rome. But Benedict felt himself drawn more and more to a life of total seclusion and prayer.

A life of prayer, fasting and penance, far away from all the corruption and distractions: this was what Benedict felt was God's will for him. The elderly governess who lived with him would miss him, he knew, but his desire to leave was so strong that one night he left her a note and softly slipped away from the villa. He planned to go far into the wild, rugged countryside that we know today as Subiaco.

He walked on and on, through the night. The going became rougher and he found himself in rocky mountains. This was just the sort of country he was looking for! Benedict smiled.

Suddenly a deep, silent valley opened before him. There would be no people here, he thought. No one would want to live in such desolation except someone like Benedict, who wanted only God and wished to leave all else.

Benedict spotted a cave among the rocks that looked perfect. It seemed to him that God was guiding his steps in that direction and he approached the cavern with a joyful heart. "May you be praised, my Lord and my God!" he exclaimed.

"Now and forever, let us praise the Lord!" a voice replied.

Benedict was startled. He looked all over. He had thought that he was alone, far from any other human creature. Yet a few feet away from him stood an old man—a hermit with a very kind face!

"I wanted to live in solitude," Benedict murmured.

"You will easily be able to do that," replied the hermit. "But tell me, who are you?"

The boy told the story of his life and of his great desire to leave the world and draw close to God. The holy hermit understood this very well, for God had inspired him, too, in much the same way. He could see that Benedict sincerely wanted to withdraw from the world not because he was afraid of the world, but because he wanted to live a life dedicated to prayer. Yet, thought the hermit, Benedict is still very young...and the life of a hermit was very difficult.

"Listen," the old hermit said. "I'll leave a bell nearby with a cord attached to it. From time to time I'll come by with some food, so when the bell rings you will know that there is something to eat waiting for you outside. That way you will not have to speak or be disturbed by anything."

Benedict was very grateful; no other arrangement could have pleased him more. Happily he stood at the mouth of the cave and watched his new friend stride away along the rocky slope. The hermit turned once to wave good-bye, then he was gone.

Poverty and privation, cold and discomfort, darkness and dampness—these were to be Benedict's life. But he scarcely noticed them, so absorbed was he in prayer, in reading his Bible and in reflecting on the goodness of God and the beauty of creation. He barely noticed as the seasons changed.

―――――

Three years passed and Benedict no longer received food from the old hermit. He grew hungrier and hungrier, but no welcome jingle sounded from the bell. Perhaps the old hermit has died, Benedict thought.

But on Easter Sunday a marvelous event occurred a few miles from Benedict's cave. A good priest was preparing his holiday dinner when he heard a voice say, "While you are eating, my servant Benedict is almost dying of starvation in the cave of Subiaco!"

The priest did not hesitate. He put all his food

into a sack, slung the sack over his shoulder, and set out for the cave of Subiaco. "Good health to you, brother!" he greeted Benedict. "I come in the name of the Lord!"

What a joyous Easter feast the two men of God had. How grateful the young hermit was for God's goodness to him!

The priest returned to his parish, but Benedict was not left alone for long. Others who were also tired of the world and its empty promises came to the young hermit and asked him to tell them how he lived so that they could do the same. Benedict accepted them as brothers and formed them into communities of monks. By the year 520, twelve monasteries dotted the rugged valley. Twelve monks lived in each one, with one man appointed to govern each group as Benedict instructed them.

From the beginning, Benedict had insisted that all of the monks not only spend long hours in prayer, but that they also work hard. "Work and prayer" became Benedict's motto. In those days, many who called themselves monks lived very lazy lives and seemed to have forgotten Jesus' example of poverty and charity. One day a group of men dressed as monks came toward Benedict's cave. He could see that they were not used to climbing up hills. When they reached him, they explained that their own abbot had recently died. They wanted Benedict to come and be their new spiritual father.

Benedict thanked them for coming, but he shook his head and told them, "No. I am afraid that my way of life and yours are too different. We would not be happy with one another." But the monks insisted. At last he agreed to go with them. It wasn't very long, however, before this group of lazy men began to complain. Benedict made them work too hard and pray too much—but how could they get rid of him? At last they decided to serve him a glass of poisoned wine at the next community meal. With Benedict dead, they would again be free to live as they pleased.

The meal came and the glass of wine was set at Benedict's place. As he always did, Benedict raised his hand over the food and drink to bless it. As he did this, the glass of poisoned wine shattered. The holy man realized what their plans had been, and he said quietly, "I told you that my way of life was different from yours. Now I will no longer live among you and you are no longer obliged to live according to my teachings. Do as you please." And he left them.

This time, Benedict traveled to the hill town of Actinium. It was a beautiful place, set way up on the mountain of Cassino. A few years before it had been destroyed by the Goths. The people who lived there had returned to pagan gods and lived almost without laws or order. Benedict began to teach them about Jesus, and showed them how to till the soil and plant their fields. Soon almost everyone had been baptized and returned to Christianity. They destroyed the temple and altar which they had built to Apollos and in its place built a Catholic church. Benedict erected a monastery nearby which quickly filled up.

The men who joined Benedict were from every group of people who lived in Italy at the time—

*As Benedict raised his hand to bless the food and drink, the glass of
poisoned wine shattered.*

wealthy Romans, peasant farmers and strong Gothic warriors. Few of the men were priests; most, like Benedict, were ordinary people who had grown disillusioned with the violence and immorality of the time. They wished to live quiet lives of hard work, charity and prayer. In those days, which we now call the "Dark Ages," the monastery of Montecassino became a center for farming, refuge, learning and worship. The monks copied important literary works from Greek and Latin. The people from the countryside gathered there for prayer and learned to farm their lands and care for their herds.

It was also at Montecassino that Benedict wrote down his rule of life. This rule became the standard way of life for all of the monks and nuns of the western world, and many religious still live by it today. "Work and prayer" remains a way for many people to organize their lives and find God in the midst of everyday demands.

Early in the year 547, Benedict told his monks, "Brothers, God is calling me!" He got a high fever. With great love he received Holy Communion for the last time, and then died. Although St. Benedict has been dead for many centuries, the world has not forgotten the great example of simplicity and prayer which he left.

"Pray and work" is the secret of success. If we want to do well in something, we must work hard at it, but we must also pray for God's help.

St. Kevin
(d. 618)

June 3

St. Kevin lived about a hundred years after the great saints Patrick and Brigid, at a time when Ireland was called a land of saints and scholars. He was baptized by St. Cronan, and a legend says that angels could be seen around the font during the ceremony. Because of this, he is often called Kevin of the Angels.

Kevin's parents were wealthy nobles. They could easily have hired tutors for the boy so that he could grow up among the comforts of home and become a warrior and chieftain. But Kevin's parents knew that a good education is better than comfort, and learning to serve God is the best kind of wealth.

So they sent Kevin away to study under a wise old monk named Petroc. The boy was seven when he started school, and nineteen when he finished. By that time he was certain about what he wanted to do with his life: he would become a priest.

That meant more studying, but to Kevin it was worth it. He continued to study under the stern guidance of his uncle Eugene, a serious, hard-working priest who expected students to measure up to his standards. Kevin found it hard at times, but he didn't give up. At last the great day arrived: ordination!

After his ordination, Kevin felt a great need to be alone with God for a while. He wanted time to pray and to think about the many things he had learned during his long years of study. And he still wasn't sure just what type of work he should do now that his studies were finished.

Into the hills of Wicklow he trudged until he reached a wild valley where two lonely lakes mirrored the sky. On one side rose a rocky crag; on the other, a green mountain. The place was called Glendalough, which means the valley of the two lakes.

For seven years Kevin lived there, eating berries and nuts and wild plants, meditating and praying. He had a great love for nature, and even the wild animals came to him without fear and shared his crude hut and glowing fire.

One day a farmer named Dima came walking through the glen. He was a pagan, but he had heard that a holy hermit lived at Glendalough and he was curious. He asked Kevin to tell him about the God he prayed to out there in the valley. Of course, Kevin was eager to do so. Simply and clearly, he told Dima about the beautiful mysteries of the Christian faith. Kevin told

Kevin trudged into the hills of Wicklow until he reached a wild spot where two lonely lakes mirrored the sky. On one side rose a rocky crag; on the other, a green mountain.

Dima about the one God who made everything from nothing and keeps us in existence. He told him about Adam and Eve and their sin of pride and disobedience. He told him about Jesus, the Son of God, who became human like us and who suffered and died for our sins. He explained to Dima how God lives with us, about God's grace and the promise of life after death with God for all eternity.

Dima listened spellbound. At last he said, "Will you come down to my farm and teach my children what you have told me?"

Kevin hesitated. "I will pray about it," he said. But almost at once he heard the answer in his heart. This was what God wanted him to do with his life. The next day he went down to the farm with Dima and his children.

Soon Kevin was teaching not just one family, but dozens of men and boys from the nearby villages and farms.

"We must build a school," he decided.

Rocks were plentiful and the farmers helped Kevin build a monastery in the solitude of Glendalough. Other monks came to help teach the children of the farmers and the children of kings and chieftains who heard of the learning and holiness of Kevin of Glendalough. The rich and the poor lived and worked and studied together, and everyone was treated alike.

More buildings were added to the little settlement, including a sturdy stone tower with a cone-shaped top. It became a famous landmark.

People came from all over Ireland to tell Kevin their problems and ask his help in solving them.

Kevin's work was very demanding, and he no longer had long hours for quiet prayers. So every Lent, Kevin went up to the mountain to live alone in a cave for forty days to reflect on his life and work as a priest. He tried to do some penances for those times that he felt he could have done better, and he would make strong resolutions for the future. Then he would pray for God's help to become always more like Jesus in order to help others.

The years slipped by. Kevin's hair and beard grew white, but his eyes still sparkled, and his step was as quick and firm as ever. He watched his students grow up. Many of them he blessed in marriage. He baptized their babies. Many chose to become monks, priests or nuns, and some of them traveled to foreign lands as missionaries. Even as he felt himself growing older and tired, Kevin desired to go on a missionary journey.

"What do you think of the idea?" he asked his very good friend Kieran, bishop of Clonmacnoise.

Kieran understood Kevin's desire. But he also knew that sometimes it is better for one missionary to train many others than to leave his students and go to the missions himself.

"Birds do not hatch their eggs while they are flying," he said.

Kevin understood. Not to go was a sacrifice, but he knew that Keran was right. He would stay at Glendalough, teaching and advising all who came to him. Then one peaceful June night in 618, his soul sped heavenward to join the angels and saints around God's throne. From heaven, Kevin prays for missionaries wherever they may be.

St. Kevin knew the importance of sharing his knowledge and faith with others. If people ask us a question about our faith, we should try to give them a clear and correct answer.

St. Columban
(543-615)
November 23

It was autumn and the old monk could feel it in his bones. The leaves on the trees were still too thick for him to see what was going on in the valley, but he knew that the other monks were down there. Today they would be working in the vineyards and olive groves, gathering the figs and the almonds, getting ready for the days of icy winds and swirling snows. There wouldn't be much food this winter, but the monks fasted so often that their supplies would last until spring.

How were the other monasteries doing? the old man wondered. He thought of each one, hidden among the forested mountains of eastern Gaul. It had been years since he had seen many of them. The old monk pondered his memories in silence, and then turned back into his cave. During the past two years he had spent many hours at prayer in this retreat. Now he felt he would soon leave the cave for good.

He had lived a long and active life. Columban thought back over the years to when he was a young man in his home in distant Ireland. There he had made the decision to become a monk, and he had stuck to it all these years. He remembered the wise old hermit woman who had advised him to leave his home and follow his desire to serve God as a missionary. And he remembered how difficult it had been to leave his mother when he went to live and study at the monastery of Bangor. There he stayed until he was nearly forty-five, finally being sent out across the sea as a missionary to Gaul.

With twelve companions, Columban, who was a priest by then, had packed a few books and sacred vessels and set sail for the European Continent. From Brittany, where more men joined them, they started out for eastern Gaul, tramping along the crumbling Roman roads which were almost closed off by the thick forests.

The forests were dangerous for many reasons. In them there were runaway soldiers and slaves, wild animals and gangs of thieves. The once glorious Roman Empire had fallen into chaos, and now groups of violent men led by various warlords governed the land. Everywhere there were signs of war and destruction; there seemed to be no law or government anywhere. Christian towns now lay in ruins and many of the people had returned to their pagan beliefs.

At last, Columban and his companions were welcomed into Burgundy, the territory of King Gunthram. There, in a wild and desolate valley,

*The forests were dangerous for many reasons. In them there were
runaway soldiers and slaves, wild animals and gangs of thieves.*

they converted an abandoned fort into the monastery of Annegray and built a chapel.

The monks soon became friends with the peasant farmers in the area. Many of them remembered when they were children and their parents had been Christians. Now they wanted to learn about Jesus and receive Baptism. Several young men asked to join Columban and the others and live as monks, too.

The monks led a hard life. They spent long hours teaching and instructing the people. It had been many years since there had been any schools. For food, they gathered wild berries and roots, and fished in the nearby lakes. In between all of this, they spent hours praying together in the chapel, or off alone in the hillsides. Father Columban had found a cave overlooking the river which made a perfect hermitage for the times he wanted a few days of quiet prayer. Often, the monks would pray for long hours with their arms stretched straight out in the form of a cross. This was a life for strong and courageous people, and Columban kept a careful eye on the health of the monks.

Soon it was time to start another monastery. Father Columban followed the river downstream about eight miles until he came upon the ruins of Luxeuil, a Roman town which had been destroyed by the Huns. Here, he told the monks, they would build the next monastery.

With joy they set to work. They cut away underbrush, felled trees and hauled stones away from the garden area. They rebuilt the town walls and constructed a church, a school and a number of little one-room houses in which the monks would live. Not long afterwards, they had to build yet another monastery a short distance away, in Fontaines. Soon the three communities housed sixty monks and over two hundred students, mostly noblemen's sons. They came to the monks to study math, religion and the sciences, but they also learned self-discipline, honesty and kindness. Men and women came from the surrounding countryside to spend a few weeks with the monks. While there, they were fed and cared for by the monks. And they also received the Sacrament of Reconciliation and learned more about living as Christians. It had been many years since some of them had talked to a priest!

Now, almost sixty years since St. Benedict had written down his rule for monks, Columban wrote down his rule. Columban's rule emphasized the need for frequent fasting and other physical penances which the Irish monks and their disciples had always considered important. But the main purpose of monastic life, he wrote, was to learn to love God with all one's mind, heart and strength and to love one's neighbor as oneself for the love of God.

We must think often about God and heaven, Columban taught. Everything that the monks had or did should somehow help them to be more like Christ and help them to reach heaven. Columban was convinced of the truth of his words. His whole life had been a challenge to keep himself thinking and acting always more like Jesus. And with his stubbornness and hot temper, it had not always been easy!

As abbot, Columban was the spiritual father of all the monks. He corrected them when necessary, just as a good father does. He watched over their spiritual life and their physical health. Above all, he came to love them very deeply as his brothers in Christ. One day, Father Columban knelt in the church at Luxeuil praying and weeping because one of the monks was dying.

As he prayed and wept, he heard someone come up behind him. "Father Abbot," came the whisper, "Brother Columban is calling for you!"

The sick monk's name was also Columban, and he was one of the twelve men who had come with the abbot from Ireland. "Father," pleaded the younger Columban, "why are you keeping me in this life with your prayers? They are standing by to lead me away." The sick man glanced about as if he saw angels surrounding him. "But they are prevented by your prayers and tears. Loose these bonds so that the heavenly kingdom may receive me."

Now Father Columban realized how selfish he had been. At once he had the young man anointed and heard his confession for the last time. The younger Columban's soul sped away in peace. Sixteen more times Father Columban would witness the death of one of his spiritual sons.

About twenty years after Father Columban's arrival in Gaul, he got himself in deep trouble. Until that time he had been friendly with the many kings of Burgundy. He was friends even with those who led very bad lives. Often he had urged the young King Theodoric to change his sinful ways. Even though the young man had listened respectfully, he continued doing as he pleased. Then came the day that the abbot paid a visit to Queen Brunhilda, Theodoric's grandmother. The two had always been on good terms. But this time he said something in his usual honest way which offended Brunhilda deeply. After the abbot departed, the queen began to urge the king and the local bishop to drive Columban and the monks out of Gaul.

One day Theodoric rode up to Columban's monastery with a band of soldiers. He had the abbot seized and taken to Besancon, a city forty miles to the south. He permitted only one monk to go with Columban. Although Columban and his companion were allowed to walk freely around Besancon, the bridge and road leading to Luxeuil were guarded. People were kind to the prisoners, for they regarded them as holy and innocent men. Then, one Sunday morning, Columban looked out over the river and saw no guards on the bridge. He and his companion set out quickly for home.

Hardly had Father Columban returned to Luxeuil when a band of horsemen thundered up to the monastery gates. They had orders to search the place, they said.

The soldiers searched, but all the monks looked alike to them. The captain alone recognized Columban, seated in the doorway of the church reading a book as if nothing at all were happening. The captain pretended not to see him. "Let us go," he told his men. "This man is hidden by divine power."

The soldiers got on their horses and rode off.

A few days later, while they were singing the psalms, Columban and his monks again heard the clattering of horses' hooves and the clash of steel weapons. "Man of God," called a voice, "we beg you to obey the king's commands and ours. Leave this land and go back to where you came from." The soldiers poured into the church.

Columban replied slowly, "I do not think it would please the Creator if a man were to return to his home land once he has left it for the love of Christ."

The soldiers understood. But they knew that Theodoric could have them killed if they did not obey his orders. "Father, take pity on us," they begged. "We do not want to take you away by force, but if you do not leave Luxeuil, we shall die!"

"And yet," said Columban gently, "many times I have said that I shall never leave Luxeuil unless I am taken by force."

"Father, we do not wish to commit such a crime. These are not our wishes but the king's commands."

Columban was moved with compassion. Turning to his monks, he said, "I shall go with them." He began to walk out of the church, the soldiers pressing around him and the monks trailing behind.

Suddenly he stopped and prayed, "O Eternal

Creator, prepare a place where we, your people, may serve you forever." The monks gathered about him. "Do not lose hope," Columban told them gently. "Continue to sing the praises of Almighty God. Because of this sacrifice we are making, many others will be inspired to join us." He paused. These men were like sons to him. How could he leave them?

"If any of you wish to come with me, you may."

A clamor arose. All of them wanted to come; no one wanted to be separated from the abbot.

"No," replied the soldiers. "The king has ordered that only the monks from Ireland and Brittany shall go with him."

And so Columban left his beloved Luxeuil, accompanied by only a few monks. The soldiers went with them all the way down to the River Loire where they all boarded a small boat bound toward the sea. It was, in all, a journey of about six-hundred miles. In the cities where they stopped, many people came out to greet the monks, for they had heard of their holiness. Finally the little band reached Nantes, a port from which they were to sail for Ireland.

Columban sat down and wrote a long, anxious letter to his community at Luxeuil and their new abbot, Attala. More than anything else, he urged them to preserve their unity of spirit and charity with one another. He reminded the monks that their own sufferings were a share in the passion of Christ.

Confident that they had accomplished their mission, Columban's guards had left him. They were not present to witness the fierce storm which blew up and caught the little ship just before it was to set sail. The winds were so strong that the ship was lifted right out of the water and set down on dry ground. The superstitious captain and crew unloaded the monks and their baggage at once, and immediately the winds died down. The next day the ship sailed without Columban and his men!

To Columban this was a sign that God did not want him to go to Ireland. Almost at once he and his monks were on the road, trekking northeast toward the safety of the kingdom of Theodoric's brother—and enemy—Theodebert. They moved quickly and secretly. It was a tiring march of hundreds of miles over rough roads.

In Metz, King Theodebert welcomed Columban kindly, for he was only too happy to help the monks whom his brother had exiled. He offered them land on which to build a monastery.

"Since I have decided to journey to Italy, your Majesty," replied the abbot, "I shall look for a suitable place along the route, and build there."

In a boat loaned by the king, he set off up the Rhine with his companions. By this time, several monks had come from Luxeuil to join them. They traveled up the river and into Lake Zurich, which is in present-day Switzerland. The people were Alemanians, a Germanic tribe. Unlike their cousins, the Franks, they had never become Christians. They worshiped earth, sky, trees, mountains and rivers.

The missionaries built huts on the lakeshore,

and began to preach among the Alemanians. The people listened to the monks and became their friends, but not many of them were convinced enough to become baptized. At last one of the monks, named Gall, grew impatient. With more zeal than prudence, he set fire to the pagan temples and threw the idols into the lake. The people were furious, and a wave of hostility surged through the town. Soon Columban was told of a plot to kill Gall.

"We must move," the abbot told his men. "These people will no longer listen to us. Perhaps in the country around Lake Constance we will have more success."

They started out once again, going northeastward and traveling swiftly past one ruined Roman town after another. At last they reached the broad pale green lake which lay in the middle of wooded hills. A small Christian community lived on its southern shore. The pastor welcomed them eagerly and helped them search for a site for a monastery.

They settled on the ruins of the town of Bregenz. It was a good location, with rich soil and a lovely view. With axes and spades, the monks began to clear and cultivate the land. They built small houses for themselves. They removed some bronze idols from St. Aurelia's Chapel nearby and rededicated the church and consecrated the altar.

Gall, spokesman for the group because of his skill with languages, attempted to teach a curious crowd of pagans about Jesus Christ. He tried to explain to them that idol worship was totally senseless. At the end of his sermon, apparently having already forgot the trouble he had caused at their previous site, he took three idols, broke them and threw them into the lake. Some of the people went away angry, but others asked for more instruction.

Happy to be settling down at last, the monks built a monastery and planted an orchard. Gall wove nets and soon provided fish for the community. He also acted as interpreter for Columban as he tramped through the forest looking for more people to instruct in the Christian faith.

Two years passed quickly; then some of the pagans went to the local duke and told him a lie about the monks driving away animals. The duke flew into a rage, for he enjoyed hunting. At once he ordered the foreigners to leave the region. But before they could go, two of them were ambushed and murdered. Sorrowfully, their brothers buried them and prepared to flee.

Some of them returned to Gaul. Others started new monasteries here and there in the wilderness. And others, including Columban, continued on their way toward Italy.

Thinking of all these adventures kept Columban deep in thought for a long time. When he realized that the sun would soon be setting, he started down the hill to Bobbio. The monastery there had been built on land given them by the Lombard king of northern Italy. As Columban walked, he realized that his death was very near. He took one last glance back at his familiar cave, then leaned forward on his walking stick and continued down the mountain. Columban could not know that this monastery in Bobbio would become one of the greatest cultural centers of Europe. He did not know that within fifty years his five monasteries would have multiplied into almost a hundred, and that many bishops would receive their early training within those walls. He did not know either that on a chilly November day, Gall, who was at a monastery hundreds of miles away, would tell his deacon, "Prepare the vessels and vestments for Mass. I have learned in a vision that my father and teacher Columban has died. We will offer Mass this morning for the repose of his soul."

Sometimes we are faced with a choice between something we know we ought to do and something we would enjoy doing. When that happens, let us remember Columban and the many sacrifices he made as a missionary. He will give us courage and help us to do the right thing.

St. Dymphna
(d. 650)

May 15

Dymphna sank into her bed, totally exhausted. It had been a long week since her mother, the queen, had died. Now, at last, the funeral was over.... Her thoughts turned to Father Gerebran, the old priest and good friend of her mother. At least he had been able to secretly bless the body, even though her pagan father, Damon, had forbidden anything but the traditional druid burial rites. Dymphna shivered as her mind pictured Damon. These long months while her mother had been ill had been difficult. Damon's dark moods and unpredictable temper had grown worse and worse. Her mother had always been able to pull him out of his dark thoughts, but now.... Fifteen-year-old Dymphna felt hot tears coming down her cheeks. Fingering the prayer beads she kept under her pillow, she prayed, "Lord God, Almighty Creator of all that is good, healer of every sickness and light in every darkness, give your peace to this family.

And keep the soul of my mother in peace forever. Amen."

The next weeks were not easy at the castle in Armaugh, the northeastern section of Ireland. Damon came and went at odd hours, sometimes silent, other times hot-tempered and mean to the servants. More and more Dymphna felt his eyes following her whenever she was in a room with him. Even though Damon was her father, his gaze left her with an uncomfortable feeling. Something was happening to Damon and she couldn't figure out what it was. Then, one evening Damon came home in a dark mood, the familiar smell of strong liquor on his breath. "Dymphna," he roared, "come and sing to me, Darling."

Dymphna trembled. Damon used to call her mother to sing to him when he felt one of his black moods coming on. Slowly she went into the room. "What shall I sing, Father?" she asked, standing near the door.

"Come closer, Darling. Come, sit on my lap and sing." Damon's voice was gentle now. Yet there was an uneasiness in the air that frightened Dymphna. She thought of calling her friend, Father Gerebran, who lived in another section of the castle, then remembered that he would be gone for the next three or four days. Trembling, she slowly walked toward Damon. About two feet away, she halted. Then she gave out a terrified gasp as she saw a strange glimmer in her father's eyes. Damon stretched out his strong arm and grabbed Dymphna, pulling her onto his lap.

"Sing!" he commanded.

Dymphna swallowed hard, then started one of the familiar melodies her mother had taught her. As she sang, she felt her father's hand moving over her body, and his hot breath coming faster and faster on her neck. Frightened, she jumped from his lap and turned to face him. Damon began laughing hysterically, tears coming down his bearded face. "My darling, my darling," he gasped. "You will be mine again. The druid told me I would not lose you forever, and now you're back in my darling Dymphna. We will be married in a fort-night. The whole village will be invited and you will be dressed as my queen!"

Dymphna shrieked and ran from the room, the horrid sound of his strange laugh ringing in her ears. Dymphna finally found her way to the kitchen and sank gratefully into the arms of her friend, Siobhan, the cook. In between her sobs, she told what had happened with her father. They both knew that such marriages between a father and daughter had occurred. But they were rare now because most of the country had become Christian, and such practices were strictly forbidden to Christians. "Come, come, Dymphna," soothed Siobhan. "We shall send little Patty out to fetch Father Gerebarn. He will speak to your father. We will explain to him that you cannot marry him. It goes against the faith of your good mother. Surely, he will respect her faith. You know that she was all the world to him."

The next morning, Dymphna was relieved to find that her father had left early for a hunting party. That meant that he would be gone for a couple of days. In the meantime, Father Gerebarn would be home and together they could develop a plan to change her father's mind. Counting on her father's devotion to her dear mother, they soon had a plan carefully worked out. Dymphna now watched anxiously for Damon's return. The sooner she knew that he would not go through with his evil desire, the sooner she could rest again peacefully. But that evening, something happened that she had never even dreamed in her worst nightmare. Damon came roaring into the castle, excited from the hunt and drunk. Dymphna stood quietly, waiting for him to go upstairs and hoping he would not see her. She knew that it would be impossible to reason with him in this condition. But then a candle flickered and he turned, looking straight at her.

"My darling," his face was contorted in the shadows of the flame of the candle. "You have returned to me! Come to me...." Dymphna screamed, realizing that in his crazed state of mind he was mistaking her for her mother. Her sixteen years of living with his moodiness and temper had not prepared her for anything like this. As Damon lunged toward her, he tripped on a rough stone and fell. Quickly, Dymphna sped around him and out the castle door. She would hide that night in the barn, and in the morning, when little Patty came out to milk the cows, she would send him for Father Gerebran. Dymphna knew that she could no longer stay in her own home. She had lost both of her parents with her mother's death, for though her father was alive, his unstable mind had now slipped dangerously off into a dark world of its own imagining.

The very next night Dymphna left her homeland forever. With Father Gerebran's help, she secretly boarded a ship headed for Antwerp, in Belgium. Father Gerebran, the cook, Siobhan and her husband, Damon's elderly court jester, accompanied Dymphna into exile.

"Where have you been, child?" the little man asked in a worried voice. "It's not right for you to be out by yourself at night."

Dymphna smiled at her old friend. "Now don't you worry. My angel was with me every step of the way. When you frown like that, you don't seem at all like the jolly court jester that used to make my mother laugh."

The jester smiled then, and said, "Well, let's go in to eat. The wife has something extra special for us tonight."

Dymphna and the jester entered a small thatched hut. Beside the fire Siobhan was busily carving thick slices of meat from a roasted goose. She turned and greeted Dymphna warmly. "At last you're home, Dymphna. You shouldn't stay out so late on your visits to the sick and the poor."

Dymphna lost both of her parents when her mother died. Even though her father was alive, his unstable mind had now slipped dangerously off into a dark world of its own imagining.

"Yes, Siobhan, I know you're right, but didn't the Lord himself stay among the poor until sunset, healing them and giving them encouragement? And besides, the people here have been so kind to us ever since we came to this little town of Gheel." Dymphna was quiet for a moment as she remembered their dangerous escape from Ireland. At last they had settled in this small Belgian village near the city of Antwerp. She began to set the table for dinner.

"Is Father Gerebran back yet?" she asked.

"Father's been out on errands of mercy like yourself, I expect," the jester growled. "I never saw the like of either of you—so tender-hearted and all that."

"We're no more tender-hearted than you," she retorted. "What other than Christ's own compassion prompted you to leave a cozy position in the court of a king to flee into the wilderness with a poor old priest and the king's young daughter?"

"With a holy priest of God and with the saintliest princess I ever knew," replied Siobhan gently. "There! The goose is ready now. We'll just wait for Father to come before we eat."

"Where did you find the goose?" asked Dymphna, knowing that they had little money left. "It's the first meat that we've had in three months."

"I bought it at the market today with some of the coins we carried with us from Ireland. We still have a few left. Oh, Father, here you are!"

The old priest made his way into the hut. His eyes were glowing with a beautiful light. "How good God has been to give us the sick and the poor to comfort," he murmured softly. "I feel so much closer to him now than I did at your father's court, Dymphna."

Dymphna brought a stool. "Sit down, Father Gerebran, and rest. Tell us about your day."

As they ate beside the crackling fire, Dymphna's thoughts drifted back to that dark night when the four of them had huddled together in a frail little boat, watching the powerful oarsmen move back and forth against the mist, listening to the soft swish-thud of the oars. How good those men were to us, to bring us all the way across the sea, Dymphna thought. They were my father's slaves, and they risked their own lives to help us escape his wrath.

"Father Gerebran, tomorrow could you offer your Mass for my father? Perhaps one day he will be well again and we can return to Ireland."

"You know that I always offer the Mass for the king, your father, that he may recover his sanity."

The group fell silent, watching the flickering flames. "You deserve a better life than this, Dymphna," Siobhan said at last. "It's sad that you who have grown up in a king's court must now live in poverty like this."

"Don't be silly!" Dymphna laughed. "Why this is better than a palace and I have Father Gerebran for my director and you for my 'family' and Jesus himself for my only Husband. What more could any girl want?"

A few days later Dymphna went to the market on

an errand when she heard a voice say, "Excuse me."

A young farmer stood beside her, twisting his cap awkwardly in his big, red hands.

"Are you the young lady who came here with the good priest a few months ago?"

"Yes," Dymphna replied.

"Well," gulped the farmer, "I must tell you something. Last market day I sold a goose to the woman who lives with you, and yesterday a stranger from Antwerp offered me money if I could tell him about any Irish fugitives living in the area. The coins which he offered me were just like the ones the woman gave me—so I told him about the four of you. My conscience has bothered me ever since."

Dymphna felt chills run up and down her spine, but she managed a weak smile and said, "Now don't worry about it. I'm sure you meant no harm. God will take care of us all."

But as soon as the farmer had said good-bye, Dymphna hurried into the forest. I must tell Father Gerebran at once, she was thinking. We must flee farther into the countryside. Only one person could have sent that spy: my cruel, disturbed father!

Down the forest path Dymphna ran toward the Chapel of St. Martin. As she had hoped, she found Father Gerebran walking up and down in its shadow reading his breviary. She quickly poured out the news.

"We need to tell the others, my child," he said. "We must leave here at once."

But it was already too late. Striding down the path from their little hut came Damon. Around him was a mob of hired swordsmen. It was useless to run.

Damon stopped, motioned his men to stand still, and approached Dymphna slowly. "Dymphna, come home with me to Ireland," he said gently, almost purring like a cat. "You will be very happy there." A strange, wild light was in his eyes.

"We know your plans for Dymphna are evil," retorted old Father Gerebran. He stood tall and faced the king. "You are a sick man, Damon. And what you desire is evil. Dymphna is a Christian, and she shall not return with you!"

Savage fury twisted the king's face into a terrible mask. "Kill him!" he roared, and the swordsmen leaped forward to seize the priest. In a flash, Father Gerebran's head was cut off. He crumpled into the dust.

Again Damon's voice became smooth and gentle. "Come home with me, Dymphna. I need you. You won't be sorry."

"Never!" Dymphna's eyes blazed with fire. "You are my father but you think like the devil. I know what you want from me. I will not do it. I will never offend God in such a way!"

Now Damon was beside himself with rage. "Seize her!" he bellowed, but this time the warriors did not budge. Princess Dymphna faced them tall and straight, like a queen. They knew she was good and holy. They would not kill her.

Damon himself fumbled for his sword and wrenched it from its sheath. "Then die!" He lunged at the girl. Dymphna raised her eyes to heaven and gave her soul to God as her father cut her head off.

Damon and his men raced away from their crime and returned to Ireland. Siobhan and her husband reverently buried the bodies of their two friends. So many came to pray near Dymphna's grave that a shrine, and later a church, was built over her remains and those of Father Gerebran, who was also canonized. To this day, the mentally and emotionally ill come to the town of Gheel in Belgium, where the townspeople care for them and St. Dymphna continues to intercede for them.

Dymphna loved both her parents, but she realized that her father was not well. She knew that in order for her to live as a Christian, she had to leave her own home. But she continued to pray for her father. Like her, we can love and pray for people even when we know they are sick and perhaps even dangerous.

St. Margaret of Scotland

(d. 1093)

June 10

"Good-bye, England," sighed Princess Margaret, as she watched the rugged coastline disappear beyond the restless gray waves. "Perhaps I shall never see you again. Farewell!"

Margaret, a pretty young woman of twenty, had grown to love England deeply during the ten years she had lived there. Her grandfather, Edmund, had been king of the little island, but Danish invaders had prevented Margaret's own father from wearing the crown. Nor would Edgar, her young brother, ever rule England because Norman conquerors had now seized the throne. Margaret was going to Hungary with her mother, sister and brother, where they would live as exiles.

The king of Hungary was a relative of theirs and would take them in.

"Margaret, please come inside the cabin!" Her mother called anxiously. "A storm is coming!"

"Yes, Mother," Margaret replied, and stooped to enter the stuffy little cabin. She could hear the oarsmen shouting excitedly to one another. Their little ship was pitching and tossing more wildly by the moment, so Margaret wedged herself into a corner and held on, smiling at her young brother, who responded with a broad grin. For young Edgar, who had never been on a ship before, this trip was quite an adventure.

For many hours the sturdy ship rode the furious storm. When it finally stopped the travelers were lost completely. At last they sighted land to the northwest, but it was a far more mountainous countryside than that of Hungary. "It's the Scottish coast, for sure," explained the captain.

"King Malcolm's country," Margaret murmured to her mother. "He was exiled in England before he reconquered the land and regained his father's throne."

"In that case," replied her mother, "be prepared to meet some wild people. Don't expect the Scots to be as civilized as the people we have known until now."

However, young King Malcolm's friendly reception surprised both Margaret and her mother. He was polite and generous, and invited them to stay for a few months in his big castle. "My queen has died, God rest her soul," King Malcolm explained. "This castle is very gloomy now that there are no women to brighten it up. I would be grateful if you would stay."

Margaret and her mother certainly did

brighten up the castle. King Malcolm was impressed by Margaret's beauty and cheerfulness, but even more so by her kindness to her family, to the courtiers, to the servants and to himself. He also admired her love of prayer and recollection. It was obvious that Margaret sincerely tried to live according to the example of Jesus.

One day King Malcolm said to Margaret's mother, "Lady Agatha, your daughter Margaret is both beautiful and good. May I have your permission to marry the princess?" Margaret's mother hesitated a moment. "I am happy that the princess has found favor with Your Majesty. However, Margaret has always intended to become a nun. I believe I must speak to her first."

Margaret was upset. She liked King Malcolm, and she enjoyed the excitement of court life. But she loved God, and wanted to serve him in the best way possible. To solve the problem, she turned to prayer.

One morning after receiving Holy Communion and talking heart to heart with our Lord, Margaret knew what she must do. It was as if Jesus himself had spoken to her, saying, "This is your place. It is here that I wish you to serve me. You will have many opportunities to do good and to become holy in this kingdom."

Margaret's doubts were gone, and King Malcolm was overjoyed when she accepted his proposal! Soon, all the country was celebrating its new queen.

Queen Margaret did find many opportunities

Princess Margaret liked King Malcolm, and she enjoyed the excitement of court life. But she loved God and wanted to serve him in the best way possible. To solve the problem, she turned to prayer.

to do good in Scotland. The people were poor and
spent much of their time raiding the English.
But Queen Margaret found a solution to both the
poverty and the raiding. She asked King
Malcolm to invite some Benedictine monks from
England and the Continent to settle in Scotland.
These monks began to teach the Scots how to
raise crops in their mountainous, rocky soil.
They also built churches and monasteries, aided
by the strong men who had formerly spent their
time raiding English villages. Children living
near the monasteries began to attend the schools
which the monks started, receiving an education
which their parents never had. Many of these
children became priests, monks and nuns, and
missionaries went out from Scotland to teach the
Christian faith to the neighboring islands—the
Shetlands, the Hebrides and the Orkneys.

Since the Scottish bishops had been out of contact with the Church of Rome for years, Queen
Margaret invited representatives of the archbishop
of Canterbury to meet with them and talk about the
many difficulties within the Scottish Church at the
time. Margaret herself attended this meeting and
took part in the discussions. This led to the period
of new fervor in the Church of Scotland.

Queen Margaret's life was full of activity. Mass,
daily prayer, aid to the poor, visits to the prisons....
But the energetic queen was never too busy to
devote time and attention to her family. She was a
loving and attentive wife to Malcolm, for whom she
prayed continually. She was a firm but understanding mother to their eight lively children; the

Princes Edward, Ethelred, Edmund, Edgar, Alexander and David; and the Princesses Matilda and Mary. "I would rather that each of you died a thousand times than commit one deliberate and serious sin," she would tell them. "Pray to the Blessed Virgin; be kind to the poor; avoid all sins of impurity. Lead holy lives, and share your belief in Jesus with everyone."

Edmund became a monk, while Edgar, Alexander and David would each one day be king of Scotland. Matilda was to marry Henry I and be Queen of England.

When Queen Margaret was almost forty-seven, she became seriously ill. She felt her strength growing weaker day by day. "I think that I may die soon," she told her chaplain.

At the same time, the English attacked the Scottish castle of Ainwick. King Malcolm said a hasty good-bye to Margaret, gathered his army, and rode off to battle. Edward and Edgar went with him.

On her deathbed, Margaret prayed anxiously for her husband and sons. She offered her sufferings for their safe return, but more especially for their spiritual well-being.

One day a bruised and battered figure appeared in the doorway of the queen's room. It was her son Edgar. He was covered with caked blood, and dusty from hard riding. Weakly, with sorrow in his face, he crossed the room and knelt at his mother's bedside.

"Your father?" Margaret asked, already sensing the truth.

"Father and Edward have both been killed, Mother," gulped the boy, and he buried his face in his hands.

"Few sorrows could have been greater than this," murmured the queen.

After comforting Edgar and calling a servant to treat his wounds, Margaret sent for her chaplain. "Two things I ask of you," she said. "As long as you live, please remember my husband's soul and my own poor soul in your Masses and prayers. And watch over my children, teaching them to love God and to live as good Christians." The chaplain promised, and Margaret, the faithful wife and mother, was at peace. She made her confession, received the Sacrament of Anointing, and left her small, war-torn kingdom for the Kingdom of Eternal Peace.

St. Margaret knew that the people we should spend the most time with and do the most for, are our own families. Let us be kind to everyone, but especially to our parents, brothers and sisters.

St. Francis of Assisi

(1182-1226)

October 4

In the city of Assisi in northern Italy, about eight hundred years ago, as the wife of the rich merchant Peter Bernardone was about to give birth to a baby, a stranger came to her door and said to a servant, "If you want everything to go all right, tell Peter's wife to go to the stable at once."

A strange command—but it was carried out. And the baby was born in a stable, just as Jesus was!

On that same day, another stranger ran through the streets of Assisi crying, "Peace and happiness!" Everyone wondered what he was talking about.

The baby was named John, but when his father returned from a trip to France, he changed his son's name to Francis, because he liked France so much.

Peter Bernardone had great dreams for his son Francis, dreams of great wealth as a merchant. He started to train Francis in business while he was still young, even though this meant taking him out of regular school.

In a short time, Francis became so good at business that Peter's customers were increasing every week. Francis was friendly, courteous, and easy to get along with. He won over even those who had not planned to buy anything! Business kept getting better and better.

Francis was not satisfied just with making money though. He wanted to spend it, too! He dressed like a royal prince. But his father didn't mind. He was so happy with the way business was going. And he was happy that his son Francis was the most popular young man in the city. In fact, his friends had nicknamed Francis, "the king of parties"! Singing, dancing, hunting trips, parties—Francis never missed a thing!

Peter the merchant, who had become wealthy by working and was not rich by inheritance, nearly burst with pride when he saw how much the great nobles liked his son! He began to have wonderful ideas about his son's future. "Perhaps some day he will even have a coat of arms for himself, such as the nobles have," he would say. But his wife would only sigh and pray harder for her son.

Francis did love a good time. But he was also a very generous person. He liked to see everyone happy, and the friends who received expensive gifts from him—gifts perfectly suited to each one—were well aware of his generosity. One day, while he was handing out gifts, a poor beggar came up. "In the name of God," said the beggar, "give me some money so that I may eat." Francis pretended not to hear or see the man. But then, as the beggar limped sadly away, the young man felt so sorry that he ran after him and gave him a purse full of coins to make up for his unkindness.

When Francis was about seventeen, a war broke out between Assisi and one of the nearby cities. A thick wall had to be built around Assisi to protect it and every man was needed to help. Of course, Francis enthusiastically left his father's store to take part in the construction work. He learned how to mix mortar and lay stones in place, and he worked so hard and so joyfully that he gave courage to the other men.

But in spite of its sturdy wall, Assisi was conquered by the attacking army, and many of the citizens of Assisi were taken prisoner. Among them was Francis. He looked like a rich nobleman's son because of his fine clothes, so he was put in a special prison reserved for the nobility.

Francis, who had been used to complete freedom and good times, found prison life horrible. But soon his joyful spirit took over and he went about each day singing. "How can you sing in prison?" the others asked. Some of them were annoyed by his good attitude!

"Why, this is nothing," Francis replied. "I shall one day be famous around the world!" Francis was joking—as usual—but this time he had spoken the truth without knowing it.

After a year in prison, Francis was released. But it was not the same youth who returned to his family. His ambitions were different now. He had decided to become a soldier.

Right at that time, men of Assisi were arming for battle. Francis went out and bought the best armor and weapons he could find. His father smiled. If his son wanted to win fame on the battlefield, that was fine with him!

The night before the soldiers were to leave for the fight, Francis found out that one of the noblemen had no money to buy weapons, and would not be able to go to the battle. Generously, Francis gave him his own best set of weapons, and kept only a second-hand set for himself.

That gallant act led to a strange dream. Francis saw a golden palace, and inside it hung weapons of pure gold marked with a cross. "Whose arms are these?" he heard his own voice asking.

A mysterious voice replied, "They belong to you and to your soldiers!"

What a dream! When Francis set out with the other soldiers, he felt as if he were riding on air. What a magnificent leader I will become! he thought.

Yet while they were on the road, Francis suddenly felt very sick. He was forced to stop, while the other soldiers went on. I'll catch up later, he thought.

That night, as he was dozing off, he heard a voice ask, "Francis, is it better to serve the master or the servant?"

"The master, of course," he replied.

"Then why are you leaving the master for the servant?"

Deeply troubled, Francis asked, "What shall I do?"

"Return to Assisi, and you will find out," was the answer.

Francis then fell into a restless sleep. As dawn broke the next morning he mounted his horse and turned back toward Assisi. His heart was sad as he imagined what people would say about his return. And sure enough, everyone laughed as the young man came into the city—he who had gone so full of pride only a few days before. "Another one of your tricks?" they asked.

Francis went back into his old habits of going out with his friends, singing loudly and riding off on hunting parties. He seemed to be the same as ever, but underneath his lively behavior his heart was sad and troubled.

As he was returning from a party one night, Francis stayed behind his companions. He stood still and gazed up at the beautiful stars in the velvety sky. Suddenly, light seemed to flood his soul! "My God and my all!" he exclaimed over and over.

When his friends came back to look for him, they found him staring off into space. "Dreaming Francis?" they teased. "Who is the lucky girl?"

"A great lady," replied Francis slowly. But he didn't tell them who she was. Like every medieval knight, he would have his lady, but she was not a person. Poverty would be his lady. Poverty, because Jesus Christ had loved it so much and chosen it for himself.

How was Francis to serve Lady Poverty? He was

not sure yet. But the idea came to him one day to make a pilgrimage to Rome, and with some money which his mother gladly gave him, he set out for the Holy City.

In Rome, Francis went to St. Peter's Basilica to pray and spend the day. Looking around, he saw that the pilgrims were giving small offerings, and with a rush of generosity, he offered them all the money he had. His great charity amazed all the other pilgrims.

A bit embarrassed, Francis went out. He saw the poor, gathered together at the church entrance, waiting for donations. Francis realized that he would never really be able to understand poverty unless he himself were dressed in a poor man's rags.

Francis walked up to the poorest man of the whole bunch and asked him to exchange clothes—fine, elegant garments for a pitiful and dirty cloak! The offer was accepted. Francis shuddered when he felt those greasy and smelly rags on his skin, but at the same time a feeling of great joy filled his whole being.

He went a step further, even, and asked the other pilgrims for donations. He asked people for charity, for the love of Jesus Christ who had become poor for our sakes. Francis had given away every cent he had; now to keep from starving, he had to depend on the charity of others.

Francis returned from Rome completely taken up with this new idea, which was becoming clearer to him every day. It was not enough to give money away. He would have to give of his own self to the Lord. But no one at home could understand him. He often went riding alone into the quiet country-side to think and pray.

One day he saw a man afflicted with leprosy, and turned away in instinctive horror until an interior voice stopped him: "How can you be a Knight of Christ if you are afraid?"

Francis remembered the words of Jesus: "Amen, I say to you, as long as you did it for one of these, the least of my brothers, you did it for me." Who could be poorer than that man, sick and abandoned by everyone? Would Francis run away from Jesus? Never! Taking a deep breath, Francis turned and walked back.

When Francis came close to the man, he kissed the man's face, covered with oozing and smelly sores. Then he gave the man a generous offering. But his greatest gift was in the tender kiss and gesture of acceptance he had made. That poor man stood speechless; it had been a long time since he had experienced such respect.

Yet Francis was even happier! That experience of reaching out to another had made him realize what true joy was. From that time on, he became the comforting angel of all those who were sick with leprosy, caring for their sores, cheering them up and talking to them about the love of God.

I must begin to live a life like that of Jesus, Francis thought. He went into a little country church, dedicated to St. Damiano, to pray. There,

Francis went to pray in a little country church dedicated to St. Damiano. There, he heard these words from the crucifix: "Go, and repair my house, which is falling in ruins."

he heard these words from the crucifix: "Go, and repair my house, which is falling in ruins."

"Yes! I shall do it!" Francis answered at once. The little abandoned church was in ruins and it would take a lot of work to fix it up. The first step was to find the priest in charge. Francis hurried off to look for him.

Francis gave the priest all the money he had with him and asked him to use it to keep an oil lamp burning in the sanctuary, in front of the crucifix. The priest was surprised, for, of course, he had no idea how much that church meant to Francis!

When Francis returned home his father was not too happy to see him. Francis spent very little time in the shop and business was not going so well. But Peter Bernardone's face brightened when he saw Francis take yards of the finest cloth in the shop and load them onto his horse. "At last the boy's getting his senses back," thought Peter. "He's off to make a fine sale of that cloth!"

Francis did sell the cloth, and the horse as well! But the money did not come home to Peter Bernardone—no, it went straight to the surprised priest at St. Damiano.

At least that was what Francis had planned. But the priest regretfully said, "I cannot accept this money to rebuild the church." Francis threw the money down and went into the church to pray. For several days Francis remained there, until one day the priest came to warn him that his angry father was on his way. "Hurry, Francis," he exclaimed, "come with me! I'll hide you until your father has gone!"

After all, the priest thought, he's a sincere young man. And everyone knew how awful Peter Bernardone could be when he was angry!

Francis escaped his father's wrath that time, but not a few days later. Peter had become so angry with his son that he went to the city officials and accused him of being a thief. Francis said that he was consecrated to God and would be judged only by the bishop. And so, the father and the son were called before the bishop's tribunal.

The father was angry and excited; the son was calm and composed. Gently the bishop told Francis, "Return to your father what belongs to him. God would not want money for his church obtained this way."

"Your Excellency," replied Francis, "I'll return not only his money, but even his clothes." Francis took off all his fine clothes. Then he told the astonished crowd, "I no longer call Peter Bernardone my father; I give everything back to him, and from now on I shall say to God, 'Our Father, who art in heaven!'"

The bishop was deeply moved. He put his arms around Francis and covered him with his own robe. Peter, meanwhile, was confused and angry. He could tell that the people favored Francis more than himself. This was not the outcome he had expected! He took his money—and the clothes—and left!

The bishop's gardener had an old tunic which

he gave Francis to wear. Joyfully, the youth put it on while the bishop made a large sign of the cross over it to symbolize the young man's consecration to God. Then Francis left the city. Climbing up the slope of the nearby foothills, Francis began to sing. He felt that now he belonged completely to God!

———————

"Repair my house!" These words still echoed in Francis' ears. But now he had no money. How could he repair the ruined church? Soon an idea clicked in his mind. He could sing for money, just as the wandering minstrels did. Only instead of singing songs about romance or war, he would sing about God! So Francis began to go through the countryside, singing such hymns of praise to God that people crowded about him to listen. They were deeply moved and willingly gave donations when Francis asked them to help him rebuild the little church.

Soon he had enough material to begin the project. He had learned how to build walls during the war; now he put that knowledge to good use. The priest watched him with kindly interest, and tried to help him in every way he could. Every night he would make supper for Francis, but the young man preferred to go begging from door to door for his food.

One family would give him a dipper of soup; another, some salad or cooked vegetables; from another he would receive a piece of bread. It all went into the bowl together. Francis would eat it gratefully, thanking the people for their kindness to a poor beggar.

There was a young nobleman, named Bernard Quintavalle, who was very impressed by Francis. He decided to get to know him better and find out what it was that had changed Francis so much. One day he invited him to his home and managed to persuade him to spend the night. They slept in the same room, so Bernard was able to see that as soon as everything was still, Francis slipped out of bed and knelt on the floor. He spent the night in prayer, saying over and over, "My God and my All." Bernard breathed deeply, pretending to be asleep, but he was really watching Francis all night. In the morning, he told Francis that he had decided to join him.

Francis urged him to think it over carefully. Poverty is not an easy thing for someone who had grown up rich and comfortable. This was something that they should pray about.

After assisting at Mass in a nearby church, Francis and Bernard asked the pastor, Father Peter Cattani, to open the altar missal three times in the name of Jesus. Each time their eyes fell upon passages of the Gospel which spoke of the poverty of Jesus and his disciples.

That was enough for Bernard—and for Father Peter, too, for he also admired Francis and had wished for a long time to have the courage to join him. Now Francis knew that God was inspiring him to lead others in the life he had chosen for himself. Together, they would try to imitate Jesus in every aspect of his earthly life. "Brothers," said Francis with great enthusiasm, "the poverty of Jesus will be our rule of life. Let us go and preach."

Soon other men joined the group of "little brothers." To all of them Francis said, "God has called us not only for our own sakes, but to save our neighbors, too. We must go out into the world and bring men to do penance and to obey the commandments."

While on one of his journeys, Francis met a young soldier riding down the road. On a sudden inspiration from God, he cried out, "Angelo Tancredi, it is time for you to exchange your sword for the cross of Christ.... Follow me, and I shall make you a soldier of Jesus Christ!"

The young man knew that only God could have inspired those words that struck him so forcefully. At once he got off his horse and stood before Francis. "I'm ready!" he said.

Often during the day the brothers would go to the small shanty town where those with leprosy lived and care for the sick and dying people there. Because leprosy was so contagious, the lepers were forced to live outside of the city, and almost everyone treated them worse than animals. But the brothers treated them as they treated one another, and often spoke to the lepers about the great love of God, the death and resurrection of Jesus and the joys of heaven awaiting those who love God. If their patients had not been living good lives before, many of them converted in their ways and prepared for a holy death.

But one man, who was very sick, only cursed and insulted the brothers. He was bitter and angry that God should allow him to suffer so much. The brothers felt very upset when they heard the man speak this way about God and they wanted to abandon him. But before taking such a drastic step, they decided to consult Francis.

"Let me see him," Francis said. He went to the hut where the man lived and offered to serve him in whatever way he could. Rudely, the sick man accepted his offer. The first thing he told Francis to do was to give him a bath. The open sores of leprosy had become infected and the smell was almost overpowering.

Francis heated some water and added some sweet-smelling herbs to it. Then, taking some clean pieces of cloth, he gently began to rub the painful sores. A miracle! Little by little the sores were disappearing. But the greatest miracle was the tremendous sense of peace and acceptance that was flooding the man's heart. He felt that not only was Francis cleansing his body, but also his soul. As soon as he could, the man dedicated himself to God and spent the rest of his life caring for others.

Francis never spared himself in the hard but joyous life to which God had called him. After many years those who knew him best could see that his health was almost gone and that he would soon die.

Francis knew it, too. He asked to be taken to the Church of St. Mary of the Angels. On the way, he told his brothers to place him down on the ground, facing toward Assisi. Slowly he raised his hand and blessed the city. "May you be blessed by God, holy city, because many souls will be saved through you and many of God's servants will live in you. They will be among the elect in the kingdom of heaven!"

Francis blessed all his spiritual children, and begged them to sing the "Canticle of the Sun," which was a beautiful hymn of praise to God for his creation. He raised his weak voice and together they sang.

Death came as the sun set on the evening of October 4, 1226. Francis' soul soared home to Paradise to take its place among the choirs of angels to sing forever the praises of God.

Poverty was the special way in which Francis was called to imitate Jesus. Taking good care of our things, sharing what we have and telling others about the love of God for them are all ways that we can imitate Francis.

St. Clare

(1193-1253)

August 11

By the year 1211, St. Francis of Assisi had a small group of men living with him. They were trying to live lives of poverty and penance, exactly as Jesus of Nazareth lived. Like Jesus, they went through the cities and towns preaching the Gospel. This particular year, Francis was invited to the parish church of St. Giorgio, in Assisi, to preach the Lenten sermons. It was a time when a few people were becoming very rich, but also a time of much violence, injustice and poverty for many. The simple sermons of Francis, calling the people to be sorry for their sins and challenging them to live according to the teachings of Jesus attracted many people. Every day the little church was full. In the audience was a young woman named Clare.

Clare was the oldest daughter of a wealthy man named Faverone Offreducio. She and her two sisters grew up in Assisi and learned all the

191

things which rich girls learned in those days—music, fine embroidery and how to entertain guests. Their mother, Ortolana, was very religious and taught her daughters all about Jesus. Together they would go to Mass each Sunday, and this year they went every day to listen to the Lenten sermons. Clare's father was happy to see how gentle and religious his daughters were. But he wanted to make sure that they each married a wealthy young man who could continue his business and make even more money for the family. He already had a husband picked out for Clare, who was seventeen years old.

Clare was very popular at the parties held for the wealthy young people in Assisi. Probably she had met Francis once or twice at such events before he left everything to follow Jesus. Now as she listened to his enthusiastic preaching and saw how much he loved Jesus, she began to think about her own life.

It wasn't very challenging, and lately she had felt her conscience bothering her as she saw more and more beggars and homeless children filling the city streets while her own family was becoming richer. She enjoyed her friends and the comforts of her home, but she did not feel satisfied. Comparing the peace in the face of Francis and his companions with the tension and anxiety which often lined the face of her father and his brothers, Clare began to wonder. Could there be something more for her than a life of parties and entertainment?

After the Lenten sermons were completed

and Easter time had passed, Clare couldn't get the thoughts and words of Francis out of her mind. How had he been able to give up so much, she wondered. At last she sent a trusted servant out to the Portiuncula, a small stone convent outside the city walls where Francis lived, and asked to speak to him privately. Fearing her father, and not yet knowing what she was looking for from Francis, Clare preferred to meet him in secret. All that year they met and talked about Jesus, about the great freedom and beauty of poverty, about the need to care for the poor and the sick as Jesus had done. By the following Lent, Clare knew what she wanted to do.

That year, 1212, she again attended the Lenten sermons with her mother and sisters. On Palm Sunday she put on her finest dress and favorite jewelry. No one else knew, but she was preparing herself to "elope" that night with Jesus! After returning home, she called the same servant, who had been Clare's teacher since she was a small child, and together they went out into the black night and through the quiet city gates. At last they reached the Portiuncula and found the doorway to the chapel of Our Lady of the Angels. Inside were Francis and the friars, holding lighted candles and singing psalms. They were ready to receive Clare as their sister.

Clare walked slowly up the aisle and knelt in prayer before the altar, which was ablaze with light from the candles and decorated with flowers. Then she removed her jewelry and the velvet gown she was wearing. A rough, grey robe was

At last they reached the Portiuncula *and found the doorway to the chapel of Our Lady of the Angels. Inside were Francis and the friars, holding lighted candles and singing psalms.*

slipped on and a knotted cord went about her waist. Wooden sandals went on her feet. Francis quickly cut off her long golden hair and a long black veil was placed over her head.

Radiant with joy, Clare promised to follow Jesus in the same way as Francis and the friars—poor, chaste and obedient. Clare was no longer a rich young lady, but a humble sister with her heart set on the infinite treasures of heaven.

Right after this simple ceremony, the brothers took Clare to a nearby Benedictine convent where she would live with the sisters and learn about convent life. Later, she would be able to begin her own convent.

How surprised and angry Clare's father and uncle were when they found out what she had done! In an armed band, all of Clare's male relatives stormed down upon the Benedictine convent. The young sister saw them coming, and ran into the church, thinking that she would be safe there. She went right up to the altar and held on to it. As her relatives crowded around her angrily, she calmly showed them her shaved head. "From now on, I belong to God alone!" she said. Defeated by her firmness—and by the grace of God—the relatives retreated and left her in peace.

But Clare's father was afraid that he might lose Agnes, his second daughter, in the same way he had lost Clare. He immediately selected a suitable young man for Agnes to marry, and made arrangements for the engagement. Then he heaved a sigh of relief. Now he would not lose his good, prayerful, sweet Agnes.

At least that's what he thought. Before he knew

it, Agnes had gone to join Clare! Furious, the father rushed to his brother, Monaldo, who had a band of tough fighting-men. "Bring my daughter back!" he urged.

The fierce Monaldo needed little encouragement. He rounded up his men, and off they thundered to the peaceful convent. Pulling up sharply in the open courtyard, the men swung off their horses and rushed into the cloister of the sisters, searching for Agnes. "Here she is!" came the cry. In an instant they had surrounded the girl. Monaldo seized her by her hair, and started to drag her away, cursing all the while.

"Clare! Help me!" cried out Agnes.

Clare heard her, but she did not come out into the open. Instead, she sank to her knees and prayed. God would be their strength. As she prayed, the attackers felt themselves growing weaker and weaker and Agnes growing heavier and heavier. And it wasn't due to any resistance on her part, for Agnes had already fainted! The men trembled in fear.

Furious, Monaldo drew out his sword and raised it violently. If they could not move the girl, he would kill her!

But Monaldo could not lower his arm to bring the sword down on Agnes' neck. He stood frozen, as if he were paralyzed.

Clare arose from her prayer and appeared on the scene. She turned such fiery words on the evil men that they turned around like whipped dogs and walked away.

Word of what happened reached Francis, who

came hurrying to the convent. His words comforted and encouraged Clare and her sister. Then he said, "This was your 'novitiate,' Agnes! We'll consecrate you to God right now!" That day, Agnes received a rough robe with a cord around her waist, just like Clare's, and made her promise to live in chastity, poverty and obedience.

As time passed, the anger of Clare's relatives cooled. Other wealthy women came to join them, and Francis appointed Clare to be their superior. The women came to be known as the Poor Clares, and they lived in the convent at the church of St. Damiano.

The sisters were always busy. They grew their own food, they sewed, embroidered altar linens and provided clothes for the poor. They wore no shoes, they fasted often and slept on the hard wooden floor. In their desire to live as simply and poorly as Jesus, nothing was too difficult for them.

Clare would spend many hours each night in prayer before Jesus in the tabernacle. Yet she was always the first one up in the morning, first to call her companions, first to light the lamps and prepare everything for Mass, first to think of little things to help her sisters spiritually and materially.

Once when Clare was ill, an army of Saracens, who had invaded Italy, passed near Assisi. Seeing the convent, they came to attack it. Their horrid shrieks and battle cries terrified the sisters, who went running frantically to Clare's bedside. Clare stood up and went to the chapel.

She took the monstrance holding a consecrated Host, praying all the while with ardent faith, and carried it out into the courtyard where the soldiers—who were climbing over the convent wall—could see it.

Clare heard a voice say, "I shall always be your salvation."

The Saracens stopped where they were, shocked. Then, gripped by a mysterious terror, they turned and ran away. What had they seen in that gentle woman whose only weapons were the Host and a strong faith? Only God knows the answer.

After the danger had passed, the sisters joined Clare in singing a hymn of gratitude and love to God.

Many years passed, and so many women had come to join Clare and the sisters that several convents were opened. Their reputation spread so far, in fact, that Princess Agnes of Bohemia wrote to Clare, asking permission to live as the sisters under Clare's direction. Agnes and Clare never were able to live in the same convent, and perhaps they never even saw each other in person! But through their letters to one another they became the best of friends, and Clare called Agnes the "other half" of her soul. Soon, Agnes had women come to join her and the Poor Clares spread out across all of Europe.

Francis had died many years before, and now Clare (who had been sick for a long time), felt that her own time had come to leave this earth. Three of the first friars, who had been present on that night so many years before when Clare had left her family to follow Jesus, came to be with her as she was dying. They read out loud the story of Jesus' own death from the Gospel of St. John, just as they had done for Francis as he was dying. Clare was so well known for her holiness that Pope Innocent IV and several bishops and cardinals came to see her one last time.

One beautiful morning, as the sisters and the three friars were gathered around her bed, Clare said, as if talking to her soul, "Go forth in peace, for you have chosen and followed the good road. Go forth without fear, for the good God who created you has also made you holy and will always protect you as a mother. Blessed be you, my God, for having created me." Then she spoke a moment to her sisters, encouraging them to follow carefully the rule of life she and Francis had given to them, and to always be kind to one another. As she lay back, she peacefully died. The next day she was buried, and barely two years later Pope Alexander IV proclaimed her a saint.

To this day there are convents of Poor Clare nuns all over the world. They live in small convents and dress much the same as Clare and her first sisters. Like them, they spend their entire lives loving Jesus and his people in a special way. They pray continually for the needs of the world, and try to live just as simply and poorly as Jesus.

St. Anthony of Padua

(1195-1231)

June 13

Young Father Ferdinand hurried to put away his books and go to the dining room. This evening a group of Franciscan friars, the new group started recently by Francis of Assisi, was passing through the city of Coimbra, Portugal, on their way to Morocco. They would be staying at the Augustinian priory where Father Ferdinand lived. He had heard of these poor and rugged friars, and he was anxious to meet them and hear about their life of prayer and preaching. It sounded so different from his calm, predictable life of community prayer, study and teaching the younger Augustinian seminarians.

Two days later Ferdinand found himself wishing his new friends well as they continued on their journey. They knew that it would be dangerous preaching the Gospel of Jesus in Morocco—in parts of that land people were not permitted to be Christians. But these young friars were full of faith and convinced that a knowledge and love for Jesus was the best way to help others live in peace and justice. In the next months Ferdinand often prayed for their ministry.

How horrified he was when, almost a year later, word came that Don Pedro of Portugal would be stopping that night at the priory with the bones of Franciscan martyrs from Morocco! Ferdinand was stunned and felt tears in his eyes as he heard the story of his friends' cruel death. At the same time, how proud and joy-filled he was for them to have received the great grace of being killed for their love for Jesus! In the next few weeks, little else filled his mind. The thought of martyrdom for the sake of the Gospel strongly attracted Ferdinand, but he knew that as an Augustinian, there would be very little chance of that!

Then along came another small group of the Franciscan friars, this time merely stopping off at the Augustinian friary for some rest along their journey. Ferdinand spent long hours talking to them about their life. When they left they carried a letter to their superior. Ferdinand was asking to leave the Augustinian life to become a poor friar. It wasn't long before the arrangements were made and Ferdinand was exchanging his white habit for the rough brown robe of the Franciscans. He also took a new name, Anthony, to symbolize the new direction he was taking. With a joyful heart he joined the next group of friars on their way to Africa to preach, hoping strongly that he would also be martyred.

Instead of martyrdom, however, Anthony soon found himself bedridden in the small friary on the coast of Africa, burning with fever. The ship hadn't even arrived before he had gotten sick.It had been four months, and he was still sick. Everyone knew that as soon as the weather was good for sailing, the new Friar Anthony would return to Europe. Otherwise he would certainly die from the fever before he even had a chance to preach one sermon! Deeply disappointed, he settled in the ship's cabin to make the journey home.

The small ship encountered a terrific storm which lasted several days, and when it finally broke they were far off course. The ship was so damaged that they headed for the coast of Sicily, which was the closest land. Once ashore, Friar Anthony found a Franciscan community and went to introduce himself. Although he didn't know any of the friars there, they quickly recognized him as one of their own. And best of all, they told Anthony that there would soon be a meeting of all the Franciscans in Assisi. With a new burst of excitement, Anthony joined the Sicilian friars in their journey to Assisi, hoping that he would have a chance to meet the now famous Francis of Assisi.

It was 1221, the last year that such a great meeting of all Franciscans would take place. Although Francis was there, the younger Brother Elias ran the meeting. And Anthony, not belonging yet to any particular community, was quite lost among the three thousand friars. After the meetings ended and the various communities were getting ready to go home, one of the Italian superiors recognized Anthony. Learning that he did not yet belong to any specific community, he invited him to accompany their little group to Padua. Anthony gratefully accepted.

How different was the hard simple life of a Franciscan hermitage from the studious routine he had followed with the Augustinians! And how different customs were in Italy from those in Portugal where Anthony had been reared! None of his new brothers dreamed that Anthony was really a great scholar and teacher of the Bible. For the next few years he was left free to pray in the little hermitage which he loved so much, and spend his working time cooking and chopping wood for the friars. All this time, though, he continued to read his Bible and to meditate for hours on the teachings of Jesus and of the Church.

One day, at a meeting of priests, he was unexpectedly asked to give a little sermon, since no other priest was prepared to do so. Some of the friars were laughing to themselves, thinking of simple, quiet Anthony having to speak unprepared in front of everyone. How surprised they were by his beautiful words! All those things which he had read in Scripture and prayed over and meditated on seemed to flow effortlessly from Anthony. The Holy Spirit was inspiring him, and everyone who listened that day was filled with love of God.

After that sermon, Anthony's days of solitude

Some of the friars were laughing to themselves, thinking of simple, quiet Anthony having to speak unprepared in front of everyone. How surprised they were by his beautiful words!

and wood chopping were over. The other friars immediately sent word to Francis about this marvelous new preacher. Francis was overjoyed and he sent word for Anthony to begin immediately to go from city to city, teaching theology to the friars wherever he went and preaching the Gospel and the catechism to the people of every town.

There are many stories about Anthony and his preaching. In one town where the people had been ignoring the teachings of the Church and were no longer living according to their Christian faith, Anthony preached for several days. But instead of listening, the people either ignored him or made fun of him. At last, realizing that they were not ready to convert and follow Jesus, he went sadly to the banks of a nearby river. It was so peaceful and quiet that he began again to preach. This time there was no one to ridicule him at least, he thought. How startled he was when the fish in the river gathered near the shore and, all together, jumped into the air, bowing their heads each time Anthony said the name of Jesus. "May God be praised!" cried Anthony. "For the fish of the water honor God more than the stubborn people of this town!" At the sight of this miracle, however, the townspeople who had followed him out to the river all fell to their knees and repented. Anthony returned with them to their homes and this time they listened attentively as he preached.

Wherever he went, people who listened to him

preach came to love Jesus and asked to be baptized. Or, if they were already baptized but had not been living a Christian life, they came to Anthony to receive forgiveness and encouragement to start over again. He made many friends all over Italy, but especially in Padua, where he would return after each preaching journey. One night, Anthony was staying at a friend's house and after supper went up to his room. Much later as his friend was going to bed, he noticed a light glowing from under Anthony's door. Curious, he peeked through the key hole and gasped in surprise. There was Anthony, holding the Infant Jesus in his arms! The man watched until the Divine Child slowly faded from sight.

Not long after, Anthony returned to Padua. Even though he was only thirty-six-years-old, he felt strangely tired. Perhaps he was never strong again after the fever in Africa. Or maybe the hard life which the friars led and the strain of constant traveling and preaching had worn him out. In any case, Anthony felt certain that he would soon be leaving this earth and going to meet his beloved Jesus face to face. After some days confined to his little mat on the floor, he called for another priest and made his final confession and asked to receive the Eucharist one last time. Then he sung his favorite hymn to Mary, said good-bye to his fellow friars and softly whispered, "I see my Lord!"

Although he had been born and reared in Lisbon, Portugal, Anthony had long made Padua his home. And the city of Padua had adopted him as one of their own. Whenever he was in town, thousands of Paduans would come to hear him preach. Now that they learned of his death, they insisted that he be buried in their city. Today, Anthony is known as St. Anthony of Padua. He is called the "wonder-worker" because for centuries people have prayed to Anthony and he has interceded for many with miracles of healing and of grace.

We can learn a lot about how God works everything for our good by thinking about the life of Anthony. Even though his hopes and plans for his life were good, things often didn't work out as he expected! But he accepted the events and circumstances of his life with a generous love for God, willing to serve him in whatever situation he found himself.

St. Elizabeth of Hungary

(1207-1231)

November 19

In the land of Hungary, in the year 1207, a baby girl was born to King Andrew and Queen Gertrude. The child was named Elizabeth, which means "Consecrated to God."

The very first things Elizabeth learned were her prayers. By the time she was three, she was walking around the palace saying, "Jesus and Mary, help me to be good. Make me a saint!" Her mother knew that love for God was the beginning of a good education for her daughter.

In those days, marriages of princes and princesses were planned by their parents, often years before the wedding. The little princess would go to live with the prince's family until the two were old enough to marry. That was what happened to Elizabeth. When she was four, she went to live with the Duke of Thuringia, so that she could marry the duke's son Herman when she grew up.

Little Elizabeth was a good-natured girl and

made friends right away with the other children at the castle. Herman and his father, the duke, were especially fond of her. But not so the duchess and the other ladies of the court. "She's too holy," they remarked. "She doesn't fit in with the rest of us!" As she grew older, Elizabeth realized that these women were not her friends. Then, two very sad things happened. First came the news that her mother had died. Then, not long after that, Herman died. "What shall we do with Elizabeth now?" pondered the duke. Should they send her back to her home in Hungary? Should they place her in a convent? He hesitated. He didn't really want to see her go. She was like a ray of sunshine in his cold castle. The other women spent their time gossiping and buying new clothes and planning parties, but there was something different, something special about Elizabeth.

Finally the duke decided. "She shall marry our second son, Louis!" he declared. Although his wife and the ladies of the court were not happy, Louis was very pleased. Elizabeth stayed.

There were many poor people in those days, and hundreds of them stood outside the castle gates begging for food. Whenever she could, Elizabeth gave them all food. This annoyed the duchess and the other members of the court. "Who does she think she is?" they sneered. They scolded her and teased her, but Elizabeth did not pay attention to them. She was hurt by their words and cold attitudes, but she tried not to show it. She was content to know that in helping the poor she was doing as Jesus did. And she was

comforted by the love of the duke and of Louis.
Then another sorrow came. The beloved duke
died. Louis, as soon as he became old enough, was
made the new duke of Thuringia. Shortly after, he
and Elizabeth were married. Louis was twenty-one
and Elizabeth was fourteen.

Both Louis and Elizabeth loved God very much.
They were generous and did everything they could
to help the poor. Louis tried to make just decisions
for all the people who lived on his lands. When
Elizabeth was sixteen, their first child was born.
They named him Herman, after Louis' older
brother who had died. In the years which followed,
three little girls were born. Each child was consecrated to God while still an infant and Elizabeth
taught them their prayers just as her mother had
taught her.

She still fed the beggars at the castle gates. She
would also go out to visit the poor families and the
sick in their small huts below the castle. Near the
gates, she had a hospital built and then an orphanage. There had been wars and epidemics which left
many people without family or strength to provide
for themselves. Often, Elizabeth would go to the
hospital to care for the sick.

One day, she met an old man almost dead from
leprosy. There was no room in the hospital, so
Elizabeth carried him up to her own room and laid
him on the bed in which she and Louis slept! Soon
the old duchess found out, and she was furious. She
rushed to Louis and told him the horrendous news.
Everyone knew that leprosy was contagious!
Even the gentle Louis was concerned about this.

One day, Elizabeth met an old man almost dead from leprosy. There was no room in the hospital, so she carried him up to her own room and laid him on the bed in which she and Louis slept.

He was afraid that Elizabeth or their children would catch the disease. He hurried toward their apartment, intending to give Elizabeth a good scolding. "Elizabeth!" he stormed as he burst into the room.

Then Louis stopped. Whatever he had intended to say froze in his throat. There, on his very own bed, lay not an old man dying of leprosy, but the body of Christ crucified! Awed and astounded, Louis sank to his knees. "Guests like these are welcome, Elizabeth," he managed to say.

Another time Louis saw Elizabeth headed out into a snow storm with her apron bulging. "What are you carrying?" he called out as he hurried to catch up with her. He was thinking, It must be food for the poor, and she's going to get very sick if she keeps running around in this weather. I'm going to send her back at once.

Elizabeth turned and smiled as Louis came running to her. She opened her apron, and fragrant red and white roses came tumbling out! Well, thought Louis to himself, if God is so pleased with her errands of mercy that he changes bread to roses, who am I to stop her?

All the people knew that their duke, Louis and his wife Elizabeth, loved each other faithfully. They saw that Louis tried to care for Elizabeth, who often seemed to ignore her own comfort in doing good to others. And Elizabeth tried to help Louis stay calm and happy in the midst of all his responsibilities as ruler of Thuringia. She was obviously sad when he had to go away on business trips, and was very happy when she knew he was on the way home. Then she would take out her best dresses and fix his favorite meals, making sure the children were there to greet him when he arrived.

How holy and good she is, Louis would think whenever he awoke at night and saw her kneeling at their bedside, deep in prayer. He had the same thought as he watched her assist devoutly at Mass or return from a visit to the sick or care for their children. "Never change," he would tell her, "unless you become even more loving." And to encourage his young wife in her goodness, he wrote to the Pope and asked him to send a priest to be Elizabeth's spiritual director and confessor.

Meanwhile, important events were taking place. Many noble knights of Europe were preparing for a Crusade. They intended to go and recover Palestine from the Muslims so that Christian pilgrims could visit the holy places where Jesus had lived and walked. Many of the knights who fought in the Crusades were killed in battle. Others got deadly diseases in the foreign lands and died. It was a great sacrifice for Christian wives and mothers to see their loved ones march off to war. When Elizabeth heard that Louis intended to go with the next group of soldiers, she was frightened.

Not only frightened—she was so overcome with the news that she fainted. Sick with sorrow, Louis revived her. But she woke up pleading. "Don't go. Don't Louis. What if you never return?"

Painful though it was, Louis tried to help Elizabeth understand that he had to go. Of course it hurt him to leave her and the children. But he felt that it was both his duty and God's will. With tears in her eyes, Elizabeth agreed.

It was a sad parting, but a courageous one. Smiles and tears and shouts of "Long live Louis!" came from all the villagers. Louis' kind eyes were shining as he waved his good-byes from atop his large stallion, his armor shining in the morning sun.

Elizabeth raised her hand in a final farewell. A few moments later the band of horsemen were out of sight and the long months of waiting began. Elizabeth was busy, however, for it was her duty to supervise the castle and the village whenever Louis was away. News did not travel fast in those days, but now and then a letter would arrive, or news from the holy lands and the war would be brought via a traveler or soldier returning home.

At first the news was good. But then horrible news—the plague had struck the Christian army. And the news she had been dreading from the beginning—Louis was dead. She had feared it, but she couldn't believe it. Louis was gone!

"Dear God," she prayed, "give me the strength to bear this sorrow. My worst fears have come to pass, but I offer you this suffering with my love. May your will be done, O Lord. May Louis be with you forever in heaven!"

She was a widow at the age of twenty, with four young children to care for. Her son, Herman, was supposed to become the next duke. Until he was old enough, however, his uncle Henry, Louis' brother, would rule the land. At least, that was how it was supposed to be. But the power-hungry Henry seized the throne at once, and on a cold winter day sent Elizabeth and the four children out of the castle. Only two of her maids were allowed to go with them.

Henry was cruel. He had been among those who laughed and teased Elizabeth when they were children. And he had always been jealous of his good brother, Louis, whom everyone loved. Now he warned the villagers not to take the royal refugees into their homes or give them anything to eat.

Even though Elizabeth had given them so much help, the people were too afraid of the new duke to help her. Eventually Elizabeth found a small, smelly shelter where pigs were kept and there they spent the night. In the morning, Elizabeth woke her family and they made their way to a nearby Franciscan monastery where they asked the friars for food. She also asked them to sing a hymn of praise and thanks to God for her.

Elizabeth was now one of the poorest of the poor. Daily she walked the streets, begging scraps for her children to eat. Often they went to sleep hungry. How terrible Elizabeth must have felt to see her children suffering, yet somehow they always managed to find shelter when night came.

Elizabeth had often talked to the orphans and the sick people in her hospital about Jesus, and how he had become a poor man like them when he came to this earth. Now she rejoiced in the fact that she was living so much like her beloved Savior. She did not understand, but she accepted the circumstances in which she found herself. She had been born a princess, and now she was a poor widow. Receiving the bread she needed day by day made her realize how grateful she was to God, who cared for all his creatures and met all their needs.

Finally, the news of what happened reached some of Elizabeth's relatives. They immediately sent for her to live with them. And then, another stroke of good fortune came. Louis' knights returned from the Crusade, and they forced Henry to return the dukedom to young Herman.

Elizabeth did not live much longer after this happy turn of events. A fatal illness seized her, and consumed by a raging fever, she became weaker and weaker. Joyfully, she received the Sacrament of Anointing. Her eyes shone with happiness; after a life filled with good works, happiness and times of great sorrow, she was going home to heaven. Around midnight on November 17, 1231, she died. So many miracles were wrought through her intercession, that in less than four years Elizabeth was canonized a saint of the Church.

Generosity is a virtue which God loves very much. We can practice it by sharing our things with our brothers and sisters and friends, and by helping to care for our home.

St. Peregrine

(1260-1345)

May 1

Peregrine Laziosi was born in the city of Forli, in northern Italy, in the year 1260. He was an only child, and his parents, like most people in Forli at that time, were strongly opposed to the Catholic Church and were unwilling to live by the teachings of Jesus and the Church. Peregrine was active in politics from a very young age. By the time he was eighteen, he was a leader in the "Anti-Papal" party. This political group was so active and violent against anything and anyone Roman Catholic that most of the churches in Forli had closed and the Pope had called away most of the priests. This was difficult for those who wanted to practice the Catholic faith, but it was too dangerous for priests to remain there. Pope Martin IV, however, wanted to try everything he could to bring about a reconciliation between the city and the Church. Finally he thought of just the person to send: Father

217

Philip Benizi. He was an excellent preacher and a holy priest. Father Benizi agreed to travel to Forli, sending word ahead that he would preach in the town square when he arrived.

It was about mid-morning when he entered the city gates, and already he could hear a large crowd gathering. Fervently, he prayed to Mary, the Mother of God, to help him speak words of peace and reconciliation to these people. He prayed that their hearts would be open to hear the Good News of Jesus and that they would be willing to turn away from the sinful lifestyles which many of them were living. He also prayed for his own safety, because several of the priests who had been sent to Forli had been killed by these people!

As he entered the town square, the crowd parted and he could see a large platform which had been built for him. Father Benizi slowly made his way to the platform, wondering if the sudden silence of the crowd was a sign of their desire for reconciliation. As he reached the top of the platform, it seemed that this elderly, humble priest already had some sort of power over the crowd. A great calm met his clear gaze. Many people—probably the Catholics—had crowded into the balconies and on the roofs to hear him speak. No doubt, he thought, they felt safer there than down in the square.

Philip Benizi held a crucifix in his right hand. He raised it heavenward, while his lips moved in a quick, silent prayer. Then he began to speak, gently inviting the people to repent.

The holy priest's heart was trembling. Was God really working a miraculous mass conversion here?

But then a disturbance began at the far end of the square. A young voice hurled an insult, and the spell was broken. From every point in the square new voices rang out, new insults. While the good fled, the others moved violently toward the preacher. Leading them was a young man, probably no more than eighteen.

Father Philip stood tall and straight, holding the crucifix and looking up toward heaven. The leader of the young men bounded up the steps of the platform and insulted the holy priest. Father Philip remained silent. The youth raised his fist and hit him on the cheek!

The square was in an uproar. Insult after insult rained down upon Father Benizi as the people pushed him around. He kept the crucifix clutched tightly in his hand and repeated over and over the prayer of Jesus, "Father, forgive them, they know not what they do."

Relentlessly, the crowd drove the priest out of their city. The drawbridge was lifted behind him, and the walled city of Forli retreated within itself.

Father Philip walked painfully beside a little brook which wound its way through the countryside. The soft murmur of the waters was soothing to his pounding head, and it formed a perfect background for his prayer. Battered and beaten as his body was, the old priest's soul was as calm as ever.

"Father, forgive them," he prayed. "They are blind!"

He thought of the young man who had struck the first blow, recalling the face hardened by anger and corruption; he saw again the raised hand....

"Father, bring him close to you. He's a poor and ignorant boy."

He walked on in the evening stillness.

All at once Father Philip heard running footsteps. Could someone else be coming to attack him? Perhaps it was only his imagination.

But no. Now he heard the footsteps clearly. A voice was calling, "Father! Father!"

The elderly man turned and saw a young man running toward him. His arms were outstretched, as if in desperation, and he threw himself to the ground at Father Philip's feet. Kissing the hem of his robe again and again, he begged, "Forgive me, Father, forgive me!"

Father Philip understood everything. He bent down and raised the young man to his feet, hugging him as a father would his child.

The face of this teenager who had struck him that morning was now softened and covered with tears of repentance. His eyes, so hardened with hatred that morning, were now glowing with a soft, new light.

"Pardon, pardon!" he repeated. "I am so sorry for my horrible sins!"

"I know it; I can see it," replied Father Philip gently.

"I want to change my life. I want to leave this filth behind and spend my life doing good to others," the young man blurted out. "God is calling me, but I know that a great change must take place in me. I don't know where or what God wants of me...but I do know that everything that I found so much pleasure in until today, now makes me sick."

Father Philip consoled him and gave him some important advice. "Return home and rid yourself of your addictions and selfishness. Practice honesty and purity and humility. Listen to the voice of your conscience and do what God will lead you to. It won't be easy, but pray. The Lord is with you. Perhaps someday you will do a great work for him." He paused. "What's your name, my son?"

"Peregrine Laziosi."

Surely Divine Providence had planned this meeting between the great saint, Philip Benizi, and this young man who would one day also become a great saint!

Peregrine finally said good-bye and walked slowly back to the city. He knew that he must abandon his former companions. But as he devoted himself to prayer and meditation, he found that his old friends and amusements—the drinking, the partying, the political debates—repelled him now. The new joy that had taken possession of Peregrine's heart was to please

Jesus and his mother, Mary. Nothing else mattered.

Peregrine's old friends and family were amazed at the change. But they figured that it wouldn't last, and they tried to win him back constantly. After all, hadn't he been one of the liveliest, the quickest-witted, the most daring of them all?

"Come back to life!" they urged. But Peregrine would not. He found life, he told them, but it was the true life, that which Father Philip had come to preach about. And it seemed that he could actually feel the life of God's grace flowing into his soul.

The days passed and Peregrine felt himself growing closer and closer to God. He was cultivating, as the holy priest had urged him to do, a trusting, childlike confidence in the Blessed Mother. He prayed to Mary often, and with great love read and reread the Gospel stories telling of the birth and childhood of Jesus. Then, one day, while praying in the shadows of the darkened cathedral, Peregrine actually saw his Heavenly Mother, surrounded by angels.

Peregrine felt a trembling in his heart; his whole being was caught up in admiration of the heavenly vision. Then Mary spoke to him.

"I am the Mother of Jesus, the one whom you adore on the cross.... In Siena is a monastery of my servants, the Servites; go to Siena, for that is where you belong."

The vision disappeared and Peregrine hurried home, with only one thought in mind: to obey the wonderful invitation of the Queen of Heaven. In the silence of the night, he slipped out of the darkened house and set out toward Siena.

It would be a hard and lonely journey, he knew. It would take four days and four nights to cross the Appenine Mountains. But no. God provided Peregrine with a traveling companion, a young boy whose lively and holy conversation made the hours and the miles speed by. When they were in sight of Siena, the stranger suddenly vanished, and Peregrine realized that an angel of the Lord had accompanied him.

At last he was knocking nervously and excitedly at the monastery door. When he had been let in, he told the monks of his great desire to join them, confessed his past sins publicly and asked to be accepted into the community. Smiling joyfully, the superior, who was none other than Father Philip Benizi, received him into the Servites.

In the years that followed, Peregrine studied hard as he prepared for the priesthood. He showed great humility, recollection, apostolic zeal and a spirit of penance and self-sacrifice. After his ordination, he strongly desired to return to Forli, where he had spent the wild days of his youth. He wanted to dedicate himself to doing good in that city so filled with darkness and sin.

Permission was granted, and the young priest retraced his steps across the mountains to the city of his birth.

The rebellious city welcomed her holy son,

Armed with only a crucifix, Father Peregrine entered the forest where the gang was known to hide out. He soon found himself face to face with them.

opening wide to him the doors of homes filled with misery. The people brought him to their sick; Father Peregrine cured them. They told him their needs, their troubles, their hopes and desires, and he listened and encouraged them. His favorite places were the hospitals, prisons and the homes of those who had not yet returned to the Christian faith and way of life. He walked through the city continually, seeking to visit and comfort and instruct, by his presence, his words and his deeds, all those who needed help.

At night he prayed, and if he fell asleep through exhaustion and toppled to the floor, he picked himself up and began to pray again. Very early in the morning he celebrated Mass, and he went to confession almost every day!

One time, a band of thieves was roaming through the countryside, attacking and robbing everyone they found traveling on the lonely roads winding through the forests and hills. The city officials and police could find no way of stopping them. Then Father Peregrine decided to act.

Armed with only a crucifix, the holy priest entered the forest where the gang was known to hide out. In a short time he found himself face to face with them. They were heavily armed. If they had wished, they could have killed him right there. They could have done this, but something held them back. The priest was calling many of them by name, and their thoughts turned back to the days of their youth, when they had been Peregrine's companions! Now he was looking at them with a gaze that touched their hearts. They did not raise a hand against him, but let him speak.

Perhaps he spoke to them about heaven, or maybe he told them the story of the prodigal son or the lost sheep.... At any rate, from that day on the country roads were free from those robbers. And the story goes that most of that once violent gang entered monasteries and spent the rest of their lives in prayer and penance.

Father Peregrine was by now quite old. The hard life of poverty and repentance which he had led was leaving its mark. Long hours of being continuously on his feet had caused an ugly sore to form on one of his legs, and now it had turned cancerous. The doctors said that the leg must be amputated.

In the solitude of the night, Father Peregrine begged God, "How can I serve you, my Lord, if I can no longer walk? How will I be able to reach all those people who are waiting for me, expecting me to tell them about you and about your infinite goodness? Yet not my will, but your will be done."

His heart was full of fear. Suddenly, the figure on the crucifix above him came down and touched the painful sore, and then disappeared. Father Peregrine wondered whether or not he was dreaming. Dazed, he struggled to his feet, and discovered that his leg was completely healed! Overcome with joy, he flung himself down in front of the crucifix to pour out his gratitude. The next morning, the doctors found no trace of the cancer or the infection.

The years passed and Peregrine continued his work in Forli. But he knew that the beautiful Queen of Heaven was waiting for him as a mother waits for her dearly loved child. After his eightieth birthday, his soul left this world with complete calm and serenity.

At the funeral a great crowd of people who had known and loved him gathered around the body to mourn their loss. They knew that he had been a saint. And just as they had brought all difficulties to him in life, they now prayed for him to help them from heaven.

It was hard for Peregrine to break his bad habits and form good ones. But his love for the Blessed Mother helped him make the change. We, too, should pray to Mary, especially when we have difficulty breaking bad habits.

St. Catherine of Siena

(1347-1380)

April 29

Stephen turned around to see what his six-year-old sister, Catherine, had stopped for. Always happy and curious, she sometimes forgot her mother's directions to come straight home from her older sister's house. "Catherine!" Stephen shouted. He frowned as he saw her staring up at the sky. Looking up himself and seeing nothing, he thought she was playing a joke on him. But he had to get home and finish his chores! He ran back to her and grabbed her arm playfully. Catherine suddenly jumped and pulled away from Stephen.

"Why did you do that?" she demanded. "I was seeing the most beautiful thing! Jesus was there, and he was reaching out to take my hand!"

Stephen looked at his sister. What a wild story, he thought. But Catherine was too serious to be making it up.... Later that night Mrs. Benincasa, Catherine's mother, noticed that Catherine took an extra long time to say her night prayers. In fact, after that day it seemed like praying was the only thing that interested her. She still played with her friends, but there was nothing she liked more than praying or learning about Jesus and the saints. By the time she was twelve, Catherine had told everyone—her parents and all twenty-four of her brothers and sisters—that she never wanted to marry. She wanted to be a nun.

Catherine's father, Giacomo, was very upset. Catherine was beautiful, and he could see no reason why she should go to the convent. To encourage her to forget her prayers, her parents had many parties at their house. They invited many young men to come and visit their youngest daughter. Finally, Catherine couldn't take it anymore. Not knowing how else to convince her father that she was serious, Catherine had all her beautiful long, brown hair cut off. Since no women in the town of Siena had short hair except the nuns, her parents were horrified. At last they gave in—but they would only allow sixteen-year-old Catherine to be a Third Order Dominican. That meant that she could make the promises to live poorly, never to marry and to be obedient to their bishop, but she would stay at home instead of going away to the convent. The Third Order Dominicans were also permitted to wear the white and black habit of the community.

For a few years Catherine spent most of her time in a little room at the family's big house. Her father gave her part of their income to use for the poor people she met on the way to the church.

Since Catherine had never learned to read or write, she could not read books herself. Instead she spent most of her time praying and thinking about the sermons she heard at church. When she was twenty-one, Catherine had another vision of Jesus. This time she saw him with his mother, Mary. Together, they placed a ring on her finger, just like a wedding band. It was a beautiful experience, and Catherine knew that now she belonged entirely to Jesus forever. Jesus also told her that instead of staying in her parents' home, he wanted her to go out and help others know how much he loved them.

Immediately, Catherine started to join some of the other Third Order Dominicans in Siena to care for the sick in the hospitals. Many people were in the hospital because they were dying and had no money or families to take care of them. Catherine became well known for choosing the sickest and poorest patients. She especially liked to care for those people who were going to die soon. She talked to them about God's love for them and about heaven. She also went to visit the prisons and the men who had been condemned to death. Some of these men were real criminals, but others were innocent people who had been unjustly accused. She talked to all of them, no matter what they had done or how much they were suffering.

One young man from another city had gotten into a fight while in Siena and been put in jail. The judge had condemned him to die. He was angry and bitter at this unjust sentence and felt God had abandoned him. Catherine spent long hours talking to him and praying with him. She tried to convince the judge that this man should not die, but the judge would not listen. Finally the young man realized that no matter how mean or unjustly human beings might be toward one another, God was always merciful and just. He listened as Catherine explained how Jesus, too, had been condemned unjustly and had accepted crucifixion in order to free us from our sins. The young man began to pray with Catherine and even to look forward to being in heaven with Jesus, where there would be no more suffering. On the day he died, Catherine was right there beside him.

Even though Catherine had not gone to school she was very wise. She was very good at settling arguments between people and even between cities. Soon, business people, mayors and bishops were calling Catherine to help them settle their disagreements. In this way, more and more people came to know her. Always a friendly person, Catherine formed many close friendships. In fact, a whole group of people began to spend time with her, helping her read and write her many letters. They also wrote down the things she said about God and prayer. But many times Catherine did not feel famous or very successful in her work. And for a long time she felt that God was far away from her. She kept praying, but she didn't really feel that anyone was listening. She was even tempted to give up her life as a Third Order Dominican!

One day, as Catherine was alone in the chapel,

she had an overwhelming sense of God's presence. She cried out to him, "Where have you been, Lord? I have been having terrible thoughts and feelings!"

And then she heard God answer. "Catherine, I have been in your heart all this time. It was I who was giving you courage and strength to keep going each day!"

Suddenly Catherine understood. God was not in one place or another. And he was not to be confused with good feelings or success. But he was always present with each person, always helping us in every situation. But in order to keep close to God and remain aware of that divine presence, we must make a quiet place in our hearts for God. A place where we can stop anytime and anywhere to talk to him and love him. Catherine told many of her friends about this experience. They were happy to listen to her because many of them were busy working and caring for their families. They didn't have much time to go into the church and pray. They began to take a few minutes of quiet time each day just to speak heart-to-heart with God and to think about his great love for them.

Catherine also knew that in order to keep that quiet place for God, a person would have to live a good life. That meant being honest in business deals, being faithful to one's husband or wife, treating others justly—in other words, to know God within them, people had to really try to act like Jesus. Many of the people who heard her teaching realized the same thing. They wanted to know God so much that they went to confession and returned to Mass, resolving to try their best to live as good Christians.

Catherine's reputation finally reached Pope Gregory XI, who was having a very difficult time leading the Church. Part of his difficulties were his own fault. Instead of remaining in Rome and taking care of the affairs of the whole Church, he had spent several years in France. And much of his time was spent dealing with local affairs of the French bishops and royalty. This caused much confusion and hard feelings. Finally, though, Gregory was convinced to return to Rome. But just when things were starting to go better, he died! The cardinals gathered and elected Pope Urban VI.

Over in France, though, the bishops were still upset that the Pope no longer lived with them. Instead of accepting the decision of the other cardinals, they elected another Pope! In those days there were no televisions or radios to spread news, so it was quite a while before the confusion became clear. Urban VI was impressed with Catherine's wisdom and asked her for advice. She cautioned him to be gentle and work toward reconciliation. But he was too stubborn and angry to sit down and talk to the French bishops. Things seemed to be getting worse.

By now Catherine was thirty-years-old. She looked much older though because she so often fasted and had done so much traveling in all kinds of weather. She had another vision, but

Pope Urban VI was impressed with Catherine's wisdom and asked her for advice. She cautioned him to be gentle and work toward reconciliation.

this one was not beautiful like the others. Jesus was on the cross, and Catherine could see how much he was suffering. Suddenly, bright red rays came from his hands, feet and heart. Catherine felt his great pain of the crucifixion. It was as if she, like Jesus, had nails in her hands and feet. Other people very close to Jesus have experienced this same thing. It is called the "stigmata." In Catherine's case, people could not see the wounds, but they could see that she was often in great pain.

At last, when she was thirty-three, Catherine had one more vision of Jesus. This one was also painful. Jesus seemed to be taking her own heart and blood and pouring it out over his Church. Catherine understood. All her last sufferings and prayers she offered to God for reconciliation within the Church which Jesus had started. She died not very long after this, and from heaven she helped Urban VI and the other bishops settle their differences. In the year 1461, she was declared a saint.

Right after she died, Father Raymond of Capua, a Dominican priest who often heard Catherine's confessions, started to write the story of her life. He also helped her friends to collect the many letters she had written and her thoughts and meditations that she had shared with them. We have many of these writings today. Catherine of Siena is known as one of the "doctors of the Church." This is a special title given to saints whose writings have helped other Christians live as Jesus did. Catherine is also called a mystic because of the many special visions which she had of Jesus.

Following Catherine's example, we can try and keep a "quiet place" for God in our hearts. We can take a few minutes each day to talk heart-to-heart with him and thank him for his help in every situation. If we sin by choosing to do the wrong thing, we can tell God that we are sorry, go to confession as soon as possible and resolve to try harder to live as Jesus.

St. Bernardine of Siena

(1380-1444)

May 20

Bernardine finally said good-night to his aunt and uncle and the many guests who had come to the reception at their house. It had been an important day for him, and he wanted some time alone to think about his mother and father. How much he missed them! They had died when he was a young boy, and Bernardine had moved to Siena to live with his relatives. Now he was sixteen, and today, on the eve of the Feast of the Assumption, he had offered his candle to the Blessed Mother. This was the custom for all young men of his day, and extravagant parties often followed the candle ceremony. But for Bernardine, it was truly symbolic of his love and devotion to Mary, the Mother of God.

Fourteenth-century Siena was a rough place to live. Not even twenty years had passed since the great Catherine of Siena had died, but already the renewed fervor for Christian living and virtue was waning. Street gangs once again ruled sections of the city, and drunkenness and sexual immorality were rampant even among the youngest teenagers. Somehow, Bernardine had never felt a part of that lifestyle. When he prayed and read the lives of Jesus and the saints, something within him seemed to burst into flame. It was so obvious that Bernardine had chosen to remain chaste and did not participate in the drinking of his friends, that they were careful not to swear or tell dirty stories in his presence. He was a good friend and they respected him, but he was also a good fighter and not afraid to stand up for what was right!

That night, as Bernardine was dozing off, he heard screaming in the distance. Another street brawl, he thought disgustedly. But then the screaming grew louder, almost frantic, and Bernardine realized it was one of the boys who often joined him for prayer and in visiting the sick. He quickly jumped up and ran out the gate of his home. Heading through a narrow alley, he raced toward the increasingly frantic screams. Seeing a large crowd of boys from the next neighborhood beating his friend, Bernardine jumped into the middle of them. He quickly realized, however, that he and his friend were far outnumbered and a sick feeling settled in his stomach as he struggled to stay on his feet.

The drunken gang members were yelling loudly. "Hit the sissy! Knock him down! He thinks he's so good! Kick him!"

Just as he was losing control, Bernardine saw a group of his own friends at the end of the alley. They must have heard the noise, too, he thought. He called out, "Francis! James! Hurry, we need help!" In an instant his friends were there and the invading gang quickly disappeared into the night. They would attack one or two boys—but they would never stand up to a whole group!

"Thanks, you guys. You came just in time." Wiping the blood from his face and pulling up Robert, the boy whom he had come out to save, he added, "We've got to unite! The young men of Siena should be the city's glory, not its disgrace!"

Then he convinced them all to walk to a nearby shrine of the Blessed Virgin. Standing next to the statue of Mary, he told his friends that she, and she alone, was the "Lady of his heart."

A couple of the boys were embarrassed at this display of religious devotion and said, "Oh, Bernardine is really crazy!" But others motioned them to keep quiet as Bernardine led them in a prayer. They said, "Wait and see! Bernardine will be our next saint!"

The years passed quickly, and in 1400, at the age of twenty, Bernardine joined the "Company of the Disciplined of Mary." This group of men worked in the hospitals, caring for the poor and the sick. One afternoon, as Bernardine was outside for some fresh air, he saw the stooped form of a person walking slowly up the street. Thinking that it was an elderly pilgrim, he ran to offer food and shelter. But as Bernardine reached him, the man fell. To his surprise, the man pushed Bernardine back roughly with his walking stick. "Go away! Go away!" he gasped. As the sick man looked up and his hood fell away, Bernardine grew pale with fright. The man was dying of the plague.

The plague, a dreadfully painful and contagious disease, had not been around for some time. But recently the people of Siena heard rumors that it was again spreading in Rome. And now, thought Bernardine somberly, the plague has come to Siena. Without thinking of the danger to himself, Bernardine picked the man up and carried him to the hospital. He knew that the awful disease would spread quickly. Within a week hundreds of people of every age and class were sick. Terror-stricken, the wealthier people of Siena packed up what food they could and left the city, hoping that the fresh air of the country would prevent them from getting sick.

But Bernardine and his companions remained. They were everywhere, from morning until late at night, caring for the sick and comforting the mourning. They set up large bonfires outside the city to burn the dead, for the disease was so contagious that normal burial was impossible. One day, when it seemed that all hope was gone, Bernardine told his tired companions, "In the Gospel it says that God will not fail to reward us for all the good we do. Will you stay and help me care for the sick?"

"We're with you!" they answered. And after praying together and offering their own health and lives to the mercy of God, they went back to their work with a new enthusiasm. And the sick continued to arrive. Bernardine did all he could for them, even leading those who still had strength in singing hymns to Mary.

Finally the terrible plague was over and the people were returning to the city. Many had lost not only their families, but most of their belongings as well. Widespread looting and fires had broken out in the chaos. Worn out and exhausted, Bernardine became very ill. On the edge of death for days, his cousins kept him in their home and nursed him.

At last the fever broke, and the danger of death passed. But Bernardine was so weak that it took several months for him to regain his strength. During that time, he was doing some serious thinking and praying. One day, as his aunt brought in his dinner tray, he told her, "You have been a true mother to me. Now I must tell you before anyone else, I think the Lord is calling me; I must spend the rest of my life for him in a special way."

As soon as he was able, Bernardine was up and giving away all that he owned. Well known for his piety, chaste living and generosity, the Franciscan friars were only too happy to receive this twenty-two-year-old man into their community. He went to a small monastery, where there were a few humble friars who could not even read or write.

"We have only a little bread and some cooked vegetables," they told him when he arrived. "We are really very poor here." They were afraid that this brave young man would be expecting something more elegant or fancy.

"No, brothers, we are rich!" replied Bernardine. He meant that anyone close to God is rich. He fell easily into the routine of prayer and work of the friars. In the evenings he continued his studies for ordination, for the superiors had invited him to become a priest as well as a friar. Bernardine was supremely happy, but some of his relatives were not so pleased. He had been one of the brightest and most handsome of the young men in the city. They did not understand how he could throw every worldly thing away and choose to live in such poverty. When they met him on the streets of Siena they were embarrassed, and said to him scornfully, "You're nothing but a crazy beggar! We are ashamed to be related to you."

"Time will tell if I am crazy or not," replied Bernardine calmly. But his heart ached. So many of his own family and friends thought so little of God. It seemed that they were ruled only by their greed and passions, and knew nothing about the great love which the Lord and the Blessed Mother were ready to shower on each of them. Bernardine longed to preach sermons that would convince them of that divine love, but his sickness had left his voice hoarse and weak. Even though he was now a priest, it did not seem that the Lord wanted him to preach.

––––––––––

Years passed and the country of Italy grew more and more violent. The wealthy landowners hired foreign soldiers to fight with each other. And the poor peasants were left without jobs or decent housing as the small villages were destroyed one after another. The country seemed lawless and evil was everywhere. Bernardine's heart ached, until one day he could keep silent no longer. With two other friars, he set out on a mission of bringing peace throughout Italy.

The long hours of prayer and meditating on the words of Jesus gave him words of peace and reconciliation. And, most wonderful of all, Bernardine grew more and more confident as he realized that his once weak voice was now clear and easy for all to hear. He attributed this miraculous cure to Mary. Who desired more than she, he reasoned, that the life and teachings of her son be made known to these poor, suffering people?

From city to city they went, urging the people to burn down the houses of prostitution and bars. They burned dirty books and pictures, and even the luxurious clothes and ornaments of the wealthy, in hugh bonfires. Bernardine would instruct group after group of men and women in the Gospel. Gently, he heard their confessions and gave absolution. Everywhere he encouraged devotion to Mary, the Mother of Mercy, and to Jesus, our Savior and Redeemer.

But not everyone was pleased with his great success. After all, closing down businesses which relied on sinful habits meant somebody would be losing money. The dishonest businessmen watched Bernardine carefully, hoping to catch him doing something wrong so they could destroy his reputation. At last they had it. They noticed that everywhere in the towns where gangs had marked their boundaries, Bernardine would go and cover over the marks with the initials "IHS." He would also hold up a large banner with the same insignia and ask the people to venerate it. "Do you see that weird emblem the friar holds up after he preaches? It must be a symbol of the devil!" they exclaimed to one another. And they came up with a plan.

While Bernardine was preaching at Viterbo, a very important envoy arrived at the monastery where he was staying. They carried a message for Bernardine, the friar, from his holiness, the Pope! Why would the Pope bother to send such an important delegation to a poor friar? It must be something important, thought Bernardine, as he went to meet them.

It was a call to Rome, and Bernardine realized that his enemies must have made a serious accusation against him. Yet he prepared to leave for Rome in complete serenity. He had no idea what the charge could be, but he was confident that he had done no deliberate evil. Trusting as always in the care of Mary, Bernardine went in to meet the Pope.

Soon the two men of God were laughing together like old friends. And they spent a long time discussing the serious needs of the Church and of society at the time. When Bernardine left, he had only one demand placed on him by the Holy Father: he was to spend several weeks preaching in Rome! It was Bernardine's hour of triumph and everywhere he displayed the "IHS" insignia, which was really a symbol for the Holy Name of Jesus! In fact, to put a stop to the overwhelming amount of

In every town where gangs had marked their boundaries, Bernardine would go and cover over the marks with the initials "IHS."

cursing with the name of God, Bernardine had been spreading devotion to the Holy Names of Jesus and Mary. Now his "new devotion" had full approval of the Pope! To the warring factions and gangs he preached peace and encouraged them to unite under the standard of the Holy Name of Jesus. "Put His Holy Name on your banners and on the flags of your ships. Write it everywhere! We are all brothers and sisters in Christ!" he exclaimed.

By now tremendous crowds gathered wherever he went. And as the Lord began to work miracles through his intercession, the people were even more ready to listen to him and change their lives. The young people were so filled with love for Christ as they listened to his words that many resolved to give their lives totally to God just as Bernardine had done. The group of friars which he had joined had numbered only 130 when he was a novice. Now there were over 4,000! And so many young women were becoming nuns that new convents were being built every day.

Reaching Milan, however, Bernardine ran into trouble. Duke Philip Visconte had held a grudge against Bernardine ever since the saint had reproached him publicly for his sinful lifestyle. Now the duke called the friar to his castle and warned him, "Brother, if you don't stop preaching, I will have you tortured!"

"I shall be happy to suffer for the love of Christ," replied Bernardine. The duke was about to insult him for this answer when one of the courtiers whispered something in his ear. Then the wicked duke said in a smooth voice, "Pardon me if I have offended you. Please accept this money for your monastery." And he held out a bag heavy with gold coins.

But Bernardine knew that if he took the money the people would be confused. They all knew that Bernardine preached against wealth and riches. And there was no doubt that this money had come through dishonest means. So Bernardine answered the duke, "We don't need money. But if you force me to accept it, then allow me to bring it where I want."

Followed by the duke's curious men, Bernardine took the bag and went directly to the prison. There he used the gold coins to buy the freedom of poor political prisoners. To each one he said, "Go home. You are free, in the name of Jesus Christ!"

The duke's men returned grumbling to the castle, and Bernardine continued his travels, always on foot. He journeyed to distant places and in the worst weather. "Courage," he would say to his friar-companions. "We shall soon find shelter and someone to feed us. Even in the darkest nights, there is always a light somewhere."

Wherever he went, Bernardine was like a flame of love that purified souls and brought peace to all. Those who had quarreled with their friends or relatives went in search of them to tell them, "Come back home! Let's give each other the hand of friendship." Those who had stolen property returned it with interest, and those who had enslaved others or failed to pay employees now paid their workers in full. As the warring family groups were reconciled to one another, the whole land once again grew peaceful and everyone prospered.

But there was still work to be done, and so Bernardine, old and worn out, continued to travel. One day, in the year 1344, he and a group of friars were on their way to Aquila. The people were expecting them and there was to be a whole week of preaching and praying. They stopped to rest as they approached the city, and one of the friars asked him, "Do you remember, Father, the time you preached in this same area on Assumption Day?"

"Yes," Bernardine replied. "I do remember...." And he seemed to be living again that moment when he had said in his sermon, "Clear, precious and beautiful as a star is our most pure Virgin Mary!" And the crowd had suddenly began to shout, "Look up at the sky! The star!" Sure enough, in broad daylight a most marvelous, brilliant star had appeared in the sky.

The memory of this soul-stirring moment was too much for the poor heart of God's weary traveler and Bernardine sank to the ground murmuring, "Most Holy Virgin, my sweet Mother...." Frightened, his brothers tried to help him.

The people of Aquila who had come out to meet their beloved preacher returned with him in a sorrowful procession. For three days, they waited in suspense, hoping that he would regain his strength.

But on Ascension Day, the bells announced Bernardine's last great journey. From everywhere, people gathered to give honor to him.

Yet, though they gathered for such a holy purpose, there was fighting between the poor people and the rich people.

"Get out of my way, you fool!" a nobleman yelled at a peasant.

"We've had enough of your arrogance!" was the farmer's defiant reply. "Friends, gather around me!" A furious battle began.

Swords and clubs were being waved when someone shrieked, "Stop! Look! Look toward the church!" Terror filled the crowd as they turned to look. What was it?

From the pale face of St. Bernardine, whose body had been laid out in the church, blood began to flow—so much blood, in fact, that it was streaming out of the church onto the square in front!

"He said it," one of the friars reminded the crowd. "He said: 'I would give all my blood to put an end to fighting and hatred!'" Then all the people began to shout, "Peace, friends. Peace!"

Many miracles occurred after Bernardine's death, but the greatest miracle was his life and his mission as "Messenger of Peace."

Just as in the time of Bernardine, we live in a society in which violence, impurity and drunkenness consume many people's lives. Like Bernardine, though, we can resolve to avoid those things and give our lives and our devotion to the Holy Names of Jesus and Mary. Like him, we can talk to others about the words and life of Jesus, and convince them of the great love which God has for each one of us.

St. Joan of Arc

(1412-1431)

May 30

Eight-year-old Joan put down her heavy bundle and stared. There was the house she and her family had left just last week, but almost everything around it was ruined or burned. The barn was gone, and she could see wisps of smoke still blowing off her father's field of rye. Looking up at her father, she started to cry as she saw a large tear roll down his face. Her mother shifted Joan's younger sister from one hip to the other and said calmly, "Well, let us thank God it wasn't worse. At least we are safe. And," continued the patient and faith-filled mother, "it doesn't look like they found our underground cellar. We'll have enough food until spring."

"Yes, Papa," added Joan's older brother. "Mama is right. Thank God we are all safe. And if we plant tomorrow, perhaps a new crop can still ripen before the winter comes."

It was the year 1420, and the "Hundred Years

War" was raging violently near the village of Domremy where Joan's family lived. The Burgundians, who were fighting with England against France, often raided the border villages in the area of Lorraine. This time, the people of Domremy had received warning in time and had fled to the neighboring village of Neufchatel. They were well acquainted with war, and often, wounded men or homeless families would stumble into Domremy for shelter. Joan's family was always among the first to offer aid, and Joan frequently gave up her own bed to the refugees.

In spite of the war, the children of Domremy found plenty of time for games and dancing, and even occasional picnics in the nearby hills. As Joan grew older, the young men coming to call were more and more frequent. Like other young women in the town, Joan had not been taught to read or write, but by the time she was twelve everyone knew that her talent for cooking and spinning was unsurpassed. Her future as a bride and mother seemed pretty well set until an extraordinary thing happened....

Joan was calmly tending the garden one afternoon when a strange voice caused her to look up. A bright light was hovering between her and the village church. What could it be? Joan remained frozen to the spot.

"Joan, daughter of God, go to church often. Be good and pure. God wants you to do this."

The light disappeared. In spite of the hot summer sun, Joan shivered. What was this all about? Maybe she should rest in the shade a minute, she thought. But, no, she was sure that she had not imagined the voice. Perhaps God wanted something special of her. Be virtuous.... "My God," she whispered, "I promise you I shall go to church often, and I shall remain a virgin as long as it shall please you!"

Soon after, the voice spoke to her again. And again on another day. This time, in the bright light, she saw a splendid being whom she knew was the Archangel Michael! Around him were many other angels. They were so beautiful! When they disappeared, Joan started to cry. She wanted so much to go with them!

Soon the girl had heavenly visits from Catherine of Alexandria and St. Margaret of Antioch. Both of them had been martyrs and were often prayed to by people of Joan's village. St. Michael was a patron saint of the French royal family.

"Joan the maiden, daughter of God," the saints said to her often, "you must leave this village. You must lead the dauphin to Rheims, where he will be crowned." The "dauphin" was the young prince Charles II, who had not yet been officially crowned king of France because of the war. The saints told Joan that she would go into battle and drive the English army from the city of Orleans.

All of this was very puzzling to Joan. "I'm only

a young girl!" she protested. "I cannot fight!"
"Go, daughter of God!" was the reply. But Joan
did not even know where to begin. Four years
passed by. The voices spoke to her often. At last
they said, "Go to Robert de Baudricourt in the town
of Vancouleurs, and he will give you men to take
you to the dauphin."

Robert de Baudricourt was a well-known noble
who fought on the dauphin's side. He knew that
until the young prince Charles could go to Rheims
and receive the crown, there would be no peace in
France. The people in every part of the country
were suffering from the war.

Joan and her brother-in-law, Durand Laxert,
went to his fortress to see Robert de Baudricourt.
They had a difficult time convincing the guards to
let them in, but once inside Joan began speaking.
"Your Lordship, I have a message for you. The
dauphin must remain ready to fight. But he should
not enter the battle himself. This kingdom does
not belong to the dauphin, but my Lord wishes him
to become king in spite of his enemies, and I myself
will lead him to be anointed and crowned."

As Joan spoke, the guards around them began
to laugh. How could this young country maiden
lead the dauphin to the crown?

"Who is this Lord you speak of, and what right
has he to give orders to the king?" growled Sir
Robert.

"The Lord of heaven," Joan replied.

But Robert de Baudricourt did not believe her,
and sent Joan home.

The next year, when she was seventeen, Joan

returned to Sir Robert, again to ask his help. This time he was more willing to listen, since the French had been suffering many defeats. After a few weeks he sent her to the dauphin. She was dressed as a boy and had her hair cut short like a soldier's. She had always been a good rider, and now she rode her high-spirited stallion with ease and grace.

Word was sent ahead that Joan was coming, and so the dauphin was waiting for her arrival. But he was not dressed as the prince! He wanted to test Joan and make sure that she really came from God, so he stood among the nobles, trying to look like just another one of them. Joan went straight up to him and introduced herself, then told him a secret which only he had known. With that, he was convinced that she was truly sent by God.

Dauphin Charles had a suit of armor made for Joan and a beautiful flag, which pictured the King of heaven with angels on either side of him, bearing the names of Jesus and Mary. Now she was ready to drive the English from Orleans.

Orleans had been under siege for months. The English had built forts around it, and cut off the flow of food and other supplies into the city. One dark night, Joan and a few soldiers slipped past the enemy forts and entered the city. How eagerly the people greeted her! They waved and cheered, while their torches flickered wildly.

A few days later, Joan rode into battle. Some of her soldiers went out first, and attacked one of the forts. The fort put up a good defense, however, and no progress was made until Joan thundered up on

Some of Joan's soldiers went ahead and attacked one of the forts. The soldiers in the fort put up a good defense, however, and neither side gained until Joan thundered up on her big war-horse.

her big war-horse. The banner she carried was whipping in the wind and was a signal for the French to attack. Her troops sprang into action at once. They had heard the ring of authority in her voice and were certain that she was being led by God. They stormed the fort and took it that night.

The next day was Ascension Day, and Joan gave orders that there should be no fighting. But the day after, she and a band of fighting men stormed another English fort. Again, the French were successful!

The following day they attacked a larger English fort. While arrows rained down upon them, the French placed ladders against the strong wall and started to climb. Then an arrow came whistling down from the battlement and drove into Joan's shoulder.

Breathlessly, the soldiers crowded around her. Would she be all right? Joan wrenched the arrow free, and said, "The wound is not deep, but I should like to go to confession before I get hit again! Please, call the chaplain." After receiving absolution, she returned to the battle.

They fought on until evening. "We may as well retreat," said the French commander at last. "We're getting nowhere."

"Not so," Joan replied. "It will not be long before we take the fort." And sure enough, that same evening the French soldiers fought their way up the walls to victory.

On the following day, the English army retreated, and left Orleans in peace. This battle completed the first part of Joan's mission. In the years to come, the English would be driven back to the coast from which they had come. For now they were fighting a nation who knew that God was with them. Soon, France would again be a free and independent nation.

Joan returned to the dauphin and urged him to go to Rheims to receive his crown. But Charles was not a very brave prince. He was afraid to travel, thinking that the English (or even one of the opposing French nobles!) would capture him. "We shall clear the way for you," Joan promised. She and her army set out with hopeful hearts, and drove the enemy away from the route to Rheims so that Charles could travel in safety.

On July 17, 1429, Charles and Joan marched down the broad aisle of the Rheims cathedral. The archbishop anointed the dauphin with great solemnity, and proclaimed him king. Joan, who stood nearby holding her beautiful banner, now knelt at the king's feet, weeping for joy.

_____

What was to happen next? "Continue to fight," the voices told Joan. "But, daughter of God, be prepared, for you will be taken by the enemy!" And so it happened. About ten months later, late at night, Joan was cut off from her men during a small battle with the Burgundians. Someone grabbed the bridle of her horse and she was taken prisoner. The Burgundians quickly sold her to the English as a prisoner of war.

Joan was put on trial. For several weeks, she was questioned for hours at a time. The English clergy who were questioning her asked her confusing questions about theology and philosophy. Their purpose was to show that Joan had not been sent by God at all, but that she was a witch. If they could prove that, then the French would again lose confidence and the English would win the war once and for all.

At the end of the long trial, which lasted for several weeks, the judge declared that Joan's voices had been from the devil. He handed her over to the civil court, which declared that she was indeed a witch—and witches must burn at the stake! She was sentenced to die on Wednesday, May 30, 1431.

On the morning she was burned, Joan was taken out to stand before the people. She said to them, "I beg all of you here to forgive any harm I have done, as I forgive you the harm you have done to me." She fell silent, and remained in an attitude of prayer for some time. Then she asked, "Does anyone have a cross?" An English soldier quickly tied two pieces of wood together and handed them to her. Joan slipped the cross inside her dress, next to her heart.

Then they led her to the stake and bound her to it with heavy chains. Someone held up a crucifix so that she could gaze at it. "St. Michael," Joan whispered, "help me die a good death." The wood had caught on fire now and was beginning to whip around her ankles. She could hear it snapping and crackling, and soon she felt the heat. Orange tongues of flame were licking about her. Pungent smoke filled her nostrils and a wave of terror ran through her. Then, as the flames caught her clothing and hair, hot searing pain...

"Jesus," Joan called softly. She continued to call his name until she died.

At the moment of Joan's death, many of those who had guarded and condemned her realized that they had burned a saint. Until then, their eyes had been blinded, but now they knew. And, as a sign from God, Joan's heart did not burn.

Twenty-five years later, Joan's family succeeded in having her trial reviewed. Many of her relatives and friends came to testify on her behalf. Finally, on June 7, 1456, Joan was declared completely innocent. Her voices were not from the devil; Joan was not a witch. Many years later, Joan was canonized—not because she had won battles or because she had been burned, but because she had remained faithful to what she knew God was asking of her.

Once Joan understood that the voices she heard were from God, she bravely obeyed them. We often learn God's will for us from the voices of our parents and guardians, and through faithful daily prayer. Let us, like Joan, try to do the right thing, even when it is difficult.

St. Francis Xavier

(1506-1552)

December 3

Francis was the son of a noble Spanish family. Although he was quick, lively and athletic, he did not choose a military career as most young nobles would have done. Instead, in his late teens Francis went to Paris to study at the College of St. Barbara. Students in Paris led a carefree and active life, and Francis was always in the midst of the good times. He kept up his studies, too, for he saw a university degree as a means to fame and fortune. Although he had no definite plans for the future, he knew he wanted to do something great.

An especially close friend of Francis was his roommate, Peter Favre. One day Peter said to Francis, "Have you seen the new student? He is Spanish, as you are. His name is Ignatius Loyola."

The name did not mean much to Francis. Nor was he impressed by Ignatius' appearance when he first met him. Ignatius was an older man, and he dressed very poorly. Francis prided himself on his fine clothes, obviously marking him as the son of a noble. But there was something unusual about Ignatius, and word spread rapidly that he had once been a famous soldier. What was he doing here? Francis thought. And why was this former soldier so often in the chapel, deep in prayer?

It had come about this way: During a war in Spain, Ignatius had been seriously injured. For months he was in danger of losing his leg, and could do nothing but lay still, waiting for the infection to go away and then for the bones to heal. To pass the time, he asked his cousin, at whose house he was staying, to give him some novels to read. However, this cousin was a very religious woman. The only books she had were lives of the saints! But these, she assured Ignatius, were as lively and entertaining as any novel. And besides, they were true stories! Since nothing else was available, Ignatius agreed to try them.

The months passed and Ignatius became more and more impressed by the courage and devotion of the saints, whom he came to consider true soldiers of the great King in heaven. He felt a yearning in his soul to come to know and serve that King, too. But where could he start? Religion and prayer had never been a part of his life....

When Ignatius' leg was healed, he did not return to the army. With thoughts of men like Augustine, Francis of Assisi and Dominic, he began walking from monastery to monastery as a pilgrim. He begged for his food and did small jobs for his keep. He journeyed from Spain to Italy, and there he boarded a ship for Palestine. Ignatius remained many months in the lands where Jesus had lived and walked. At last, feeling that God was leading him to a special mission of his own, Ignatius returned to Spain to study for the priesthood.

There were many things he had to learn. First came Latin, for priests in those days had to know Latin. Sitting with schoolboys, thirty-three-year-old Ignatius stumbled over the verbs and noun declensions, trying not to take the boys' laughter at his mistakes too seriously. This was God's will for him at the moment, he knew that. With determination, he learned all the lessons required before he could enter the seminary.

Ignatius' mind was so fixed on God by this time, that when he had to conjugate the Latin verb *amo*, to love, he would say to himself, I love God, I am loved by God.... And then he would stop and reflect on this great truth!

To learn logic and theology Ignatius traveled to Paris, where he met Peter and Francis and their friends at St. Barbara's. Peter began tutoring Ignatius, and Francis teased his friend about this. He didn't mind the tutoring so much, but it bothered him that Ignatius spent so much time with his friends talking about God that it seemed they never had time for going out anymore. One day he was making fun of them at the dinner table, when Ignatius asked with a smile, "Tell me, Francis, 'what does it profit a man to gain the whole world and suffer the loss of his soul'?"

"I didn't ask you to preach to me," retorted Francis.

But, although Francis would admit it to no one, God was working in his soul. He could see that many of the other young men had been going to talk to Ignatius privately, and he had seen that their lives were changing. Little by little, Francis also felt the attraction to prayer and the spiritual life—but he would fight it all the way!

Finally, the Lord took matters a step further. Francis' friend, Peter, had to leave St. Barbara's. Everyone knew that Francis was the best choice to replace him as Ignatius' tutor. Reluctantly, Francis agreed. He soon found that he was more of a student than a teacher, however. He went with Ignatius to the hospitals and was impressed with the gentleness and love with which he treated the patients. He walked with Ignatius through the filthiest sections of the city, where misery was stamped on every face, and watched the older man ease the sufferings of the poor, the sick and the starving. Ignatius thirsted for sacrifice, while Francis had become almost bored with his comfortable and lazy life. Feeling challenged to match the enthusiasm for life which his older pupil had, Francis at last submitted to grace and asked Ignatius to permit him to join the community of religious which he was forming.

The little group of men who gathered around Ignatius took the name "the Company of Jesus." In an age when many young men took up the sword to fight for earthly lords, these men vowed to take up the banner of the Gospel and fight for souls for the Heavenly King. They would be the army of God. They made their first vows on the Feast of the Assumption, 1534. Four years later their way of life was approved by Pope Paul III, and they were asked to go to the lands outside of Europe and spread the Gospel of Christ. The little band grew, and became known as the Jesuits.

Seven years had passed since Francis had asked to join Ignatius, and the two had become as close as father and son. Now, Ignatius was asking him to leave their house in Paris and go to India. He was to join the few priests already there in instructing the people in the Christian way of life, baptizing and celebrating the sacraments, for Francis was now Father Francis Xavier. He had often dreamed that he was carrying an Indian on his shoulders. Now that dream would be fulfilled as he carried thousands of Indians through the waters of Baptism into eternal life.

The ship plowed through the blue Atlantic, rounded the tip of Africa, landed at Mozambique, and then crossed the Arabian Sea to Goa, on India's southwest coast. It was a year-long voyage, in an unhealthy climate. The food was very different from what Father Xavier and the other Europeans were accustomed to and, as always happened on these long voyages, many of the passengers became ill and some died. Frequently seasick himself, Father Xavier was always among the passengers and crew, washing and feeding the sick, giving them medicine, preaching sermons and preparing the dying for a holy death. Even the rough sailors, whose confidence he won with his sincere friendliness and gentle ways, stopped using bad language and attended the prayer services which he led.

Everyone who met Father Xavier noticed how

friendly and cheerful he was. He seemed to attract people like a magnet. And having drawn them to himself, he turned their thoughts to Christ, who loved them with such infinite love that he had shed his last drop of blood for them. Many people became kind and considerate of others because of Francis' kindness to them!

Goa was an Indian seaport which the Portuguese had conquered not long before. Many of the natives had been slaughtered or mistreated, and the Portuguese Catholic settlers were leading lives of cruelty and sin and greed. Father Xavier found conditions so bad that he once wrote, "It would be far better for me to be massacred by those who hate our holy religion, than it would be for me to live on as a powerless onlooker to all the outrages which are committed daily against God despite all our efforts to prevent them. Nothing saddens me so much as my inability to end the terrible scandals given by certain important persons."

Yet the poor were not beyond his reach. It was to the poorer Portuguese and the Indians that Father Xavier finally directed his efforts in Goa.

Each morning he would walk through the streets, ringing a bell, calling out, "Faithful Christians, friends of Jesus Christ, send your sons, your daughters and your slaves, to Christian doctrine classes, for the love of God!" People would crowd around the black-robed priest, who would lead them into a church. He recited each catechism lesson in rhyme and encouraged the people to sing it. In this way, the Creed, the commandments and lessons on the sacraments were being sung by people everywhere—in the streets, on the ships, in the fields. Other priests began to follow Father Xavier's example.

It was difficult to convince the Indians that God loved each person equally. In their culture, everyone was born into a certain social class, or "caste." People of one caste were not permitted to associate with those of another caste. And it was impossible to move out of a caste. Because they believed that it was a person's fate to be born into a certain caste, the rich people had no sympathy for those who were poor; those who had power used it harshly over those who did not. Goa was a most challenging place to bring the Christian message of unconditional love!

Even with all the work to do in Goa, Father Xavier was eager to visit the poor fishermen who lived along India's southeastern coast. As soon as possible he sailed from Goa, and traveled six hundred miles to Cape Cormorin, at the southern tip of India.

From the Cape he walked northeast, from coastal village to coastal village, teaching the basic truths of the Catholic faith to the Paravas, who were pearl divers. These people had been baptized many years before, but because there was no one left to continue their religious instruction they had returned to their former pagan beliefs. When they understood why Father Xavier had come to them, however, they welcomed him warmly and were eager to learn more about Jesus. Many were baptized, and those who were most eager to learn came for extra classes. These were appointed official catechists who would spend their time instructing and baptizing the people after Father Xavier moved on.

Father Xavier soon became a familiar figure. The people called him "Black Man," because of the long black robe he always wore. Together with Father Xavier, each small village built a chapel out of sticks and mud where the people would gather each day for prayer. When Father Xavier was in a village, they would bring all those who were sick for him to cure or bless before they died.

Upon returning to Goa, Father Xavier found a letter had finally arrived from his spiritual father, Ignatius. It was the first word he had heard from him in over two years!

Back again in the coastal villages a few months later, the missionary found trouble brewing. Rumors of raiders passed from village to village. One dark night the people came running up to Father Xavier screaming, "Save yourself, Father! They will kill you!" A gang of outlaws had swarmed into the area, burning and killing.

Father Xavier breathed a quick prayer and with steady courage went out to meet the raiders. "They are human beings, just as we are," he told the frightened villagers. He held the crucifix before him and grew enraged as he heard the screams of women and children being attacked all around him. Determined to stop the violence, he marched right into the middle of it all.

The outlaws were astonished. What powerful charm was this which the black-robed stranger had? What kept him from fleeing in terror? Why, the other villagers trembled just to hear the word "raider," and this man was facing their cruel knives quietly, with no sign of fear!

This was too much for them. It was better not to know where this man received his power! Slowly, the outlaws withdrew into the night.

News of such great heroism spread fast. Soon, it reached the Rajah of Travancore. He welcomed Father Xavier into his territory. There the missionary found people who were eager to learn about Jesus and the Christian understanding of God. Often as many as six thousand people would gather to listen to him, and since the country was flat he found it necessary to climb up into a tree so that everyone could hear. In that part of India alone, Father Xavier baptized thousands of persons and built many small chapels.

Meanwhile disturbing news came out of northern Ceylon, where a priest sent by Father Xavier had made many conversions. A crafty rajah who hated Christians had ordered all of them to renounce their faith in Jesus. The new Christians remained faithful, though, and many of them were martyred.

Anxiously Father Xavier followed reports of a struggle taking place between the rajah and another claimant to his throne. If only that cruel ruler could be driven out before he murdered the rest of the people! The revolt failed. Father Xavier heaved a sigh of disappointment and looked to the future. Perhaps he should sail to the East, for the remainder of India was closed to Europeans.

He took a small boat going north to the village called St. Thomas of Meliapor, where according to legend the Apostle Thomas had been buried. A priest and a small community of Christians received him happily, and the missionary set about preaching and baptizing. One day he sought out a rich man whom he knew had been avoiding him for some time. The man's name was Jacinto, and he was the object of gossip for miles around because of the sinful life he led.

"Good evening, Jacinto," Father Xavier greeted him. "I trust you will forgive me for calling upon you at this hour!"

Here it comes! thought Jacinto. He's going to give me a sermon! But there was no getting out of it. It was time for the evening meal and not to invite the priest to eat with him would not be polite. Glumly, Jacinto ushered Father Xavier into the dining area.

They chatted amiably. Father Xavier joked a good deal, and Jacinto found himself loosening up a little as they talked and laughed together. But he was still waiting for the sermon.

At last Father Xavier said, "Thank you very much for your kindness, Jacinto. It has been an enjoyable evening. I should return to my lodgings now."

"It was a pleasure having you, Father. Please, do come again," the rich man mumbled. He watched the slim figure of the priest stride away into the dusk. Not a word about changing my ways, he thought. Has he decided that I am a hopeless case?

Jacinto did a lot of thinking that night. He paced from one room of his fine house to another, pausing now and then to stare out into the velvety tropical darkness. "I have gone so far that Father Xavier will not say a word to change me—he who has converted the most wicked of sinners!"

Father Xavier was not at all surprised when Jacinto approached him the next day and blurted out, "Father, I have something to tell you!" Jacinto made a full confession of his sins, and promised to perform all the penances and employ all the remedies Father Xavier prescribed for him. From that day on, he was a new man!

———————

At the tomb of Thomas, the apostle, Father Xavier prayed earnestly, "My Lord, please show me your divine will, to which, with the help of your grace, I shall be faithful no matter what!" And God, who had given Francis the desire to serve him, now gave him the answer to his question. Suddenly, deep in his heart, Father Xavier knew that he must go to Malacca. That Maylayan seaport was the crossroad of the East, where merchants from Arabia, Persia and India traded with those from China, Japan, the Philippines and the Spice Islands. The city was a Portuguese stronghold, having been conquered thirty years before, and its people had fallen victim to the same vices of the cruel Europeans which Father Xavier found running wild in Goa.

The missionary's fame went before him. As he stepped ashore, he was greeted by a large crowd, especially children, eager to see the famous priest who loved people so much. Father Xavier greeted them warmly, and he started right away to teach them about Christ. He took up residence in the hospital, where he cared for the sick by day and prayed by night, allowing himself only two or three hours of sleep. Many times he was fasting and praying for the conversion of the greedy Europeans who had conquered this beautiful land and people. Often he went into the soldiers' barracks, into the prisons, into the homes of the poor and destitute, becoming a friend and an inspiration to all. Malacca was gradually becoming a more humane and just place to live and was no longer famous for its immoral entertainments.

Two thousand miles to the east, the Moluccas and the Spice Islands began to attract him. These islands lay along the equator between Celebes and New Guinea—22,000 square miles of dense jungles of marshlands and sunken reefs, of treacherous channels where pirates lurked, of steaming volcanos and spouting geysers. The heat was terrible; the storms were fierce; the sins of the Portuguese and natives were horrible; it was a challenging mission territory indeed!

And Father Xavier loved it. During all his years in the East he was never happier than he was on his voyage through the Moluccas. He went from island to island, preaching and baptizing, curing the sick and exhausting himself in the process. The heat was so unbearable that it seemed to drain all his energy. Yet he loved the people, they came to love Father Xavier as well. Through his love many came to believe in Jesus' love for them also.

From the Moluccas, Father Xavier returned to Malacca, where he stayed a few months before sailing for India. He landed in Cochin, and hastened to revisit the fishing villages of the Paravas. His old friends rejoiced to see him again, but he did not stay long, for he was anxious to make his way back to Goa as soon as possible. From Goa, he sailed far north to Basein, and returned to Cochin ten weeks later, having sailed over 1,600 miles in that space of time. Settling down at last, he spent the winter in Goa, where he devoted much time to the College of St. Paul which was training Indian seminarians for the priesthood. He also made some changes among the little groups of missionaries he had assigned throughout the vast territory, and appointed local superiors in the Jesuit communities there. He wished to have everything functioning well without him, for who knew what his next voyage would bring him?

He hoped to go to Japan.

The "Land of the Rising Sun" had a strange fascination about it, ever since the thirteenth century when Marco Polo first wrote of a mysterious island empire which lay somewhere east of China. Since that time a few Portuguese traders had set foot on Japanese soil, but they had not ventured inland and could report practically nothing about the land or its people. There was, however, a firsthand source of information in the person of a young Japanese named Yajiro, whom Father Xavier had met in Malacca and whom he had catechized and baptized. Yajiro told Father Xavier of the religion, government, customs and philosophy which his nation possessed. These people sounded like they were ready to learn about Jesus!

"Father, do not go!" urged one of his friends, a priest in Goa.

"It is too dangerous." exclaimed another. "The voyage is long, and pirates sail the waters!"

"And if anything goes wrong on your voyage, there would be no refuge, for the Chinese will let no Westerner into their harbors," reminded someone else.

Father Xavier just looked from one to the other and smiled.

Seeing that he was having no effect, the first priest continued. "There are still people here in our own islands who have not yet been catechized—no need to journey thousands of miles to find souls!"

Father Xavier laughed kindly. But then he said, "So, one of you can stay and preach to them. I will go east, to the Land of the Rising Sun."

Before embarking for Japan Father Xavier had to pay another visit to his beloved Paravas. Always searching for new souls to win to Christ, he could never abandon his concern for those whom he had already baptized; he was constantly writing letters of detailed advice to the priests he had settled in various regions, to make sure that they were caring for their communities lovingly and faithfully.

One more quick visit to Goa and Father Xavier was in Cochin once more. He wrote to the Jesuits in Rome: "It is true that we shall find ourselves in the midst of pagans...but we have only one thing to dread; that is to offend God. One delightful thought fills us with enthusiasm and strength; it is that God sees and knows our hearts, that he reads in the depths of our souls that our one aim is to make him known and served, to extend his empire, to procure his glory."

During a stopover at Malacca, Father Xavier wrote more letters to his charges. One of them, a note to a young Jesuit novice, shows clearly his own virtue and spirit of sacrifice: "Whatever you do, whatever the situation, strive always to gain mastery over yourself. Subdue your passions, embrace what is most unpleasant to your senses; above all things repress the natural desire for glory, and give yourself no rest in that regard until you have torn the pride out of your heart by its very roots, and you are content to be considered less than everyone else, even rejoicing to be despised. Without such humility and mortification you cannot grow in virtue, nor be an instrument for saving souls, nor persevere in the Company of Jesus."

Late in June 1549, Father Xavier set sail for Japan in a bulky Chinese junk, skippered by a Chinese pirate. He was accompanied by Father Cosmas de Torres and Brother John Fernandez, and by Yajiro, who had taken Paul as his Christian name. It was a three-thousand-mile voyage,

which would take two months. On the way, the
three Jesuits studied Japanese earnestly.

The southernmost island, where the missionaries landed, was Kyushu. The people were skillful
warriors, daring and brave, like some of the noblemen Father Xavier had known in Europe.

Eagerly the missionaries began to teach them
the Creed, the commandments and simple prayers
which they had translated into Japanese.

The bonzes, or pagan priests, were learned and
intelligent. They asked Father Xavier questions
which most Christians could not have answered,
but the studies of years before came to the
missionary's aid, and he answered the bonzes'
arguments with a thorough grasp of logic and
philosophy.

In comparison with other lands, the people of
Kyushu were slow to commit themselves to the
Christian God and receive Baptism. But those
who did were strong as steel in their new faith.
They clung to the truths they learned in their
catechism classes and recited the prayers and
commandments frequently—in fact, they re-
tained everything Father Xavier taught them for
ten years, which was when the next Christian missionary would come to their island. Three-hundred years later, after bloody persecutions, a faithful band of Japanese Christians again welcomed
missionaries to the shores of Kyushu.

———

The largest of the Japanese islands was called

Late in June 1549 Father Xavier set sail for Japan. It was a 3,000 mile voyage, which would take two months.

Nippon. The four missionaries landed at Yamaguchi, a major seaport, and began a three-hundred-mile trek inland to Miyako, the capital. On their backs the travelers carried coarse blankets, a few books and a portable altar. Winter was beginning. Sleet pelted them and snow choked the road in front of them; icy winds made it bitterly cold. By night the missionaries huddled in a little glen or by the side of a lonely pagoda. By day they trudged northeast, their bleeding feet leaving red marks in the snow.

When they reached Miyako they approached the emperor's palace.

It was Father Xavier's idea to catechize the emperor first. If he believed and embraced Christianity, or at least gave them permission to preach the Gospel to his people, then their path throughout Nippon would be clear. Praying earnestly for that grace, Father Xavier approached the palace guards and requested an audience with the emperor or with the commander of his armies. Little did he know that both men were only tools in the hands of powerful feudal lords!

He was not granted admittance, in spite of all his pleading, in spite of all his prayers. For eleven days he waited at the palace gates in the rain and snow, listening to the jeers of the people. Then he realized how futile his attempt was.

"It is not the will of God," he finally told his companions sadly, and they returned through the snow to the coast and Yamaguchi.

In Yamaguchi Father Xavier debated skillfully for many hours with the bonzes. Twice they became so angry that they attacked him, beat him and would have killed him had not a terrible thunderstorm arisen. Yet some of the people were asking for Baptism, not by the thousands as in India and the Moluccas, but by ones and tens until they numbered around a thousand. And those converts were well grounded in their new faith and fervent in their prayers. They were faithful years later, in the face of the horrible persecutions that would come upon them.

Having baptized people in several other cities as well, Father Xavier left Brother John Fernandez, a tireless worker, in charge of the Japanese mission. Two and a half years had passed, and it was time to check on conditions in India.

On the island of Sancian, off the China coast, Father Xavier met an old friend, a merchant named James Pereira, who invited the missionary to accompany him back to Malacca. Father Xavier accepted gladly. As the two men stood on the deck of Pereira's *Holy Cross* watching Sancian fade from sight, Pereira remarked, "I have a problem, Father. Look at this letter I've received."

Father Xavier opened the letter carefully. It had come from a Portuguese merchant imprisoned in China for smuggling goods. Since the Chinese emperor had forbidden all trade, everyone caught smuggling was held in prison and tortured cruelly. Several men were there now, the letter stated, and would remain there until they died, unless some kind of agreement could be made. Would Pereira ask the Portuguese government to appoint him ambassador to the emperor? By means of costly presents, he might be able to obtain the prisoners' freedom and reopen China's ports to trade.

Father Xavier folded the letter slowly. His eyes were glowing.

"Well?" asked Pereira. "What do you think I should do, Father?"

"I think," replied the priest slowly, his eyes on the China coast, "that this is the opportunity we've been waiting for. All China bows before one man—the emperor. If he became a Christian, the entire nation would be open for evangelization. And the Japanese, who look up to the Chinese in matters of religion, might soon follow."

"Yes," Father Xavier continued, "let's try it. You, as ambassador, to beg the prisoners' release and the resumption of free trade; I, as your companion, to bring the emperor the treasures of heaven."

As the sturdy ship sailed toward Malacca, the two friends made their political and financial plans. "Our first aim must be to free those poor prisoners!" Father Xavier exclaimed. "And yet," he added strangely, "I'm afraid the devil will cause our attempt to fail." He repeated that fear several times in the next few days.

Finally Pereira replied, "Surely you are mistaken, Father; we are bound to succeed."

"You will see," murmured Father Xavier. "You will see."

Goa welcomed him joyfully. It watched with admiration as he plunged into a round of administrative duties, reorganizing, encouraging, appointing. One of the appointments was that of a priest to be vicar in his absence, and who would carry on if anything happened to him. Before departing for Malacca he knelt at his new vicar's feet and renewed his religious profession.

Father Xavier arrived in Malacca before Pereira. He was waiting eagerly when the merchant's sturdy ship came into view and dropped anchor in the harbor.

Almost at once the blow fell: the governor of Malacca placed an embargo on the *Holy Cross* and had her rudder removed by force so that she could not leave the harbor!

Why did the Portuguese governor deliberately oppose the noble plans of his countrymen? We do not know, but oppose them he did—in spite of pleas from Father Xavier, from mutual friends and from his own brother.

"Let's seize the rudder, and may no man stand in our way!" roared one of Pereira's sailors.

"No!" said Father Xavier firmly. "There must be no bloodshed."

Father Xavier was confident that the Lord would work in his own way and in his own time. Besides, Francis had a power which he seldom thought about: he happened to be the Pope's official representative in all the East. That meant that anyone who prevented him from fulfilling his duties—and bringing the Gospel to China was his duty—should be excommunicated. Father Xavier did not want to use that power, but he knew that justice demanded him to do so. He pronounced the sentence.

The governor howled with rage. Excommunication was a serious offense to the Portuguese! "Why you..." he burst, in a fit of insults and rage. Then he ordered, "The embassy to China shall embark. But Pereira and his crew will remain here and a new crew will be placed aboard the *Holy Cross*. The ship may proceed to China, and you, Father, may sail with her." Only two of Father Xavier's old companions were permitted to sail with him: Christopher, a Malabar Indian, and Anthony, a Chinese.

The *Holy Cross* made her way northeastward to Sancian and anchored offshore. It was a barren island, its only inhabitants being Portuguese traders who were trying to smuggle goods in and out of China. Father Xavier approached them and asked them to help him reach the mainland.

"Impossible!" they exclaimed. "It means death, or torture in the prisons of Canton. You cannot take the risk, Father, nor can we!"

Father Xavier knew they were right. But China lay before him, its millions of people completely unaware of the Redemption. He could not leave.

For two months the *Holy Cross* lay at anchor off Sancian while Father Xavier awaited his chance. At last it came. A Chinese trader asked for a huge sum of money. Father Xavier had powerful friends; he knew he could borrow the money. The deal was soon set.

But when the appointed day came, the Chinese trader did not appear. Nor did he come the next day, nor the next. As the hours slipped away the missionary who had labored so tirelessly for years felt his strength ebbing away. Such a fever seized him that his companions took him to the shore and placed him on a rough pallet in one of the traders' huts. Through its doorway Father Xavier could see the China coast.

The fever made the priest's mind wander, but he prayed almost continually, "Jesus, Son of David, have mercy on me! Mother of God, remember me."

There was no priest to hear his confession, to give him the Sacrament of the Anointing or the Eucharist. Except for Anthony and Christopher, Father Xavier was entirely alone. What a strange end to his heroic labors for Christ! And yet, what did apparent failure matter as long as all had been done for God? "In thee, O Lord, have I hoped," he exclaimed with some of his old joy. "I shall never be confounded!"

In the early hours of December, Father Xavier raised his eyes to the crucifix. "Jesus," he whispered—and his soul passed peacefully into eternity.

Word of the heroic missionary's death spread quickly throughout the Orient. It passed from ship captain to cabin boy, from merchant to townsman, from missionary to Indian villager. From the far-flung Moluccas to the coast of the

Paravas, from Malacca to Goa, the East mourned the passage of its greatest benefactor.

In Goa, where his body was brought, crowds swarmed to the beach to meet the ship; for days people filed past the body, which showed no sign of decay in spite of the heat. Father Xavier had passed in and out of those people's lives in a few short years, but not even centuries would erase his memory from their hearts.

One burning desire filled St. Francis Xavier's soul—to do something for Christ, who had suffered so willingly for him. We, too, can do something to show our Lord that we love him. We can do unpleasant duties willingly and offer them all to Jesus.

St. Stanislaus Kostka

(1550-1568)

November 13

"Paul, pay attention to me. You are sixteen now, and your brother Stan is only fourteen. I want you and Mr. Bilinsky to keep an eye on him in Vienna. You know how much I love your little brother." Count John Kostka's voice softened a bit with this last statement. It was not easy to send his two sons all the way to Vienna for their schooling. But there was no college near the family castle in Poland where they would receive such a fine education. As much as he disliked the Jesuits, he knew they were the best teachers in Europe.

Meanwhile, Paul Kostka felt his throat tighten and his fists clench, but he knew better than to interrupt or contradict his father. His ears burned as he listened. Why was Stan always the "favorite"? After all, he, Paul, was the oldest son. Just because he knew how to have a good time while his lazy little brother.... Startled, Paul broke out of his angry daydream as his father grabbed his arm. "Paul, are you listening? Here, this is an extra two hundred dollars. I want you to use it on Stan. Bring him out with you at night and teach him how to enjoy life. I don't want him spending any extra time with those priests."

Paul smiled as he felt the bag of coins. Well, he thought, now Father is talking my language! "Yes, Father," he replied. "You know Mr. Bilinsky and I can teach Stan how to have a good time!"

Early the next morning Paul, Stan and Mr. Bilinsky set out on the journey to Vienna. Their horses were frisky and ready to run along the misty road. Paul and the stout middle-aged tutor, Mr. Bilinsky, traveled together, a bit ahead of Stan. They laughed coarsely as Bilinsky told Paul crude stories about his own days as a teenager away at school. Stan was happy to lag behind. Ever since he was a small boy, he had felt such a great love for the Blessed Mother and for the Holy Child, Jesus, that any sort of impurity or bad language actually caused him physical pain. One time he had become so upset at the stories told by some of his father's friends that he had fainted! How angry and embarrassed Paul had been that day! Stan bit his lip as he thought about his "secret desire." He was inwardly excited to be going to Vienna. There he would surely have a chance to tell the Jesuits of his desire to join them.

That night the three travelers stopped at a roadside tavern to rest. It had been a long day, and Stan was tired. He slipped quietly up stairs as Paul and Bilinsky ordered another round of drinks for everyone. They are certainly free with Father's money, thought Stan. I wish they would have given at least a dollar to that poor family we met on the road.... Stan knelt beside his bed and began his Rosary. At least he would have a chance to say all his prayers in peace tonight.

On the third day they arrived in Vienna. What a glorious sight! Stanislaus couldn't help but marvel at the magnificent buildings and churches. Everywhere there seemed to be crowds of people armed with shopping baskets, and venders with carts full of flowers, fruit and fresh vegetables shouting out their prices. By the time they found the college and settled into their apartment his head was spinning. As usual, Paul and Bilinsky had wasted no time in scouting out the nearest bar. Stan felt his head hit the pillow and had a fleeting moment of anxiety as he thought of the following day. Then he was sound asleep.

The days at school went by quickly. Stan rarely saw Paul and Bilinsky, as they had no classes together. But he was embarrassed to hear how soon word got around that "for a good party" all one had to do was contact Paul. And Paul, for his part, was equally embarrassed by the reputation his younger brother was achieving. Several of the boys had noted Stan's piety and dedication to studies. Most nights, in fact, there would be a small group gathered in Stan's room to study—and, most embarrassing, they would end their evening by praying the Rosary!

*Many nights a small group of boys gathered in Stan's room to study;
they would end their evening by praying the Rosary together.*

No wonder the priests here can't praise him enough, Paul thought bitterly. The way he acts you would think he wanted to be one of them. Wouldn't that upset Father!

Eight months into the school year brought an unexpected turn of events for the Kostka brothers. The emperor of Austria, Ferdinand, died. His successor, Maximilian II, asked the Jesuits to give him the building which served as the students' living quarters. That meant that the students had to find lodging of their own in the city. Bilinsky and Paul set off the day after the news to find suitable quarters. Since their father was a wealthy and important count of Poland, their lodging had to be in keeping with their social position. At last they came across a gentleman who had an entire apartment for rent, complete with a cook and individual studies for the boys. When they came to pack their things and told Stan of the arrangements, they forgot to mention that their new landlord had a vicious hatred for the Catholic Church.

While they were living on the campus, surrounded by the Jesuit priests and the other students, Stan had been able to carve out his own little circle of friends. And he had also been close to the chapel where he could go early each morning for Mass and have some time for spiritual reading and meditation. Their new quarters did not allow for such things. Now he had to follow Paul's schedule and ride with him each morning in the carriage. Often they were late for the morning prayer service, which annoyed Stan. One time he brought up the matter with Paul, but his brother had become very angry. So angry, in fact, that he hit Stan hard on the side of his head. As the weeks passed, Stan became more and more worried. Paul and Bilinsky were out drinking almost every night. When they were home, Paul was often violent and insulting toward Stan. But Stan only kept silent and tried to avoid annoying his older brother. The trouble was, it seemed that just his presence was annoying to Paul.

That winter the situation between the brothers was worse than ever. Paul would often insist that they eat out at one of the local bars. Stan would not go with him. Besides the rough company and drinking, he knew that Paul never came home in time to finish his studies. Often Stan would end up with a piece of leftover bread from his lunch and a bottle of water for his evening meal. And frequently, Paul would come into his room late in the evening and kick or punch Stan. Three weeks before Christmas, Stan could take it no longer and he developed a high fever. The doctors were called in, and much to Paul's annoyance, said that Stan was seriously ill. What would he tell his father? Paul wondered anxiously.

Three days before Christmas, Stan woke up feeling worse than ever. Feeling that his life was being sucked away by the fever, he called in Bilinsky and Paul. "Please," he asked them, "call in one of the priests for me. I am afraid I am dying. I want to go to confession and receive Communion one more time." His eyes were glazed and his forehead hot and dry, but he saw no pity on the face of Paul. Tears slipped silently down his cheeks as the two men turned and left the room.

"Paul," Bilinsky started, hesitating, "perhaps we should call a priest?"

"No!" exclaimed Paul. "You know the landlord made us promise never to bring a priest here. Besides, I should not be so lucky that Stan would die...." The bitterness in the young man's voice shocked even Bilinsky, but fearing Paul's temper, he said nothing. The two companions avoided Stan's room for the next two days, sending up the housemaid with a bit of broth in the evening. But the Lord was keeping his own watch over Stan. On Christmas Eve, when Stan was certain that he would not live until morning, an extraordinary thing happened. Just after the bit of candle stub had burned out, a soft light filled the room. Too weak to sit up, Stan opened his eyes and was startled to see a lovely woman standing at the foot of his bed. As he saw the beautiful infant she was holding, he realized that it the Blessed Virgin. Holding out his arms, she lay the Child Jesus on his chest.

"Stan," said the Holy Mother of God, "you will not die from this illness. You will soon be well. God wishes you to become a Jesuit, but you must go soon to join them." With that, the infant was taken up from his arms and the vision disappeared. Stan felt health and peace flood through his entire being. Sure enough, the next morning he woke up completely well.

That week, Stan approached one of the priests at the college and told him of his desire to join the Jesuits. The rector of the college had been expecting this, as Stan's piety and goodness were apparent to everyone who knew him. But equally well known was Count Kostka's opposition to almost anything related to the Catholic Church. What would he do if his son were to join? Having thought it out carefully, the rector advised Stan to go to their German province and ask admittance there. Father Peter Canisius was the provincial of the German Jesuits, and he was a priest of good judgment and some influence.

That night, Stan put on his oldest set of clothes, took a few coins from his purse and left a note for Paul. He did not say where he was going, but asked him to say good-bye to their dear father and not to worry. "Not worry!" exclaimed Bilinsky the next morning. "The boy is only sixteen, and he knows he is the favorite child of his father—and he asks us not to worry now that he has run off! Hurry, Paul, we must overtake him and bring him home at once!"

The two set out, asking the horse keeper in which direction Stan had gone. For two days they traveled up and down the roads leading out of Vienna, but with no luck. At last they resigned themselves to the inevitable. With a trembling heart, Bilinsky wrote a note to the count. It was obvious that young Stan had gone off to join one of the Jesuit communities.

Meanwhile, Stan traveled three-hundred-miles

to the German town in which Father Peter Canisius lived and gave him the note from the rector in Vienna. Father Peter read it and looked thoughtfully at the tired, but happy young man sitting before him. "Stan," he said at last. "Stay with us a few weeks and rest. Then, if you still desire to join us, I will send you on to our house in Rome. Father Francis Borgia, our Father General, is there. He will take you, I am sure. And it is just far enough away that perhaps your father will not pursue you."

Stan nodded. The thought of his angry father only seemed to strengthen his resolve to obey the inner voice telling him that to be a Jesuit was not only his will, but God's will. The next three weeks flew by. Stan was asked to help the cook and to clean the rooms of the Jesuit novices. Everyone was impressed by the quiet kindness and obvious piety of this young man from Poland. As he set off for Rome with two companions, they followed him with their prayers.

In Rome Stan lost no time in finding the Jesuit novitiate and contacting Father Francis. He had been expecting Stan, as Father Peter had sent word ahead. Everyone in Europe knew the power and wealth of the Polish Count Kostka. Receiving his son into the Jesuit novitiate was not a decision to make lightly. But after their first interview, Father Francis was convinced that Stanislaus was certainly gifted with a vocation. He would enter the novitiate immediately, and together they would face the opposition of the count.

Within weeks, a letter arrived from Poland with his father's seal on the envelope. Stan opened it, and read it slowly. He had expected this. His father was demanding that he return immediately, or he would see to it that the Jesuits would be kicked out of Poland forever! It was not a threat to ignore, but Father Francis only said, "God has brought you here, Stan. God will protect you here. Let us have faith and pray for your father."

Relieved and with great peace in his heart, Stanislaus fell easily into the routine of the novitiate. At last he could pray and study to his heart's content and no one said a word of reproach. In fact, the Jesuit community was so fervent under the leadership of Father Francis Borgia, that there was almost a holy competition to see who could become a saint first! But if a vote were taken, Stanislaus would surely have come out in first place. He was observant and kind to all; he was so obviously happy to be a religious that just his presence in a room was enough to inspire good thoughts and desires in his fellow novices. He was soon a favorite companion of young and old alike.

But the years of stress and abuse from Paul, and the long trip to Rome, had taken their toll on Stan's health. Now, in the hot, humid summer of Rome he again developed a high fever. He had only been there for nine months, but Stan knew this was his last home on this earth. He told his novice director, Father Fazio, that he felt ready to die and go to heaven. But the energetic priest laughed and gave him a pat on the back, "Stan," he said, "don't joke so! This is just a typical 'Roman fever' that you have. As soon as the cooler weather comes you'll be as healthy as ever." But that evening Father Fazio went to speak with the infirmarian, Father Ruiz. They both knew that their favorite novice was gravely ill, and decided to move him at once into the infirmary.

In the early hours of August 15, 1568, Stan suddenly woke up. Father Ruiz was by his bed, as he had been for several nights, placing cool towels on the boy's head. Now he grew worried as he saw Stan sit up with a soft, supernatural glow on his face. Then he heard him say quietly, "I see the Blessed Virgin Mary! And she is surrounded by beautiful angels!" Then Stan lay back down and died. Father Ruiz rang the bell, telling the other priests and novices that the young novice, Stanislaus Kostka, had died. Sadly, they gathered around his bed to recite the Office of the Dead and to prepare his body for burial. Even though he had been in Rome for only a short time, many people had come to know and esteem this holy novice from Poland. The Jesuits' chapel was filled for the funeral, and many of the people were speaking of the "new saint." It was no suprise to Father Francis when, a few days later, he was told that Stan's brother, Paul, and a Mr. Bilinsky were in the parlor to see him.

Father Francis opened the parlor door, and held out his hand to greet Paul. But Paul ignored the gesture, and asked roughly, "Where is Stan? I demand that you bring him to me at once!"

Shocked, Father Francis realized that the news of Stan's death had not yet reached Paul.

Sitting on the chair for a moment he looked up at the two angry men and said quietly, "I am very sorry. Your saintly brother, Stanislaus, died this very week."

A long moment of thick silence filled the air, then Paul let out one long agonized scream and dropped to the floor in front of Father Francis Borgia. "My brother, my brother," he cried. "My brother was a saint and I have killed him with my jealousy and abuse and meanness!" As the young man continued to sob, Father Francis looked up at Bilinsky, and was surprised to see that he, too, was crying shamelessly.

"But, what can you mean?" asked the priest. "You did not kill Stan. He was very happy here, but he died of a prolonged fever...." But soon the story came pouring out of Paul and Bilinsky. They told Father Francis of their hatred for the gentle and pure young Stanislaus, their jealousy of his good reputation and self-control, of the many times they had left him hungry and alone at night and of the nights they came home and beat the young boy as he was sleeping or trying to study. Slowly, Father Francis realized that Stanislaus had been more than just a "good novice." In fact, the young man had practiced heroic virtue and patience for many years. He was a saint.

Father Francis explained to Paul and Bilinsky how Stan had always spoken well of his parents and family. Certainly, he was aware of how much his father disliked the Church and opposed his vocation. But Stan prayed fervently that the Lord would grant his family the grace to accept him. Never had he indicated that he had been in any way mistreated by Paul. Within a short time, Father Francis Borgia petitioned the Vatican to open the canonization process of Stanislaus Kostka. His parents and Paul and Bilinsky were among those who spoke of the boy's innocence, love for purity and goodness with everyone. Paul himself spent many years struggling to reform his life, and at the age of sixty he entered the Jesuits as a novice.

St. Stanislaus always longed for heaven. In spite of suffering persecution and abuse for his resolve to remain pure and close to Jesus and Mary, he did not become bitter or give in to peer pressure. We can pray to Stanislaus Kostka to help us in our resolution to be good and pure.

St. Benedict the Moor

(1526-1589)

April 4

"Good night, Benedict! Sleep well, my son!" Diana blew out the candle and lay down beside her husband, Christopher. They were Ethiopian Christians who had been captured many years before by the slave traders and brought to the island of Sicily. They had been bought almost immediately by Signor Manasseri, who owned a large farm near Messina. It was a difficult life, and being slaves was a great sorrow for them. But they had come to be grateful that at least Signor Manasseri was a just man and treated all of his workers well. He was so pleased with the work that Christopher and Diana did that he had not only appointed Christopher as foreman, he also promised that their first-born child would be a free man. That child was their son, Benedict.

Benedict, now eighteen, walked quickly through the cool night toward his own hut, outside of the slave quarters where his parents lived. He was still thrilled with the news he had come to share with them. Having worked the past two years for Signor Manasseri as a free man, he had saved enough money to buy his own team of oxen. Tomorrow he would begin to plow fields for good pay. That money he would share with his parents and the other slaves, whose lives were so often filled with sorrow and poverty. For the next three years, Benedict worked every day. Every farmer knew that for the straightest furrowed rows and cleanest fields, Benedict was the man to hire.

"Hey, there goes the 'holy moor'!" "Hey, blackie!" Another voice called out. "You'd better get on home to your plantation—and give those oxen back to whomever you stole them from!"

Benedict tried to ignore the taunts. These were just some of the local young men, out like himself looking for work. Only they were white, and they thought that somehow made them better than Benedict. In his mind, Benedict thought of the Gospel of St. Luke, which the priest had preached about last Sunday. It was the story of Jesus before the crowds of people yelling "Crucify him!" Jesus had said nothing. He had not defended himself. Benedict decided to do the same, and continued on.

The young men, however, had other plans. It irritated them that this young black man was getting more requests for work than they were.

Of course, they did not want to consider the fact that he did a better job than they did. They began to pick up clods of hardened dirt and stones to throw at Benedict. But just as the first round was leaving their fists a strong voice broke into the early morning breeze: "Stop that! Stop, I command you!"

The men froze. They recognized the voice of Jerome Lanzi, once one of the wealthiest noblemen in the country. He was now a well-respected Franciscan hermit. "You are making fun of this man now because he is black. But I tell you, before long, all the country will be saying great things about him!"

The seriousness of his tone, and his reputation, warned the men to say nothing. Looking once more at Benedict, who was as surprised as they were, they turned around and went on their way. "Thank you, Brother Jerome," stammered Benedict. "What did you mean by that?"

"Come with me, Benedict. The Lord wants you to join us in the hermit's life. You are already similar in spirit to our gentle father, St. Francis. Come." Jerome held out his hand and smiled. Benedict had never considered the life of a religious. He was not educated; he didn't know any blacks who were religious. Yet something in Lanzi's eyes and voice attracted him.

"Yes. Yes, I will come," Benedict replied. "What must I do?"

"Sell your oxen," commanded Jerome. "Give the money to the poor, to your family. Then come, join us in the forest. We'll be expecting you."

As Jerome turned and walked quickly back into the woods, Benedict felt his heart leaping. What had happened? He had never felt such joy, such excitement! He turned the oxen around and prodded them back to the village. The man he had bought them from would surely buy them back. With that money, his parents would be able to care for his younger brothers and sisters. The next evening, he walked into the forest where the small band of hermits lived, and found a small hut ready and waiting just for him.

The years passed quickly, and the life of the hermitage suited Benedict well. He was an excellent cook, and the other hermits were happy to give the duty to Benedict. Besides, he always managed to have some extra to give to the beggars who came to them for food. Jerome Lanzi was a good leader and a holy man. His group of hermits was not attached to any large community of Franciscans, but lived the rule as an independent group. Often, they would be forced to move as new farmers came in and cleared the forests where they lived. Eventually they ended up near the city of Palermo. Just when they were settled, however, their beloved leader, Jerome, died.

Sadly, the brothers buried their spiritual father. The next day they gathered to decide who should take his place. Benedict had been deep in thought all night. Who would it be? Brother James was wise, and had studied theology. Father Timothy was the community's priest; surely he would be a good choice.... Benedict was startled out of his thinking by the voice of Brother Stanley. "We have elected you, Benedict. You were the most faithful son of Jerome. Now you will take his place as our spiritual father."

"What? Me?" Benedict was shocked. Perhaps the brothers were teasing him. Racing to the clearing where they had gathered, he began to protest. But Father Timothy came up to him and gently motioned for him to kneel for the blessing. Humbly, Benedict obeyed. And they had made a good choice. In spite of never having studied in school, Benedict had a keen mind and an excellent memory. He could quote Scripture better than anyone, and he knew the rule of St. Francis as well as his own name. Most important, Benedict was a man of great prayer and had compassion for all who came to him.

Life for the little group however, was not to continue in peace for long. It was 1562, and because there were so many independent groups of friars roaming around Europe—some holy and some not so holy—Pope Pius IV had ordered that they all disband. Their members could freely join any of the already established and approved religious orders, of which there were plenty around! Saddened by the news, but maybe not entirely surprised, the hermits said their good-byes. Each friar went to where the Spirit led him. Benedict headed for the nearby Franciscan community of St. Mary of the Angels. The community of St. Mary welcomed him at once, for already his reputation for holiness and wisdom had spread throughout the region. They asked him if he would be their cook, a job which he readily accepted. This involved not only cooking for the friars, but also distributing food to the poor who came each day to the convent gate. The friars relied totally upon what food they could grow in their garden and what the neighboring farmers and bakers donated. The community soon noticed that even though more and more people were coming to the gate, they never ran out. It was no surprise to anyone but Benedict when he was elected their next superior!

As superior of St. Mary of the Angels community, Benedict had the added responsibility of guiding the other Franciscan groups in the area. At the last meeting of the various convents, the friars had decided that some of them had become lazy in their observance of the Franciscan life. They had chosen St. Mary of the Angels to be a model community for reform, and they recognized Benedict as the man to lead them. The next three years saw dozens and dozens of Franciscans coming through St. Mary of the Angels to talk and pray with Benedict. No one even noticed that he was "uneducated," so great was his wisdom and knowledge of Scripture. By the end of his three year term all of the friars realized that a good and holy novice master was needed to train the youngest and newest members. No one had any doubt but that Benedict was the man for the job.

As superior of St. Mary of the Angels' community, Benedict had the added responsibility of guiding all the other Franciscan groups in the area.

Always ready to do the simplest and the most difficult task; always kind and generous in helping the poor; always on time for the community prayers—Benedict was a good model for the younger men aspiring to the hard life of the friars. Nine times each year there was a forty-day period of fasting. In those days, these periods were all called "lent." During that time the friars would eat only one meal a day. In addition to their long hours of daily prayer, they also worked in the fields and preached in the nearby churches. The life of a friar required not only physical strength, but a lot of self-control and generosity!

Benedict was a wise guide for the novices. Often he was able to perceive what was bothering them even before they told him! As his reputation continued to spread, more and more people came to seek his advice. Princes, bishops, the wealthy and the poor, all came to Benedict. And he treated everyone with equal dignity and respect. When his term as novice master ended, the community asked him to again be their cook. Joyfully he accepted. Only this time, an assistant was necessary. So many people continued to come to speak with him that Benedict had little time left for potatoes and broccoli!

By this time Benedict was over sixty years old. His many years of hard work and responsibilities had caused his shoulders to stoop a bit, and his fingers were bent from arthritis. But he had become such a part of the life of the friars that no one even noticed these things. Instead, people noticed the miracles that resulted from his blessings, and the reconciliations that occurred through his mediation. It was a surprise for everyone when they gathered from Mass early one morning, as they did every morning, and Benedict's place was empty. Hurrying to his room, they found him lying there in great pain. All knew that this would be his final day with them.

Kneeling beside him and around him, the friars prayed with their brother, their mentor and their friend. With tears in their eyes they heard him ask them for forgiveness for any wrongs he had committed. He looked fondly into each face that he knew so well. At last, his gaze fixed upward, he smiled and said, "Father, into your hands I commend my spirit." And Benedict, the son of slaves, the "holy moor," the superior and friend, passed into eternal life.

People loved Benedict because of his humility and kindness. Benedict loved people because in each one he saw the image and likeness of God, the Creator of all. He saw the beauty of each person whom Christ had died for. We, too, can see Christ in each person, regardless of their social position or their race or the religion they practice.

St. Aloysius Gonzaga

(1568-1591)

June 21

Five-year-old Aloysius was sleeping next to his younger brother, Ridolfo. Their father, the marquis of Castiglione, was already dreaming of an exciting future for his oldest son.

"We'll make a great soldier of him!" he proudly said to his wife, Marta. As the oldest son, Aloysius would someday inherit his father's fortune and carry on the name of Gonzaga. The marquis was certain that Aloysius would be the bravest of fighters, among the bravest of men in all of Italy.

Aloysius' mother, Marta, was of a very different character than his father. She was gentle and was one of the closest friends of the wife of King Philip II of Spain. Marta and her husband were often invited to dinner parties or dances held at the royal courts. But Marta was a very religious person and made sure that her sons learned their prayers before anything else.

Even when he was still a toddler, his mother

could see that Aloysius was more like her than the marquis. Little Al was bright and full of mischief, but he was also gentle and sensitive. At night he said his prayers with so much attention and fervor that she often wondered if he was destined for the army of the king or the army of God. But since Al loved playing toy soldiers with his little brother and friends, and because of her husband's dreams for their oldest child, Marta didn't bring up the subject of her own hopes for a priest in the family.

When Al was almost six, his father decided to take him along to inspect the troops of soldiers camping across the Italian countryside. The young boy felt proud to be with his famous father. He soon became the mascot of the soldiers, and from them he learned bad language and habits which made them laugh. One afternoon, while the soldiers were resting, little Al went to look more closely at the cannon they had fired that morning during their drill. All the equipment was still sitting beside it. Al was a strong boy, but he could barely lift the cannon ball to push it into the barrel. Once it was in, he had to stop and think what the soldiers had done next. Spying the fresh wick sticking up from the barrel, Al quickly found a branch, lit it at the nearby cook's fire and lit the wick. He ran back and covered his ears, just as he had seen the soldiers do that morning.

The big gun jerked backward, and there was a big, booming shot. The force of the jolt sent the boy spinning away, and his father and a soldier who had seen all this were afraid that he was seriously hurt—even dead. They ran over to Al, only to be met by a big grin. Al was as calm as if he had been playing with a toy.

Of course, his father was delighted. "What a fine soldier we will make of him!"

As Al grew, his father's hopes grew higher and higher. One night, when Al was twelve, a candle toppled over and set fire to his bed curtains. The brightness of the flames awakened Al, who jumped up and found something to throw on top of the blaze to smother it. The entire household was impressed by his calm, quick thinking.

"Ah, yes," exclaimed Marquis Gonzaga. "My son will make a splendid soldier indeed! Certainly he will be captain of the troops someday!"

In order to educate his sons properly for their future lives at court and in the service of the king, the marquis sent Al and Ridolfo to study in Florence. Even though they were only eight and nine, they had lessons in language, mathematics, fencing and dancing. The dancing was most important, because as sons of the marquis they were required to attend all kinds of parties. Both boys were soon favorites at the court. In those days, marriages were arranged by the parents while the children were quite young, so many mothers at the court parties were keeping a close eye on Aloysius and Ridolfo.

Both boys were popular, but there was something about Aloysius that set him apart. For one thing, he took his studies much more seriously than the other students. And everyone noticed how attentive he was to the sermons given at the Sunday Mass. When it was time for him to receive his First Communion, the famous preacher Charles Borromeo was chosen to instruct Al and Ridolfo for the Sacrament. On the lovely morning in May, Al knelt in complete adoration after receiving Jesus in Holy Communion. For him, the Lord was so truly present that he wanted to stay and talk to him in his heart for as long as he possibly could. "I am yours—completely yours. And I always will be," he whispered over and over. It was about the same time that he was allowed to consecrate his virginity to God and asked the Blessed Virgin to protect him. In the society of his day, especially at the wealthy courts, virginity was not a very popular subject. Many young men had sex with older women and girls long before marriage. But Al knew that this was not the way Jesus had asked his friends to live. He would have to face some teasing and misunderstanding from his peers, but he was determined to keep his promise to the Lord.

When Al was thirteen, his father decided it was time to send him to the Spanish court of Philip II. There he would learn even more about the art of warfare and chivalry, which was necessary if he was to become a great captain in the military! Even though Al already felt attracted to the life of a priest, perhaps even a monk, he knew that until he was older he had to obey his father's commands. So off he went, again accompanied by Ridolfo. Intelligent, good looking and polite, young Al was soon the talk of the Spanish courts. But he also made some enemies among those who liked to drink too much and sleep with young women from the nearby villages. In fact, Al would not tolerate anyone cursing or blaspheming God's name in his presence. Ridolfo, of course, was also religious and devout, but he certainly wasn't always pleased with the fights which his brother's attitudes sometimes caused. And he did not understand why Al refused to eat the best food or wear the best of clothes. But his older brother was happy, and Ridolfo soon had his own friends and interests.

At about this time Al came across the writings of some of the first Jesuit missionaries who were bringing the Christian faith to India and Japan. Filled with admiration for their courage and great learning, he felt in his heart that this was what he also wanted to be. But what could he do? He had already been through the first of many ceremonies which would mark him as heir to his father's fortune and royal titles.

Soon, though, Al became so sick that it looked like he wouldn't have any future at all on this earth! A severe kidney disease left him permanently weakened and unable to eat many of the rich foods served at the court. This gave him a good excuse not to attend all of the parties, and he was also able to convince his father to transfer the

Ridolfo did not understand why Al refused to eat the best food or wear the best clothes. But his older brother was happy, and Ridolfo soon had his own friends and interests.

rights of inheritance to his younger brother, Ridolfo. A few years later, when Al was almost eighteen, he knew he had to finally break the news to his father. He had been accepted into the Jesuit novitiate in Rome.

Surprise, anger, blind rage—that was the reaction of the marquis to his son's news. "I forbid you to become a priest!" he screamed. When Marquis Gonzaga's temper cooled a bit, he began to make plans for Al to go on one business trip after another for him. Al had always been good in business, and even though he was young, his father wanted worldly experiences to keep him from entering religious life.

Obediently, Al agreed to spend several months traveling for his father. And he did run into every sort of temptation along the way. But far from discouraging him from his desires to remain pure and live devoutly, the disgusting examples of the immoral court life caused him to become even more strict with himself and to spend even longer hours in prayer each day. Whenever he could, he would fast on bread and water; he would wear his oldest clothes and avoid as many of the parties as he could.

At last, Ridolfo and his friends were convinced of Al's sincere desire to be a priest and began to help him avoid the many distractions of court life. One day his exasperated father asked him, "Will you obey me and forget this foolish talk of joining the Jesuits, or not?"

Al looked sadly into his father's eyes. Lately the

older man had been drinking more and more. Worse, his mother had told them that the family fortune was greatly depleted because of the marquis' weakness for gambling. Al put his arms around his father's sunken shoulders and gently said, "No, Father. It is not foolishness; it is what God is asking of me. And when I go, you must let Ridolfo begin to run the family affairs. He is old enough, you know."

The marquis knew he was beaten. "The Lord wants him?" He asked Marta that night. "Then the Lord shall have him. Tomorrow he will go to Rome."

How happy the young man was as he put aside forever the fine clothes of his noble rank, and put on the plain habit of a Jesuit novice. Now he was truly poor, and he looked like any other novice in the community. No one could tell that his was a wealthy and noble background! In fact, Al was careful to choose the most disgusting and annoying duties—cleaning the toilets, dumping the garbage from the kitchen, anything at all which would make him forget the comfort and wealth of his boyhood. For the rest of his life, he was determined to be as poor and humble as Jesus.

Aloysius settled quickly into the routine of classes and prayers and work. His spiritual director in Rome was the holy priest, Robert Bellarmine, who would also be canonized as a great saint. Because Al was not very strong the Jesuit superiors would not allow him to continue with his frequent fasting. And he had to go out every day for some fresh air and exercise with the rest of the novices. If he wanted to go to the missions, Al would have to build up his strength. And he was so prayerful and generous, that he was fully expected to be accepted as a foreign missionary.

But in 1591, the chance for heroism came unexpectedly as the plague broke out in the city. Thousands of people were sick and dying within a matter of days. The hospitals and doctors were not able to care for all the people who were sick. The Jesuits decided at once to open their own hospital. All the priests, brothers and novices were free to leave for the country, or stay and care for the sick. The plague was so contagious that anyone caring for the sick usually got it, too. But most of the men stayed, including Al. Day after long day he joined the others in cleaning, cooking, feeding and burying. All night the wails of people mourning the dead and the cries of pain from the dying split the night silence. One by one, many of the Jesuits also became sick and died. Not until the plague had almost run its course did Al become sick. For a few days it looked like he, too, would be among its victims. Instead, he pulled through and the immediate danger passed. But he was left with a low fever that continued to eat away at his strength.

The spring was quickly turning into a warm summer, and his superiors decided to send Al to one of their country houses to recover his strength. The night before he was to leave, though, he asked to speak with Robert Bellarmine. Al knew that he was dying, and he asked to receive the Sacrament of the Sick. Father Bellarmine knew how serious and fervent a religious Al was; if he felt that he was dying, the experienced priest believed him. Al stayed in Rome and his brother Jesuits took turns staying at his bedside. Another few weeks passed and Al seemed to be in no immediate danger. But it was the Eve of Corpus Christi, the night on which Al knew he was to go to his eternal reward and live with Jesus forever. After again receiving the Sacrament of the Sick, he was left with two of the brothers for the night. Around midnight he became restless, and within a short while Aloysius breathed his last breath, the name of Jesus on his lips.

Aloysius Gonzaga understood how difficult it is to remain pure in a society where drunkenness and immorality are common. He understands what courage it takes to insist on attending Mass on Sunday and receiving the sacraments regularly in a family which does not share one's fervor or desire for God. For that reason, in 1726, Aloysius was canonized a saint of the Church. And in 1926, Pope Pius XI declared him to be the patron of youth. Now, from Heaven, he watches over young men and boys who desire to give their lives to Jesus.

St. Philip Neri

(1515-1595)

May 26

Florence, Italy, in the early 1500s, was an exciting and sometimes dangerous place to live. The period of history called the Renaissance was at its peak, and Florence—as well as Rome—was at the center. The arts, music, architecture and learning seemed to occupy almost everyone's attention. The Church, too, seemed to be more intent on the affairs of this world than in preparing people for eternal life.

Young Philip Neri's family was no exception. Though they were not wealthy, Francis Neri had great plans for his four children, especially Philip, whom everyone affectionately called "Pippo Buono" (Good Philip). Philip was educated by the Dominicans until he was sixteen. They hoped that this friendly and intelligent young man would join them. But his father had other ideas. Philip was sent to live with his wealthy uncle. Because his uncle had no children, it was obvious that Philip had been chosen to be his heir.

Philip obeyed, and went to live with his aunt and uncle in the country. He was so cheerful and generous that his relatives liked him right away and treated him as if he were their own son. They put him in charge of the men who worked in the fields. Philip enjoyed long hours beneath the wide blue sky, planting and harvesting. The countryside was beautiful and he lived in a fine house—yet Philip felt that something was missing from his life.

Something was missing, but he did not have to look far for it. Against the skyline loomed the great stone monastery of Montecassino. It called him gently, but irresistibly. Philip began to visit the monks in the evening, after the day's work was done.

"Why don't you join us, Philip?" the monks began to ask after they had known him for a while. "Come here, and you will know true peace."

Philip wished he could say yes, but he knew deep down that his call was to another type of life. God wanted him, yes, but not as a monk meditating in his room or as a farmer working the fields under the clear blue sky. God wanted him to go to the poor, the sick, the prisoners, the confused teenagers—all the suffering people—and bring them food, clothing, tenderness and mercy. Philip bade an affectionate farewell to his uncle and aunt, and set out for Rome.

Rome was a city in trouble when Philip arrived.

A few years before in 1527, it had been attacked by the powerful armies of the German emperor Charles V. In only eight days, thousands of churches, buildings and homes had been destroyed. Once the center of Renaissance learning and culture, the city was now trying to rebuild and recover.

In those days, the Pope was ruler not only of the Church, but also of the civil property which it owned. This meant that the Pope and cardinals were concerned with things like armies, taxes and construction. By the time Philip arrived, the people were disillusioned with the Church. And many of the clergy were so discouraged or caught up with worldly affairs that they no longer even said their daily Mass.

Philip found himself a small room in exchange for tutoring the two young children of some friends of his father. At night, he studied philosophy and theology and spent long hours in prayer. Almost two years went by like this. Philip was almost a hermit. Then one day he felt that God was asking him to go out among the people and begin to speak to them about God's love. And he also went out to show them God's love by caring for the sick, the homeless and especially the many gangs of teenagers who roamed the streets all day and all night.

Each day, Philip would go out and talk about Jesus Christ to anyone who would listen. He would tell them about the crucifixion and how Jesus, after dying for our sins, had risen again that we, too, might have eternal life. He would preach to the people about the Ten Commandments, and the need to pray and trust the Lord. Then, in the afternoon, he would ring the bell of the church and call the people to join him in prayer. Little by little, more and more people came to pray with Philip. And those who didn't come to pray, came so they could hear the beautiful music and singing which Philip always provided!

After the prayers, he would teach them about the scriptures, history and the lives of the saints. His prayer group became known as the Oratory. Often, he would gather its members together to do some good work for the poor, or they would go off together to the mountains for a picnic. The teenagers especially began to gather around Philip, and he would usually greet them with the words, "Well, my friends, when shall we begin to do good?"

Philip encouraged the people to go to confession and to receive the Eucharist often. He knew that if people received these sacraments they would no longer be bound by their sins and bad habits. But Philip himself was not a priest! After almost eighteen years of this ministry, his confessor convinced him that God desired him to receive the Sacrament of Holy Orders. Philip had such a great respect for the priesthood, and felt such pain seeing so many priests in Rome not living according to their consecration, that he had always objected to his own ordination. He simply did not feel worthy. As soon as he was convinced that it was God's will, however, he immediately began to study again and was ordained at the age of thirty-five.

Within a few years, a small group of his penitents were also ordained. Desiring to follow the example of Philip's life and ministry, they went to him for direction. He had them promise to live together, sharing everything in common and supporting one another in prayer and by good example. Soon this little group grew and the Pope gave them an abandoned old church to be their home. They became known as the Congregation of the Oratory. Like Philip, they went about among the working class and teenagers, to preach, teach and care for their spiritual and material needs. Daily, they would ring the bells of their churches and gather the people together for prayer. Father Philip continued to preach, too, but so many people were coming to him for confession and spiritual direction that he often spent the whole day and most of the night in the confessional!

One day Philip was approached by a teenager who had sinned so much that he did not have the courage to admit his troubles to anyone.

"Come on," Philip urged him. "You'll feel better soon."

"Father, I've made so many mistakes and hurt so many people...."

"All your sins will be forgiven."

"Maybe, but I am afraid of the penance I might have to do!"

"Nothing exceptional!" Philip assured him. "Only this: every time you sin, come back right away and put yourself in the state of grace."

The young man promised. He confessed, received absolution and went on his way happy.

But he returned almost at once, head down, humiliated and discouraged.

Philip Neri comforted him and encouraged him one, two, three, many, many times; every time he returned with bowed head, weary and dejected.

But eventually he began coming less frequently. Philip's smile, which had never faded, now grew brighter as he saw that the boy, aided by God and his desire to live as a Christian, was becoming a virtuous and holy person.

———————

There was another young man who had lived in the streets for a very long time. "Father, I am tangled up in so much sin, I don't know if I can ever change!"

"Never fear," replied Philip. "I will help you get out of your life of sin."

"But what must I do? Where do I start?"

"Just this: say the 'Hail, Holy Queen' seven times every day, and kiss the floor saying, 'Tomorrow I might be dead!'"

The young man put the priest's advice into practice and little by little began to lead a holy and happy life, thanking God and Father Philip.

———————

Philip also had the gift of prophecy. One day, one of his young friends told him that he planned to take a trip to Naples.

"It would be best for you not to go," the priest advised at once.

"But, why not, Father? It's a pilgrimage trip, and Naples is a beautiful city. I don't see anything wrong with going."

"Listen to me; don't be stubborn."

"Father, I really want to go."

"All right, do so if you wish. But you will be ambushed by the Turks and almost drowned."

The youth decided to go anyway, and set sail with the others for Naples.

At sea, the Turkish pirates attacked the ship. The boy, not knowing what else to do, flung himself over the side and struggled to keep himself afloat in the water. He went down once, and again....

"Father Philip!" he screamed, "Father, save me!"

Philip Neri, who was miles away in Rome, appeared before his eyes, seized him by the hair and carried him to safety. What a miracle! Philip was one of the saints who had the gift of being in two places at the same time.

———————

Philip always acted according to the needs he saw in those who came to him. He was gentle with one person, stern with another, playful with another. In everything, he tried to follow the leading of the Holy Spirit, who helped him see what each person needed the most.

Philip always prayed for guidance, relying always on God's grace. "Lord, watch over me this day," he would pray. "Without your help, I may betray you!"

Father Philip Neri showed people God's love by caring for the sick, the homeless, and the many teenagers who roamed about in gangs all day and night.

No matter how distinguished Philip's visitors were, they found him doing ordinary tasks. Often, he would greet them with an apron on and his shirt sleeves rolled up, scrubbing pots in the kitchen. Philip was careful not to let his fame make him proud. Often, when he was to meet with the most important people, he would dress in a fantastic costume, or with his clothes inside out and long white shoes on his feet. Sometimes he would walk through the streets carrying a huge bunch of weeds in his hand. He would hold the flowering weeds like a bouquet of roses, stopping every now and then to sniff them. He would do anything to make people think he was foolish. This not only hid his holiness but it also made people laugh—and that was important to him.

Philip Neri felt that people could not make progress in the spiritual life, or conquer sin, unless they were cheerful. "Never commit sin, and always be cheerful," was his favorite advice. "A cheerful soul becomes holy more quickly." He was convinced that a happy heart, is sign of purity and innocence.

When boys and young men played games in the courtyard, bouncing a ball against the wall of Philip's room, the other priests complained about the noise. "Don't listen to them," Philip responded. "Go on playing."

"How can you put up with that racket?" asked a visitor.

"They could chop wood on my back and I wouldn't mind," answered Philip, "as long as they keep out of sin."

The celebration of Holy Mass became an almost continuous ecstasy for Philip. Often he was seen suspended in the air, as if he wished to ascend to heaven. Often, he would burst into tears or start to tremble from head to foot; at other times he would become as still as a statue, his gaze directed upward.

When he was nearly eighty, Philip became sick. Cardinal Frederick Borromeo, brother of Charles Borromeo, came to anoint him and give him Viaticum. Philip received the Eucharist with great joy, saying, "Anyone who wants anything but Jesus, does not know what he wants. All else is vanity."

One of his friends looked worried. "Are you afraid that I am dying?" asked Philip. "Well, I am not afraid."

May 25, 1595, the Feast of Corpus Christi, he went to confession and celebrated Mass. Then he spent the day praying, reading the lives of saints and hearing confessions. But by six o'clock that evening he was dying.

"If you don't have any more medicines," he joked with his doctor, "don't worry about it. I can't use them anymore."

With tears in his eyes, his friend asked him, "Father, will you leave us without saying anything? At least give us your blessing."

Philip Neri opened his eyes, raised his gaze to heaven and then looked around at his friends. He lifted a hand and blessed them weakly.

This was his last act. When his hand fell, his great heart stopped beating. That heart had known heavenly joys even on earth—so much so that at times Philip had cried out: "No more, Lord, no more; I cannot bear so much joy!" Now that same Lord drew near and opened new floodgates of joy.

True joy comes from avoiding sin and doing good deeds. Joy is the mark of a Christian. We, too, will find joy when we make heaven our goal and try to imitate Jesus in the way we treat others and pray to our Father in heaven.

St. Germaine

(1579-1601)

June 15

Laurent Cousin rubbed the shoulders of his young wife, Marie. Here, in the small house they had shared for the past year, they were now preparing for the birth of their first child. "How do you feel now, Marie? Is this helping?"

Marie turned and looked up at Laurent's worried face. Her pregnancy had been difficult, and now that the time for birth was near she had to stay in bed almost the whole day. "Don't worry, Laurent. I want this baby so much that no pain or discomfort is too great. Besides, I think this might be the night.... Perhaps you should go get your sister after we eat."

Laurent ate quickly and ran out to the neighboring farm house where his sister Monique lived. She had four children and had promised to help Marie when her time to give birth came. "Monique! Monique!" As Laurent ran up the path he thought his heart would burst with excitement. "Monique, come home with me. Marie thinks this is the night!"

"Calm down, Laurent." Monique was laughing at her brother. "This is her first child. It will be a long time before she is ready for me to be her midwife!" But Laurent convinced her to come back with him right then. And it was a good thing, because by the time they arrived at Laurent's house, Marie was already starting to give birth.

Monique flew into action, directing Laurent to bring water and clean cloths, and then sending him out of the house because he was so nervous that he was no help at all! As the hours passed Monique began to worry. Marie was having a very difficult time and was growing weaker by the minute. At last, however, a little baby girl was born. But as Monique picked up the small baby she gasped. Besides being far smaller than usual, the tiny girl clearly had a crippled right hand and there were two large lumps on either side of her neck—a sure sign of a tubercular sickness called scrofula. Monique sadly handed the infant to its mother.

But Marie hardly noticed the deformity or sickness of her little child. Nothing could take away her love for this small baby. She smiled, then laughing and crying all at the same time, she called out for Laurent to come and welcome their first child into the world. Laurent's face showed his disappointment. Though he had been hoping for a boy, a little girl was just as welcome. But a little girl who was sick and deformed. Laurent felt like someone punched him so hard he couldn't breathe.

"Laurent, what's wrong?" Marie asked. "So what if her hand is deformed? I can see already that this little girl will be beautiful and kind. Come, let us thank God for her. What shall we name her at the baptism tomorrow? How about Germaine, after my mother?"

And so the baby was named Germaine the very next day. The neighbors came, bringing gifts of food and small blankets which they had woven from the fine wool for which their village of Pibrac was famous. But as they met together to gossip they all said the same thing: "Too bad. That child will not live long. And Marie, she looks terrible. Do you think she'll live?"

Laurent cared anxiously for his wife. Never a very religious person, he now found himself begging God not to let her die. But day by day Marie grew weaker. She had to let another young mother in the village nurse Germaine, who was growing surprisingly quite strong. Soon enough she took her first steps. And it was clear that she had a joyful and calm disposition like her mother. Little Germaine would come tumbling into Marie's bedroom with a bunch of wildflowers clutched in her chubby fist. Laughing and smiling she would plop the bouquet onto her mother's lap. But one day, Germaine went in with her flowers and her mother was not there. Marie had died the night before, and Laurent had already buried his beloved wife.

During the next few months, Germaine was sent from the house of one relative to another. Her lymph glands would often swell and even though she was only three-years-old, her joints were already growing deformed because of the scrofula. Many of the people of the village were sure that the child must have "evil spirits" in her to be so sick so young. It was the year 1580, and people then did not know very much about sickness or birth defects. Germaine's father didn't want anything to do with her. He wanted to marry again, and was afraid that no woman would marry him with a sick child to care for. Eventually, though, he did find a new bride and Germaine went to live with her father and stepmother.

By this time Germaine had become a favorite of the parish priest in Pibrac. He had never known a child so quick to learn her prayers and so eager to learn about God. Why, Germaine was not yet ten, but she knew her catechism well enough to teach the younger children! One day he went to pay a visit to Laurent and his new wife. "Laurent," the priest began. "I wanted to tell you how well Germaine is doing with her catechism. Why don't you allow her to come to the school and learn to read and do math with the other children?"

"Never!" growled Laurent.

"Never!" snapped the stepmother, who by now had two young children of her own.

"Where is Germaine?" the priest asked. "She is too small, surely, to be out working in the fields...?"

"Her size has nothing to do with it! She is a naturally lazy child. It's all I can do to get her to watch the sheep in the field!" said the step-mother. "In fact, she should be grateful that I allow her to sleep with the sheep. With her sickness, I live in fear that she will contaminate the flock!"

"Sleep with the sheep!" exclaimed Father.

"Surely not! Why, Germaine's sickness is not contagious...and you have plenty of room in the house, don't you?"

"And risk having my own two dear children get sick! She will *never* sleep in my house!" By now Germaine's stepmother was furious. Just the sight of Germaine was often enough to send her into a rage, and almost daily she beat and kicked the frail girl for one thing or another.

"Calm down, my dear," purred Laurent. Then turning to the priest he said roughly, "I don't come to the church and tell you how to mind your affairs. I would appreciate it if you don't tell me how to mind mine!"

"Maybe you should consider coming to church, my friend," said Father. "In any case, I beg you, be kind to the child. I can see from her eyes and gentle manners that the Lord has a special place in her life. Good-day."

That night as Germaine finished herding the sheep into the stable, she thought of the children whom she had taught that day. There was a regular group of almost a dozen village children who came to her after their school classes to learn about God. Even though Germaine was not pretty, and sometimes her neck was swollen so badly that she could hardly speak, there was something about her that made the other village families realize that she was special in many ways. And when she spoke about God and his love for each and every person, it was with such conviction that even the saddest listener went away encouraged and peaceful. It seemed everyone loved Germaine except her own father

Germaine spoke about God's love for each and every person with such strong conviction that even the saddest listener went away encouraged and peaceful.

and stepmother....

"Germaine!" shrieked her stepmother. "Stop dawdling and get over here. Did you finish spinning the wool I gave you this morning?"

"Yes, Mother," said Germaine. "I finished it, and here it is." As she handed the large woman the bundle of wool, Germaine couldn't help but cringe. Her stepmother's violent moods were so unpredictable. And by now Germaine had received so many beatings that just hearing the woman's voice made her small body tense up and her stomach knot. Every morning and evening she said special prayers that God would soften this woman's heart, and that her father would love her as his daughter. But so far, her prayers seemed to go unheard.

This night proved to be no different. As Germaine was walking down the back steps with her supper of bread crusts, her stepmother said softly, "Germaine, turn around. Let me see that face which the priest likes so much."

As Germaine turned she could just see the broomstick coming at her, but didn't quite duck in time. Falling down the steps and dropping her bread in the muddy path, the stepmother's voice came cackling out, "That will teach you to make something of yourself in front of the villagers! You might act holy in front of them, but I know what a wicked child you are! Now get away from my house and my children!"

Germaine limped away into the barn. Later, as she lay gazing up at the stars, she prayed, "Dearest Father in heaven, dearest Mother Mary, I am your child. You give us every good blessing and I thank you. Please soften the hearts of my father and stepmother. They are so unhappy, and they don't even realize it! Let them recognize the love you have for them through my patience and goodness. I offer my whole self to you, I wait for every good thing from you." Saying the Rosary on a string of knots, Germaine fell sound asleep.

She was now over twenty-years-old, but because of her small build and the ragged clothes she wore, Germaine didn't look more than twelve. Although she still slept in the barn, her stepmother rarely beat her anymore. She didn't dare! For one afternoon when Germaine had come home from the fields she had met an old beggar. Knowing that her crusts of bread would be on the kitchen table, Germaine had crept quietly into the house to take them and give them to the old man. But just as she was closing the door, her stepmother appeared. "Germaine! What do you have in your apron, you thief?" The stepmother picked up the large wooden stick used for rolling the bread dough and began chasing Germaine into the village, shouting, "Thief! Thief! I have been raising a thief, and now everyone will see the truth of what I say!"

And indeed, almost the whole village had come out to see what Madame Cousin's latest rage was about. Seeing Germaine trying to outrun the angry woman, they gasped. "She'll kill that child someday!" some exclaimed. "But wait," said others. "Maybe the child really is a thief. After all, how else could she have survived on the little bit of food Madame Cousin tosses out to her?"

By now the strange looking group had reached the village square and Germaine could go no farther. "Well," she thought, "if I let go of my apron and let the bread spill out, I will receive a beating for taking it. If I refuse, I shall get a beating anyway." With that, she stood facing her stepmother and calmly let the apron drop. Immediately she heard the crowd of peasant women gasp and many fell to their knees. In amazement, Germaine looked down. Instead of crusts of old bread, beautiful flowers of a kind no one there had ever seen were laying in a pile at her feet.

"A saint!" she heard someone say. "She is a saint!" another agreed. One by one the crowd came up to gather some of the miraculous flowers to bring home. At last, only Germaine and her stepmother were left. With a shamed look on her face, Madame Cousin could only say, "Well, I never. Well, it is late Germaine. Come home, let us begin the evening's work." The lady was too proud to apologize, but too smart not to realize that never again could she beat the girl who was clearly so blessed by God.

Even though Germaine was now welcome to eat in the house, she preferred to sleep out in the stable with the sheep. There she could gaze up at the star-filled sky and think of the beauty of God who had made so many wonderful things. And there she was also free to pray, as she often did, into the early hours of the morning. Her joints were always stiff and painful now, and she could no longer stand up straight. But dozens of children still came to her in the fields to learn their catechism and prayers. And she still left the flock of sheep in the care of her guardian angel each day as she went to Mass and Communion in the village church. Her friend, the village priest, tried to have food to give to her each day, knowing that she would probably give it away before she ate it.

Then one evening, two monks who were traveling through Pibrac on their way to Toulouse saw bright lights and what looked like angels hovering over the farmhouse of Laurent Cousin. Stopping to watch, they stayed there until morning. When Madame Cousin got up and saw that the sheep were still in the stable, she ran out, calling, "Germaine! Germaine, are you sick?" As she entered the stable, she gasped and tears ran down her face as she picked up the small body of her stepdaughter. Germaine had died peacefully during the night. The two monks told everyone in the village of the lights and angels which they had seen. At Germaine's funeral the villagers were convinced that they were burying a saint. From that day, people have prayed to Germaine and received many miraculous cures and graces. From heaven, the little shepherdess of Pibrac continues to love and assist all who come to her in their need.

Even though she was sick all her life and was born with physical disformities, Germaine allowed God's love to shine through her and touch the lives of hundreds of people. Let us be confident that no matter what our physical appearance may be, we are all beloved children of the Heavenly Father.

St. Camillus de Lellis

(1550-1614)

July 14

John and Camilla de Lellis had been married for almost forty years, and as much as they had hoped to have a large family and even see grandchildren, Camilla had never become pregnant. Now, long after most of their friends and relatives had given up hope for them, Camilla realized that she was expecting a baby! At almost sixty-years of age she took every precaution to make sure nothing would go wrong. Early one spring day in 1550, when the hills of central Italy were bursting with flowers and fresh grass, she gave birth to a perfect little son. They decided to call the baby Camillus in honor of Camilla. Everyone said that he would be the blessing of his parents' old age.

Soon, however, most of the small town was wondering if Camillus would live long enough to be a blessing to anyone! He wasn't sickly—far from it. In fact, the boy was soon almost six feet tall and solid muscle. He was also uncontrollable—rebellious, quarrelsome and impulsive. His father was ready to throw him out of the house by the time he was twelve! John de Lellis was a captain in the army, and he would not tolerate disobedience. He and Camillus would have fights that scared the neighbors and caused Camilla to spend whole nights crying. Her husband tried discipline and force; she tried prayer, persuasion and pleading. But at sixteen, Camillus found himself out on the streets.

Free at last! he thought. He went immediately to the part of town where there were many bars, dance halls and gamblers. Everyone knew he was the young son of John de Lellis, but Camillus was so big and strong that no one questioned his right to be in such places. He soon learned the thrill of winning a bet, and before he knew it he was an addicted gambler. But he quickly learned that all he had to do when in debt was challenge some unsuspecting stranger to a fight. His friends would place their bets, and Camillus would come up with money to spare. That is, until his luck ran out—and his friends also. Camillus was so proud and quarrelsome, that the other men just didn't want to be around him anymore. At eighteen, Camillus found himself alone. He decided to join his father's army.

There was a war going on with the Turks and strong soldiers were needed. Camillus was moving fast up the ranks because of his size, strength and courage. But an infection developed on his foot that became so bad that he couldn't walk. Fearing for his life, he was sent to the hospital of St. James in Rome. St. James was a hospital for people with "incurable" diseases and many of its patients were destitute. Camillus was accepted as a patient, but was also required to work part-time in

the wards. For a few months all went well and the
infection was clearing up. But the longer Camillus
was there, the more he got into fights with the
other workers and patients. For Camillus there was
only one way to do anything—his way. And when
others didn't agree, there was trouble. At the end
of nine months, Camillus found himself once again
out on the streets.

"Free" again, he went back to gambling and
drinking. This time, though, something was different. He was no longer able to control his
decisions about when to gamble or when to
drink. All he had to do was wake up in the
morning and he was soon at a card game or in a
bar. He would end up in trouble in one town after
another. Camillus moved farther and farther
south until he was in the lively port city of
Naples. For several weeks he was the talk of the
taverns as he won fight after fight, bet after bet.
The more he won, the more he would risk on the
next game. One day he lost it all, even the shirt
on his back! He woke lying in a gutter, bruised
and sore from being beaten and robbed while he
was drunk. Realizing that he could not stay in
Naples, he headed east and didn't stop until he
reached the shore of the Adriatic Sea, at the town
of Manfredonia. In the clear fresh sea air he
could feel life coming back into his system. Tired
of begging for scraps of food, Camillus decided to
look for work—temporary work, of course.

At that time, a community of Capuchin friars
were enlarging their monastery on the outskirts of
Manfredonia and were in need of construction
workers. Camillus was hired right away and for

his pay he accepted room and board with the friars. Humbled by his circumstances and ashamed of himself for having reached such a deplorable state, Camillus was a loner. He did not join the other hired workers for drinks after work, and he was careful to avoid card games on his lunch break. His reputation had not spread this far, so everyone assumed that he was just a quiet, sad young man.

The Lord, however, knew Camillus' heart. And slowly, grace was breaking through the hardened crust of his soul. As so often happens, grace was working through ordinary human events. Whenever the friars were in the chapel chanting the office, Camillus felt irresistibly attracted. He would move closer to the chapel walls and sit beneath the window so that he could hear better. "O Lord, come to my assistance," one group of friars would sing. And then came the response, "O Lord, make haste to help me."

"Lord, make haste to help me." The ancient prayer echoed in his head morning and night. He also noticed the great peace with which these friars went about their daily duties. He especially noticed how kind and wise Father Angelo was. Father Angelo was the community "guardian," or superior. It was Father Angelo who assigned the work each day and distributed the week's wages. He had noticed the quiet young man on the construction crew. Father Angelo could see the lines on Camillus' face that betrayed his sinful past, and his heart ached for the sadness that surrounded the giant of the construction crew. Day after day, Father Angelo patiently waited for the moment of conversion to come. He did not approach Camillus but waited for Camillus to approach him. And sure enough, the day came.

"Father Angelo," stammered Camillus, "may I talk to you, please?"

"Camillus, isn't it? Yes, I've been waiting for you." Father Angelo stood up from his desk and gently took Camillus' arm. Looking up at the young man's red face, realizing how difficult this must be, he said, "Let us go out into the gardens. We will be alone and can talk freely."

Three hours later, Camillus felt like a new man. He began joining the friars for prayer. No one was surprised when, a few weeks later, he appeared dressed as a Capuchin novice. Camillus felt that he had to make up for all the pain and hurt he had stubbornly inflicted on his family, on his friends and on the Lord. There was no novice so devoted as he to performing the most humble tasks and to keeping the many fast days of the Capuchin rule so strictly. Camillus had never in his life known such freedom and joy.

One afternoon, Camillus received a message to go at once to Father Angelo's office. He felt a pit growing and gnawing in his stomach as he limped toward the main house. Was Father calling him to tell him he would soon be able to profess his vows? Or was he calling him because of the disgusting sore that had reappeared on his foot? Before he reached the guardian's office, he felt sure that he knew what he was about to hear....

"I'm truly sorry, Brother Camillus," Father Angelo said. "There is nothing wrong at all with your behavior, far from it. But we cannot admit someone to profession who will not be able to keep our strict way of life. And with that foot of yours, well...let's pray that another stay at St. James will cure you for good. Then you may return."

Sadly, Brother Camillus took off his novice robes and accepted the offer of a ride to St. James. He was so big and so strong, why should such a small thing as a foot infection keep him from fulfilling the only dream he had in life? Yet he was to come and go three times between St. James and the Capuchin monastery. At last, Father Angelo had to tell him that it seemed the Lord was leading him to another way of life. Not knowing what else to do, Camillus returned once again to St. James. But it was not the same Camillus who had been expelled from the hospital so many years before! Indeed, everyone was talking about the way Camillus was acting. He treated everyone with such kindness and respect that several of the "incurables" had recovered and gone on to live normal lives! What was the gentle giant's secret?

Camillus had come to think of each patient as being Christ himself. Hadn't Jesus said, "What you do to the least of my brothers, you do for me?" And to govern his own attitudes and behavior, he reflected often on the words, "Truly I tell you, unless you change and become like children, you will never enter the kingdom of heaven. Whoever becomes humble like this child is the greatest in the kingdom of heaven" (Mt. 18:3-4). But while he was trying his best to treat each patient with kindness and respect, he couldn't help but notice that many of the attendants were rough and even abused the sick and poor. In fact, he was horrified

Everyone was talking about Camillus. He treated each patient with such kindness and respect that several of the "incurables" had recovered! What was the "gentle giant's" secret?

when he realized that some of the people were being buried before they were even dead!

Gradually, Camillus began to figure out which of the attendants were concerned about the patients and were trying to live good Christian lives, and which were not. For those who were caring for the sick with Christian compassion, he started a support group. They met together for prayer and to talk about the particular needs of each patient. They also began the custom of praying at the side of dying patients. To avoid burials of live people, Camillus instructed his followers to keep praying for at least fifteen minutes after they thought the patient had died, and to avoid covering the body for a while after that. Not everyone was pleased with Camillus' ideas—indeed, some of the attendants who were used to abusing the poor were quite angry—but others took notice and soon Camillus was appointed administrator of the hospital.

By this time, Camillus had organized his life in such a way as to schedule regular periods of prayer and attendance at Mass. And his confessor and spiritual director was none other than the famous St. Philip Neri! Philip could see God working in Camillus and guided him eventually into considering priestly ordination. At thirty-two, Camillus began studying and in 1584, he was ordained a priest. For an ordination gift one of his relatives granted Camillus a large annuity. This guaranteed him a steady and substantial income for life. It also set the stage for Camillus' dream of the religious life to come true.

Camillus left his administrative role at St. James and, gathering his closest followers, began to live a common life of prayer and service of the sick. They would go out to the ships which had been quarantined and care for the plague victims. They would go to the leper colonies, and to the shanty town where no other doctors would venture. They called themselves the Ministers of the Sick. When a war broke out between the Venetians and the Croatians, Camillus sent his best men to care for the wounded soldiers. This was the first time that there was a medical corp for the battlefield! In 1591, Pope Gregory XIV gave canonical approval to the group, making them an officially recognized religious community. Camillus was seen everywhere, accepting new members, encouraging and instructing the older members and always caring for the sick wherever he was.

His brothers all knew, however, that Camillus himself was in need of medical care. The sore on his foot never healed completely, and there were times when the infection was so bad that he was confined to bed. And as he grew older his health declined in other ways as well. But he never allowed his physical ailments to be an excuse for special treatment. He shared everything with his community, and was always available to give his advice and settle the inevitable disagreements. And this once reckless and quarrelsome youth had become so patient and gentle that no one feared to approach him.

Soon his community numbered in the hundreds and the burden of governing them all was clearly too demanding for the ailing Camillus. He knew it was time to step down and turn the duty of authority over to another. In 1607, a new superior was appointed. Camillus was free to serve his beloved sick. In 1613, he attended the General Chapter of the community, and after a new superior general was appointed the two men set out for a tour of all the communities. They went slowly, for Camillus' health had again taken a turn for the worse.

By the time they reached Genoa he was seriously ill. They stopped for a few weeks of rest, but then Camillus insisted that they continue because he sensed that this was his last chance to see the members of his community. At the end of the tour he collapsed, and everyone knew the end had come. At sixty-four, the gentle giant and servant of the sick received his last Communion, gave a final sermon to the brothers gathered around his bed and passed into eternal life. From there he prays and intercedes for all those who care for the sick, especially the members of his community who continue his work even today.

St. Camillus was so good to the sick because in them he served the suffering Christ. If we dislike a person, or are afraid of someone because of a disease or handicap, we can pray to St. Camillus to help us see Christ in that person.

St. John Berchmans

(1599-1621)

November 26

Thirteen-year-old John Berchmans quietly slipped into the door of his father's cobbler shop and up the back stairs. It was just about dawn, and his father was heading down to his cobbler's bench to begin the day's work. "Good morning, John," he said. "Did you pray for your mother? She is not feeling well yet. You will have to wake up your brothers and sisters and prepare their breakfast before you go to school."

"Good morning, Father," answered John, kissing him lightly on the cheek. "Yes. I always pray for Mother when I serve Mass. I will be very quiet so that she does not wake up."

John tip-toed up the rest of the stairs and set the water on the wood stove to boil. Then he went to the bedroom where his two younger brothers were sleeping. His mother and the new baby were sleeping quietly in the other room of their small apartment. Their father was the shoe-maker for the little village of Diest (in what is now Belgium). Like most of their neighbors, they lived above the family's workshop.

At last the children were fed and brought to their aunt's apartment where they would stay while John was at school. Later in the afternoon, he would stop for them on his way home. This had been his daily routine for the past two years, ever since his mother had become sick while pregnant with the last baby. He loved his mother very much, and she was always at the door waiting for him when he arrived home. This evening, though, his father stopped him on the way in.

"Wait a minute, John," he said. "I would like to speak with you before you go upstairs. Send the other children on ahead."

After making sure the smallest child was safely up the steep stairs, John went back into the cobbler's shop. His father asked him to sit beside him on the cobbler's bench. As he sat, he could smell the sweet odor of leather mixed with sweat and linseed oil on his father's work apron.

"John, I must ask you to make a sacrifice."

"What is it, Father?"

"With your mother not well, and another child to feed, I no longer make enough money for our family to live on."

"What shall we do? Can I help you in the shop after school?" John looked up at his father's worried face. Although he loved his father very much, he rarely spoke with him about serious matters.

"John, I think you must decide on a trade to learn and become an apprentice to one of the other shops in the village. I have spoken to several of our neighbors already. The baker and tailor have both promised to take you in. Besides teaching you their trade, they will also pay you a small wage. You can decide which one you would like to learn and let me know this Sunday afternoon. You will start Monday."

John felt like he couldn't breathe and almost fell off the bench. Becoming an apprentice meant that he would have to quit school! And if he quit school, how could he ever realize his secret dream of becoming a priest? But from the way his father had turned and started working again on the shoe in his hand, John knew that further discussion was not possible. With a heavy heart he went upstairs and began to prepare the family's evening meal.

That Sunday, after Communion, John prayed, "Please Jesus, you know that I want nothing more than to be a priest and a saint. And if I do not become a saint while I am young, I never will. Help my father and I to know what your will for me is."

The next day John trudged off to Mr. Miet, the village tailor, and began his apprenticeship as his father had asked. But on the way home he stopped at the village church and knocked on the door of Father Peter Emmerich. "Please, Father," he began. "I want to become a priest. But I must quit school and work at Mr. Miet's so that my father will have enough money to feed us. What can I do?"

The old priest looked silently at the boy. John Berchmans had been a faithful altar server for almost eight years already, and he had often accompanied the old priest on pilgrimages to nearby shrines. Often he had wondered if this oldest son of Mr. Berchmans would not one day be a priest. But what could be done if he had to quit school?

"John," he finally said. "You must obey your father for now."

With that, the priest turned and left John alone in the church. John knelt for a moment before the Tabernacle and prayed again. "Jesus, help me to be a saint. Show me the way to the priesthood."

Disappointed that the old priest had not been more helpful, John nonetheless continued his work at the tailor's and learned the skills of sewing quickly. In the evenings he tried to study his Latin, or went with his friends to practice the play they would perform on the first Sunday of Advent. In those days, the young men and boys of the villages often put on plays based on stories from the Bible or the lives of the saints. These shows were called "mystery plays" and were a popular form of entertainment. John was one of the best actors in his group, and people from distant villages would travel to see their shows.

The weeks passed and John continued to pray and to work. One evening as he arrived home he met a tall priest walking down the street. It looked as though he had come from his father's shop, but John did not remember seeing him before. As he walked in, his father called him over to the cobbler's bench and made room for him to sit beside him.

"What would you say, John, if I told you that you

could both earn a wage and study for the priest-hood at the same time?"

"Father! What do you mean? How can I do that?" John could feel his heart beating faster. Although he had not discussed the question of being a priest with his father a second time, he had often hoped that his father was still thinking about it.

"Well, Father Froymont just left the shop—you may have passed him on the street just now. He is looking for a young person to be his servant. Father Peter told him to come and see me. John, if you want, you can go with him tomorrow. In exchange for your work for him, he will give you the same wage as Mr. Miet and let you continue your studies besides."

John looked closely at his father's face, and thought that he saw a tear creeping down one of the heavy lines around his eyes. "Where will I live, Father?"

"You will have to go to the city of Malines. You will not be able to come home very often, John. The choice is yours."

With that his father turned back to his work. John sat quietly. It had not dawned on him before that becoming a priest would mean leaving his home, leaving his mother and brothers and sisters. Yet wasn't this the opportunity he had been praying for? By the time he was up the stairs, John was fairly jumping up and down for joy. As soon as his mother saw him, they both knew that this would be his last supper at home. Father Froymont was to leave the next morning for Malines, and John would go with him.

———————

Father Froymont was very different than old Father Emmerich. And certain things about his life surprised John at first. For one thing, instead of visiting shrines on his free days, Father Froymont liked nothing better than to go duck hunting. John was put in charge of the dogs and quickly learned to train the pups for hunting. Among his other duties, he was assigned to wait at tables. Father Froymont was one of the priests assigned to the Cathedral of Malines, so guests and important people often ate with the priests. During the day, though, John was free to attend the seminary and continue his study of Latin and Greek in preparation for ordination. Even though it was still a long way off, he dreamed of the day that he would be able to celebrate Mass and make the Body of Christ present on the altar.

In 1615, when John was sixteen, the Jesuits came to Malines and opened a college there. John was one of their first students. Almost immediately, he was attracted to the life of these young and dedicated priests, many of whom were preparing to go to faraway missions. After much prayer and asking the advice of his spiritual director, John decided to ask to join the Jesuits. Father Froymont and Mr. Berchmans were both upset at the idea and tried every argument they could think of to make John change his mind. But in the end, John was accepted as a postulant and within a few months, he began his novitiate. His joy was broken only by the death of his mother a few weeks later.

As a novice, John lived most of his days in much the same way as he had before. Mass and meditation every morning, long hours of study, assigned chores around the house, and, for entertainment, the ever popular plays that John loved so much. One of his favorite phrases which he wrote in his personal notebook was, "Set great store on little things." John had quickly realized the importance of doing each thing well. He was especially careful to make every conversation with his brother Jesuits holy—by being cheerful, honest and thoughtful. By far, he was one of the most popular young men in the novitiate.

Two years passed quickly and it was time for John to make his first profession as a Jesuit. His joy on this happy day was dampened by the sorrow of his father's death just the day before he would have come to Malines for the celebration. John was angry at his relatives for not having told him that his father was ill. But he finally realized that they had not wanted him to worry. John wrote a letter to Father Froymont, asking him to watch out for his younger brothers, and then set out for Rome where he would begin studying philosophy. There were still several years of study before he could be ordained, and John was eager to begin.

Soon after arriving in Rome, John's teachers realized what a brilliant student he was. John found that he could take several difficult classes at the same time and still study for them all. Father

Soon after arriving in Rome, John's teachers realized how brilliant he was. Yet, in spite of his reputation for studying, John was very popular among the other students.

Massucci, the spiritual director for the senior students, wrote: "After Blessed Aloysius Gonzaga, with whom I lived in the Roman College during the last year of his life, I have never known a young man of more exemplary life, of purer conscience or of greater perfection than John." Yet, in spite of his reputation for studying, John was very popular among the other students. He enjoyed playing ball games on their free afternoons, or putting on miracle plays for the older priests. The time passed quickly, and in May of 1621, he was ready to take his final exams in philosophy.

Although the exams were very difficult, John passed easily. His teachers were so impressed that they chose him to take part in a public debate of the Catholic faith. Only the most learned and skilled debaters were allowed to participate. All the townspeople would come to watch and listen, and the debaters had to be prepared to speak on many different topics. John did not have time for even a short vacation before he began studying for the debate. Even though that summer was unusually hot, he stayed in Rome and worked hard to get ready.

August 6, the date of the debate, was very hot and humid. John had not been feeling well for several days, but had not said anything. He thought that he would be able to participate in the debate, then take a few weeks to rest in one of the Jesuits' country houses. The debate went well, and everyone agreed that John Berchmans was one of the most brilliant young men they had heard in many years. But the next afternoon, before he could even leave for the country, John was too sick to move.

Somewhat embarrassed by his sudden illness, John tried to joke with the fathers who were attending him. But the doctors were not laughing; John's illness was serious, and they did not know what was causing the fever and pain. Within a week he had become very weak, and even though he remained cheerful, John knew that he was dying. The doctors had no more ideas and the best they could do was try to keep the fever down by bathing his temples with old wine. When one of the Jesuits told John what his "medicine" was, John smiled and said, "Well, it's lucky that they don't expect me to last long—that is very expensive medicine!"

On August 11, Father Cornelius a Lapide (a famous Jesuit biblical scholar) asked John if he had anything to confess. They both knew that the end was very near. In Latin, John answered peacefully, "*Nihil omnio.*" (Nothing at all.) On the morning of August 13, John Berchmans quietly died. John had died young, and he had died a saint.

One of the beautiful things about John Berchmans was his cheerfulness. Whether he was at home helping care for his younger brothers and sisters, or in the novitiate doing chores or studying, he was always kind and pleasant. His strongest desire was to be a saint—to be like Jesus—and his one goal was to be a priest. With John Berchmans, we can pray, "Jesus, help me to be holy. Help me to be a saint."

St. Martin de Porres

(1579-1639)

November 3

Young Martin de Porres skipped up the stone steps of Holy Cross Church and slipped into the cool, dark sanctuary. There, where no one could see him, he gazed up at Jesus on the crucifix. "O, Jesus," he whispered, "the beggar looked so happy when I gave him the bread and fruit. He was so thin.... Please help mother not to be angry with me. I know you will not let us go hungry." Martin had felt dizzy with joy when he gave the food to the beggar. He still felt happy as he knelt in the church. But as he walked out of the church into the hot, busy street of Lima his stomach felt slightly knotted. Sometimes his mother was not pleased when he came home from the market with empty hands.

Martin darted in and out the dirty streets until at last he reached the small cabin on the outskirts of Lima where he lived with his mother and his little sister, Juana. He quietly slipped through the narrow door. His mother was cooking dinner. He paused for a moment to listen to her quiet, low voice as she sang to herself. How he had missed her last year when he was at school in Venezuela. He was grateful that his father, a wealthy Spanish nobleman, had paid for his schooling. Life with his cousins had been exciting, and he had not gone to bed hungry even once that year.

"Martin! Martin!" His mother's angry voice broke into the boy's daydream. "Martin, how could you do it? You know how hard I work to feed you and your sister. How can you tell me you gave away our food again?" Martin's mother was very upset.

"But, Mama, didn't you explain to me last night that Jesus said 'Whatever you do to the least brother we do for him'? How could I walk by and not give the beggar what I had?"

Anna Velasquez could only sigh. At times she did not know whether to be proud of her gentle, generous son, or totally disgusted. Looking into his sensitive young face she remembered her life with the Spanish nobleman, Don Juan de Porres. She, a poor black slave girl, had given birth to two children, Martin and Juana. Don Juan left Anna when he realized that his black children would never be accepted by his Spanish family and friends. The pain of rejection was softened only by Anna's deep conviction that in the eyes of God all people are brothers. If Martin was overly generous it was because she so often taught him about Jesus, who suffered the deepest humiliations without bitterness or hatred. No, Anna could not remain angry tonight. Besides, she had good news for her young son.

"Sit down, Martin. I have something to tell

you—something more important than the bread and fruit you've given away."

Martin sat on a short wooden stool. "What is it, Mama? Is Papa coming? Did he send money again so you won't have to work so hard?"

"No, Martin, no. Something more important than gold from your papa. Señor Rivero, the barber on Calle de Fuentes, stopped by this afternoon. He heard how well you did in school last year and he wants you as his apprentice. Imagine, Martin, he will pay you for your help while you are learning from him!"

In the sixteenth century, barbers did much more than cut hair and trim beards. The local barber was expected to know the remedies for fevers and other sicknesses. His shop was full of the herbs and powders then used as medicines. His long sharp knives were used to drain infected wounds as well as to pull teeth. His gentle hands were expected to set broken bones and ease pain.

Twelve-year-old Martin's first duty was to learn the names and uses of the medicines. Carefully he would dust the shelves of bottles that lined the walls of the shop. Señor Rivero taught him to recognize the valuable herbs and leaves of the Peruvian countryside. As the boy gathered them and spread them out to dry, he dreamed of the day when he would be able to treat the sick and injured himself. As his mother had taught him, Martin tried to see the wounded and suffering Christ: "Whatsoever you do to the least of my brethren, you have done to me."

Dr. Rivero was pleased with his young apprentice. Martin learned quickly. His long fingers were steady and firm. After a year or so, the doctor left Martin to tend the shop while he went to visit the sick in the hospital or in their homes. One afternoon Martin was preparing a batch of herbs when screams and shouting broke his quiet thoughts. A fight! Martin couldn't stand the constant fighting among the Peruvian Indians, the black slaves and the proud Spaniards.

Suddenly the shop door burst open and angry men dragged in a wounded and bleeding Indian. "Where's the doctor! Boy, quick, call the doctor! This Indian can't die or I'll be charged with murder!"

The panicking man roughly shoved Martin aside as he ran through the shop looking for Señor Rivero. The other men yelled at Martin to get out of the way. After all, what could this black youth do for a dying man? But Martin already was heating water to clean the wounds as he ripped up strips of clean cloth for bandages and pulled bottles of medicine from the shelf.

The wounded man relaxed under Martin's care. The other men began to calm down. In a few moments they were watching in awe. The relieved attacker, a rough Spanish soldier with a fiery temper, was grateful that his victim would not die. He tried to slip some gold pieces into Martin's hand. But Martin would not accept them.

"No," he said. "I have done nothing for you and I do not need your gold. You should give it to this Indian whose children will go hungry while his wounds are healing and he cannot work."

Ashamed, the soldier tossed the coins into the Indian's lap and fled the shop.

Word of Martin's skill and generosity spread

throughout Lima. Señor Rivero was pleased when people came and asked Martin to care for them. After all, he was growing old and another doctor was needed in this rough section of the city....

———

Ventura de Luna crept quietly up the stairs. For the third time in a month her newest boarder, fifteen-year-old Martin de Porres, had asked her for the stubs of candles. Every evening as she went to her room to sleep she saw a dim light under the door of Martin's attic room. What could he be doing? She had already searched the room for books, but the only books Martin had were his Bible and a small prayer book. He could not be writing—paper and ink were a luxury that few could afford. "Well," she murmured to herself, "I run a fine rooming house. If that lad is doing something wrong, I need to know about it."

Peering through the large key hole, she gasped in surprise. Señora de Luna straightened up, rubbed her eyes and peered in again. "Good Lord," she muttered. "Have mercy on me—the boy is a saint!"

There was Martin, kneeling with arms outstretched in front of his most treasured possession—a small wooden crucifix.

Early the next morning she served Martin's breakfast with a new sense of respect. She had already heard of the young man's skill in medicine. Now she saw him no longer as a poor black youth, but as a mature person. She knew that only a person of deep conviction could pray as she had seen Martin praying.

Indeed, Martin's reputation as a holy and skillful doctor was spreading throughout the city. It was very difficult for a black man to earn a living in Lima; most blacks were slaves. But Martin had been born free. He could easily earn a good living by practicing medicine. Everyone came to him: the poor and abused Peruvian Indians; the despised and often mistreated black slaves; the Spaniards who had conquered this vast land of the Incas. Martin's brown skin and African features didn't matter when people were in need of his care. And to Martin, the color of a person's skin made no difference. He was firmly convinced that all people were created in God's image and that Jesus Christ had suffered and died for all. By the time Martin was seventeen, however, he knew that he would not be the one to take Señor Rivero's place. Instead, Martin felt certain that God was inviting him to become a Dominican laybrother. After saying good-bye to his friends, and making sure that his patients would be cared for, Martin packed his few clothes and set out for the Dominican monastery of the Holy Rosary.

Father Juan de Laranzana sighed. He had heard of the young man in front of him: Martin de Porres, son of a slave woman and of a Spanish nobleman; Martin, the apprentice surgeon of Lima; Martin, who would give away his own meal if a hungry person walked by. Father de Laranzana knew that Martin refused to accept payment from the poor. Most of all, the priest recalled the young man's reputation as a devout and holy person. Yet Martin was not well educated in reading and writing.

Father Juan smoothed the front of his long

white habit while he thought about what to say. "Martin," he finally began, "do you know what you are asking? We Dominicans are an Order of *preachers*. We are teachers, Martin. Scholars. What do you hope to accomplish by joining us?"

Martin was not disturbed by the priest's question. Before this meeting, Martin had spent long hours praying and thinking. He desired to live as much as possible like Jesus, and for this he felt he must choose the most humble work. "Father, you are right," Martin responded. "The Dominicans are great scholars, and I am barely able to read. You are great preachers, and who would listen to me? But I am not asking to become a preacher or a scholar. I want only to be a lay brother in this holy monastery. A *donado* who would serve the brothers and fathers here and share in their life of prayer."

Martin's sincerity could not be denied. To accept him as a lay brother seemed reasonable enough, thought Father Juan. "Very well, Martin," the priest said, "you may live as a postulant in our monastery."

After weeks of "trying out" this new life, Martin was allowed to wear the long white tunic and black cloak of a Dominican lay brother. Father Juan appointed him assistant in the infirmary. Martin was also appointed the community tailor and barber. Brother Martin felt right at home in the monastery. It was like a dream come true!

In those days, when a young man entered the monastery to become a priest, he would receive a special haircut called a *tonsure*. His hair would be cut short all around, and the middle of the head would be shaved. Everyone who saw the young man would know that he was on his way to becoming a priest.

Brother Martin had great respect for the priesthood. He especially liked to cut hair for the tonsure because it was so symbolic. Martin was careful to cut the hair very even and to make the shaved spot perfectly round. Most of the young men were pleased to have their hair cut so well. They were proud to have everyone know that they were on their way to ordination. But one day a different sort of man came for his tonsure. He was from a very rich, noble family. He was not happy about having his carefully groomed head shaved. He had a plan all figured out.

"Listen, Brother," he said boldly. "You don't need to cut my hair quite so short, nor shave it to the skin."

"Oh?" replied Martin kindly, "Aren't you coming for the tonsure?"

"Yes, I am," answered the proud young man. "But I am a Spanish nobleman studying for the priesthood and you are nothing but a black boy dressed up in Dominican robes. Therefore, you must cut my hair as I say."

The other young men expected Martin to become angry at the unjust remark. Instead, Brother Martin said nothing. Martin simply motioned for the man to be seated, and then proceeded to cut his hair in the usual manner.

When the haircut was over, the young nobleman put his hand on his head. How upset he was! "You stupid boy!" he screamed. "Didn't I tell you how to cut my hair? Why didn't you do as I said?"

Brother Martin waited a minute, then calmly said, "My friend, look at the robes we wear. It is made of white and black cloth. Both colors contribute to the Dominican habit. And if you are pleased to wear the Dominican robes, should you not be pleased to have your hair cut in the Dominican style?"

All the young men clapped and cheered. Martin's humility and common sense had won their respect. Soon Martin became a wise friend to many of the seminarians and novices who came to confide their hopes and fears to him. Martin helped many (including the proud young nobleman) to improve their attitudes and to follow God's call with joy.

"Brother Martin, we won't have enough food," whispered Brother Sebastian.

"Have we ever run out?" Martin asked.

"Well, no. But I've never seen so many people lined up at mealtime. The pot was not even full when we started. Don't you think we should serve each person a little less, so we don't send some away with nothing?"

Martin looked up. There were people sitting on the ground, eagerly eating their soup and bread. Others were still waiting in the late afternoon sun for their portion. There were old men bent over their walking sticks, young mothers with babies and toddlers, teenagers with vacant eyes. Poverty in Lima seemed to spare no one. Martin thought about Jesus, who had miraculously multiplied loaves and fish to feed a hungry crowd. Quietly, Martin said to his companion, "Tell me, Brother, is anyone here less hungry because we have less food? No. The Lord knows how many people depend on us. Let us serve generously."

Brother Sebastian talked about that afternoon for years to come. In spite of his fears there was plenty of food for everyone. There had even been some left over for Martin's animal friends, the dogs and cats of the neighborhood.

The next day was Martin's day off. Martin was grateful for the chance to spend some time with his best friend, Brother Juan Masias. And so Martin set out, walking across the city to the Dominican monastery of St. Mary Magdalen.

"Brother Martin!" exclaimed Juan as he saw his friend coming up the monastery walk. "I was hoping you would come today. I have the whole day free."

"Yes, Brother Juan. So do I. In fact, I came to propose an idea to you."

"I'd be excited to hear it," Brother Juan said sincerely. "Why don't we go into the orchard to discuss it?"

Once they had found a shady spot, Martin began. His deep brown eyes were gazing across the orchard, but it was obvious that his mind was far away from the pleasant monastery yard. "Last night we had more people than ever in the food line. And so many children. It seems they have no place to go, no one to care for them."

Brother Juan twisted a blade of grass between his fingers, studying Martin's face as if to find an answer there. Like all big cities, Lima had a large number of abandoned children. The luckier ones became apprentices to craftsmen or servants in large households. But many faced a hard life of stealing, jail and hopeless drunkenness.

Martin looked up. There were people sitting on the ground, eagerly swallowing their soup and bread. Others were still waiting in the late afternoon sun for their portion.

"If we do not help these children," Martin said, "I fear for their future. How will they ever learn that they have a loving Father in heaven?"

"Martin, what can we do? There are so few of us, and so many needs. We have too much to do already!"

"I know, Juan," Martin said. "But I have an idea, and I am sure it will succeed. We will need a building, and teachers, and maybe some dedicated women who will be able to care for these young ones." As Martin spoke, his face and eyes lit up.

"Martin, you're incredible!" Brother Juan shook his head. "You'll probably have the building ready by the time we go for evening prayers!"

Martin laughed. "That would be quick work, wouldn't it? It's time for evening prayers *now!*"

A month later, Juan visited Martin. "So, Brother, how are the plans coming along?"

Martin smiled, as he motioned his friend to a chair. He had good news. "Last Wednesday, the archbishop visited our monastery. He asked to speak to me." Martin's eyes glowed with the memory.

"Well? What did he have to say to you?" Brother Juan was sitting straight up, eager to hear the news.

"Oh, Juan," Martin exclaimed, "truly the Lord does hear the cry of the poor."

"Martin, what did you tell the archbishop? What did he say?" Brother Juan was beginning to wonder if he'd ever hear the news.

"I told him about the children, and about our hopes." Martin stood and put his hands firmly on Juan's shoulders. "And the archbishop said that he knew a good family who would surely contribute enough money to build a house and a school!"

Juan clutched his friend's arms. It was almost too good to be true, but there was still more. Martin continued. "The archbishop will ask some good women to come to care for the children. The school even has a name already: the College of the Holy Cross. It will be for any homeless or orphaned child who comes to its door."

Together, the two brothers sang a hymn of praise to God. Their dream was on its way to becoming a reality. And even today, Holy Cross is a home for the homeless youngsters of Lima.

———————

Martin lay back on his hard bed and closed his eyes. He had another high fever. His head felt light, but Martin was calm. He knew the signs of the fever, and he knew it would pass. It always had.

"How is Brother Martin?" the Father Superior asked the infirmarian.

"Not well, Father. But he won't move off his hard bed onto one of the infirmary beds. And you know how little he eats! Brother Martin may be a great doctor, but he is a very stubborn patient!" The Brother threw his hands up in the air with a sigh.

"Well, don't force him," said Father Superior. "The other day I went to see him and he told me he would be back on his feet by Sunday. Somehow he always seems to know how long this fever of his will last."

Martin was up by Sunday. But many years had passed since Martin had put on the habit of a lay brother. After nine years, his superiors had invited him to make religious profession and he became a full member of the Dominican Community. What a joyful day that had been! Brother Martin was soon known all over Lima, and even beyond, for his good works and charity. And his own brothers thought of him as a saint. Now it was January of 1639, and Brother Martin was sixty-years-old.

That summer the archbishop of Mexico City became seriously ill while visiting Lima. Even though he had the best doctors in Lima available to him, the archbishop had heard of Martin's fame as a healer. Fearing that he would die, the archbishop asked for Brother Martin to come to him. Sure enough, the archbishop was well soon after Martin's visit. The archbishop was so pleased that he invited Martin to return with him to Mexico to be his personal physician.

Sadly, Martin's superior gave his consent, grateful that the archbishop would not leave with Martin until after the end of the summer. Martin seemed unaffected by this sudden change of plans in his life.

One day while Martin was cleaning the monastery a young priest asked him, "Brother Martin, won't you be glad when you get to the archbishop's palace in Mexico? There you will be well treated and will probably even have servants waiting on you!"

"No, Father. Servants will not wait on me. And as for this work I am doing now, there is nothing I'd rather be doing at this moment than cleaning our beautiful monastery."

A few days later the whole community took notice when Martin showed up wearing a crisp new habit. Martin had not worn a new habit since he had entered!

"Surely you must be planning to wear that habit to Mexico soon, Brother Martin," commented the Superior.

"No, Father. This is the habit I shall soon be buried in," Martin said simply.

Father Superior was greatly upset by this. He counted on Brother Martin for the work that he did, but even more so for his friendship and sound advice.

Later, Martin met one of his friends who was often sick. "Please pray for me when I die, Brother Martin," he said. Martin put his hand on his friend's shoulder and said quietly, "I shall die first. Please pray for me."

Sure enough, within a week Martin was in bed again with the fever. He knew that soon he would die and go to meet the God whom he loved so much. One by one his friends came to visit the brother who had been their physician and friend for so many years. Each day Martin grew weaker until one evening the community was called to begin the prayers for the dying. Gathered around his bed in the small room, the entire community sang the *Hail Holy Queen* and chanted the Creed. As they neared the end of the Creed, Martin sighed, smiled and died peacefully.

It seemed that the whole city of Lima came for Martin's funeral. Thousands and thousands of people passed silently by the coffin. From that day and in the years that followed miracle after miracle was reported in Martin's name. Among his own Dominican brothers and from all over Peru people were cured of incurable diseases and wounds. From 1639, until the present day, St. Martin de Porres remains as a friend to all who suffer. He is the special patron saint of American blacks. His feast day is celebrated on November 3.

Martin de Porres is famous for his great charity to all people and also for his gentle love for animals. But Martin is especially known for his love for prayer and his ability to be a good friend. We can be like Martin when we try to accept every person as a son or daughter of God, without distinction or prejudice.

St. Jane Frances de Chantal

(1572-1641)

August 21

Young Jane, holding her infant son in her arms and with her three little daughters hanging on her skirts, waved good-bye to her husband and his friends as they rode off. Baron Christopher de Chantal was an officer in the French army and was home at last for a few months. Today he was going out hunting with his good friend, Monsieur d'Aulezy, and some of their neighbors. Jane was laughing as she led her children into their large home. How much she loved this home in Bourbilly, France, with its lovely gardens, stable and farm lands. Jane's mother had died when she was a small child, and so often as she cared for her own young children she prayed that her mother would watch over and guide her from heaven. Little did she realize just how much she would need those prayers in a very short while!

As Jane put the children down for their nap she heard her good friend, Madame d'Aulezy ride up to pay a visit. Opening the door, Madame d'Aulezy hugged Jane, then looked at her. "Jane!" she exclaimed. "That dress and your hair look beautiful! What's the occasion?"

"Christopher is home, and you know I always like to look my best for him," replied Jane.

Jane's friend smiled. She and her husband were only recently married, and she wanted nothing more than to be as much in love with her husband in ten years as Jane and Christopher were. "Jane, don't you think we should have a party and dance to celebrate Christopher's return? We can plan it for next week—and perhaps the men shall catch a young deer for the feast."

"I think that's a great idea! Let's do it," Jane replied. But as the two friends sat talking and laughing, they heard the clatter of horses running at top speed and men's voices shouting. "What could be wrong?" Jane exclaimed, running out to the front porch. Then, crying out, she saw Christopher's body slumped over his horse as Monsieur d'Aulezy and the other men led it up the drive.

"Jane, my God, forgive me! Forgive me!" Monsieur d'Aulezy was almost hysterical, but the others pushed him aside as they helped Christopher to the ground and led him, bleeding, into the house. By sheer accident, his best friend had shot him in the leg, badly wounding him. Jane fainted as she saw her husband's face already ashen white.

"We've already sent for the doctor, Jane," one of the men was saying as she came to again. "I'm afraid it doesn't look good...." It was the year 1601, and there was little that could be done to prevent infection. The doctor did his best to dig out the bullet, but within a week it was clear that Christopher would not survive. A devout Catholic, he gathered his small family around and called for the priest to come and celebrate Mass. He received the Sacrament of Anointing, accepting his death without bitterness. He forgave his friend over and over, and begged Jane to do the same. But Jane was already so overwhelmed with grief that she could barely get up each morning to care for the children. When it was time for the funeral, she could not even attend the whole thing without fainting.

Four months passed and Jane was in a deep depression. She laid in bed and cried day and night. Her young daughters and infant son were left in the housekeeper's care. At last her father, a wealthy politician from Burgundy, wrote Jane a strong letter, urging her to consider her love for her children and to care for them—at least for Christopher's sake. The letter stirred something within her, and little by little the young widow regained her strength. Although she had been left a large amount of money from Christopher, the estate belonged to her father-in-law, and the old baron asked Jane and the children to move to Chantal and live with him. Sadly, Jane packed their belongings and said good-bye to the home she had loved so much.

Life with the baron was not always happy. He was almost eighty, and often grumpy. The children had to keep very quiet and not disturb him. He had a housekeeper whom he trusted, so Jane had to obey the woman's rules and had little control over her own life. More and more Jane turned to prayer and to reading the scriptures to find strength and encouragement. She fasted often, and begged God to send her a spiritual director who would lead her in doing God's will. Without realizing it, she had become very strict with her children and rigid in her manners.

Then one Lent she went to stay with her own father in Burgundy where the famous bishop, Francis de Sales, was preaching. The first time that she saw him and heard him preach, she was certain that he was to be her director. Since Father Francis was an old friend of her father it was easy enough to arrange a meeting. Father Francis was immediately impressed with Jane. Although she had a certain sadness about her, he could see that she was also a brave and generous person who sincerely wanted to do the very best she could for God and for her family. He spoke with her often, and they wrote many letters when he was away from the city. Little by little, he encouraged her to be less strict with her children and to spend more time relaxing with her friends. It was okay for her to pray and fast, he said, but her first duty was to be a good mother to her children, daughter to her father and friend to her friends.

Under Father Francis' direction Jane felt alive and happy again. While she had many friends and lots to do, she still loved her times of prayer and meditation. In fact, as she watched her children grow up and prepare to start their own families, she found herself thinking more and more about becoming a nun. Finally she presented the idea to Father Francis. As usual, he showed no surprise at what she said, but neither did he encourage her. Instead, he told her, "Jane, this is no small matter you are considering. Let me think about it and pray about it for a while. I will let you know what I think when I return to Chantal this spring."

Jane sighed. Father Francis would be away for at least four months. But trusting his wisdom and concern for her, she agreed to say nothing to anyone else, but to pray daily for the Lord to guide them. Eagerly she waited for his return, and when spring finally came, so did Father Francis. She invited him over for dinner one evening. After they had eaten he called her to take a walk with him. "Jane," he began softly. "I have something to ask you."

Jane could only think that he was going to tell her that she should not join the cloister—but she desired it so strongly! "What is it, Father Francis? I am prepared to obey your guidance."

"Jane, I have plans to begin a new community of women in the diocese of Annecy. They will not be cloistered, but will be able to go around the city and countryside to help all who are in need. Their model will be Mary, who traveled to visit and assist her cousin Elizabeth." They walked a few steps more in silence. Then Father Francis contin-

Jane sighed. Father Francis would be away for at least four months. But she trusted his wisdom and agreed to say nothing to anyone else.

ued. "And I would like you to be the first member and the guide for those who will join you."

With her head spinning and her heart pounding, Jane could only exclaim, "Yes! Yes!" She had always helped her neighbors in times of need and when they were sick, and often she had thought with sadness that joining the cloister would end that work. But now—why, she could live a life of prayer and community even while helping her neighbors!

At first, Jane's family was not happy with her plans. But they began to soften when her oldest daughter announced her engagement to Father Francis' younger brother! After all, now at least the holy bishop was part of the family.... Jane's heart ached as she thought of leaving her father and the other children. She finally decided that her two younger daughters should come with her to Annecy. One would soon be married anyway, and the other had always suffered poor health. (In fact, she died soon after the move.) She was most concerned for her fifteen-year-old son, Celse-Benigne. But at last she arranged for him to live with his grandfather, whom he loved deeply, and finish his high-school courses with a tutor. Even so, the day she left was emotional indeed.

As she prepared to leave, Celse-Benigne laid across the door post and dared her to step over him. With tears in her eyes she knelt in front of her elderly father and asked for his blessing. Gently he put his hands on her head and said, "You go with my consent, and I offer you to God, a daughter dear to me as Isaac was to Abraham. Go where God calls you. I shall be happy, knowing you are in his house. Pray for me."

"Go where God calls you." Those words became the strength and guiding force of Jane's life as the years passed. Women joined her and Father Francis opened one convent after another. There were many difficulties, and they had a very hard time convincing people that the sisters did not have to live in a cloister. Finally, they did have to restrict their activities in some ways, but their initial spirit and desire to serve all in need continued. Jane traveled constantly, from one house to another. Encouraging the sisters here, helping them out of troubles there, praying for them and guiding them all along. Almost without realizing it, Jane's once rigid and sometimes harsh character had softened. Father Francis' constant words, "Be humble. Be meek," had had an effect. Everywhere, Mother Jane Frances was known for her kindness, serenity and wisdom.

Mother Jane Frances' life was never without its trials and sorrows. Only the year after receiving her religious habit, her father died and she had to return home for several months to settle his affairs. Then only a few years passed and her beloved friend and guide, Father Francis, died. Five years later, in 1627, her son died in battle, and shortly after that the plague struck France. This horrible disease killed many members of her family and also of her religious community. Courageously, she led her sisters in caring for the sick and instructing the children who were left orphaned. By 1636, there were over sixty-five communities of Visitation sisters. In 1641, the queen invited her to Paris to open a community, which she gladly did. But on her way back to Annecy, Mother Jane Frances de Chantal died. All of France mourned the woman that so many of them had come to know through the good works and prayers of the Visitation sisters. In 1767, she was canonized a saint.

From the time that her mother died when Jane was a small child, she had to face many difficulties and sorrows in her life. Even though she often must have felt like giving up, or that God must have forgotten her, she kept trying to do her best in the situations that she was in. As a wife, as a widow, as a mother and as a foundress of a religious community, Jane Frances de Chantal never quit loving God, believing in his love for her and sharing that love with others.

St. Isaac Jogues (1607-1646)
St. Rene Goupil (1593-1642)

October 19

In the middle of the seventeenth century, when the first Europeans were exploring North America, several Jesuit missionaries from France settled among the Huron nation in what is now southeastern Canada. They lived with the Hurons, learned their language, ate their food and shared their lives of hunting and fishing. Their purpose? To fulfill the command of Jesus to the disciples: "Go out to all the world and tell the Good News; baptize in the name of the Father, and of the Son, and of the Holy Spirit."

One of these missionaries was Father Isaac Jogues. A young, active and strong man, he was accepted by the Hurons. He could walk for miles carrying a heavy load without stopping—and he shared the Hurons' food, which was very different than what he was accustomed to! The Hurons gave him the name Ondessonk, or Hawk, and considered him to be one of their favorite "blackrobes." The Hurons called all priests "blackrobes" because of the long black cassocks which they usually wore.

One summer, Father Jogues was traveling between Quebec and a Huron village with a band of Huron Christians and three other Frenchmen. The thirty-five men traveled in twelve canoes, under the command of their fiercest chief, Ahatsistari. He was a famous warrior who had taken the baptismal name Eustace. Other leaders among the Huron Christians who were on the trip were Charles, Stephen, Joseph, and Eustace's nephew, Paul. Among the Frenchmen were Rene Goupil, a young doctor, and William Couture, a woodsman.

One morning, they approached a stretch of river where hostile Iroquois war parties might be lurking.

"If we are attacked, brothers," said Father Jogues, "remember always to be faithful to God who has given his life for you!"

The Hurons nodded in agreement; one by one each pledged loyalty to their baptismal promises. Eustace was the last to speak.

"Brothers," he said, "if captured, I will tell the Iroquois that no matter how severely they torture me, even if they try to tear the soul from my body, they will not be able to tear from my heart the consolation that after death I shall be supremely happy. I shall tell them that while they are burning me. Charles, my brother, if God should decree my capture and your escape, go to my kinsmen in the Huron nation and tell them that if they love me, if they love themselves, they must accept the Christian faith and adore the Divine Majesty which is invisible to our eyes but makes Itself felt in the very depths of our souls when we don't close our eyes to his truths—when we obey his commands. Tell them I am convinced of this. Warn them that I fear we shall be separated forever unless they become followers of God, who alone is my hope, and in whom, wherever I may be, I wish to live and die."

Of all the Huron Christians, thought Father Jogues, Eustace has understood the Christian faith the best. He will make a fine catechist soon....

With strong, sure strokes, the Hurons paddled their canoes in the choppy water. They paddled steadily, hour after hour. By nightfall they had covered almost thirty miles.

"Brothers," said Eustace, "we must decide what route to follow tomorrow. We may travel in the open waters, safe from an ambush, but that way is long, as you know. Or we may pass through the north channel—a shorter route which holds many dangers."

"We have heard of no bands of Iroquois nearby," said an older brave. "Let us take the channel."

At the end of the discussion, the northern route was chosen.

In the stillness of dawn, the men gathered about Father Jogues as he led them in prayer. Then they boarded their canoes and slipped cautiously through inshore reeds until they reached open water. The entrance to the northern channel lay a short distance beyond.

Suddenly, one of the braves clucked a warning. Each Huron seized his bow and arrow and gazed at the shore intently. In a patch of clay by the water's edge were marks which could only have been made by canoes!

Eustace and some of his men paddled over to examine the markings and the fresh footprints next to them. "Iroquois," Eustace decided. "But only three canoes. There are enough of us; let us continue without fear."

The twelve canoes stroked on into the channel, where they had to string out single file. Anxiously, the men watched the forested island to their left and the dense mainland to their right. When a stretch of weedy swampland opened up between the channel and the shore, everyone sighed in relief.

Then war whoops filled the air. The swamp suddenly came alive with painted bodies. While guns blazed and bullets whistled overhead, Eustace and his men shrieked and paddled their canoes toward the enemy.

The chief thundered, "Great God, to you alone we look for help!" Father Jogues raised his hand and pronounced words of absolution over his people. Then he turned to a young brave in his canoe who had been hit by a bullet. He was a catechumen who was almost ready for Baptism.

"Would you like Baptism now, Atieronhonk?"

"Yes."

The priest cupped some water in his hand, and sprinkled it on Atieronhonk's head, baptizing him Bernard. Then the canoe rammed into the weedy shore.

Only half of the Huron canoes had come within range of the Iroquois guns. The others turned around swiftly and shot back down river to safety. Eustace was left with about fifteen braves, plus Rene and William, to face thirty Iroquois. The Iroquois had retreated to the forest's edge while the Hurons crept toward them through the swamp grass.

Another blood-curdling shriek—this time from the river! Eustace turned. There were eight canoes of screaming Iroquois! The Hurons were completely surrounded.

Soon the men were engaged in hand-to-hand combat—about five Iroquois to each Huron. One by one the Hurons fell. Charles, Stephen, Paul, Bernard, Joseph.... The Iroquois roared in triumph at each new victory.

In the tall river grass crouched Father Jogues. As a priest, he was forbidden to join in the battle. Christ had given his life for the Iroquois just as much as for the Huron. All he could do was wait and pray.

Yet what could he wait for? Now, almost all the Hurons had been captured; Eustace, still fighting valiantly, had vanished in the trees; William also had disappeared.

If I crept through the weeds to that thicket on the right, he thought, I could go through the forest and escape down river....

But how could he leave the Hurons alone? The Christians among them were only recently baptized. And among the captives were some who were almost ready to receive the Sacrament. Trembling, Father Jogues rose to his feet and picked his way through the weeds back to the Iroquois who were guarding Rene. The braves stared at him in amazement, waiting for some kind of attack.

Trembling, Father Jogues rose to his feet and picked his way through the weeds back to the Iroquois who were guarding Rene. The braves stared at him in amazement, waiting for an attack.

"Don't be afraid!" the priest shouted. He stretched out his arms as a sign of surrender. Several Iroquois cautiously approached him—then leapt upon him, kicking him and beating him, tearing off his long cassock. Then they dragged him over to the other prisoners.

"Do not tie me up," Father Jogues told his captors. "I won't try to escape as long as these Hurons remain your prisoners. They are my bonds."

The Iroquois were shocked at his words, but they did not tie the priest up. Father Jogues approached Rene and said, "My brother, God is our Lord and Master. What he has permitted can only be for our good. So be it."

"Yes, my Father," the young doctor replied. "God has permitted this. May his holy will be done. I love and cherish God's will with all my heart."

Father Jogues next turned to his Huron friends. "Take courage, brothers. The torments we will suffer now are as nothing compared with the glory to come. God will not let us suffer anything beyond our strength."

He turned to the unbaptized catechumens among the Huron captives.

"We are near death, brothers. Do you wish to be baptized in the name of the good God of whom we have spoken so often?"

They said they did, and Father Jogues used drops of water squeezed from his own torn, wet garments to baptize them in the name of the Father and of the Son and of the Holy Spirit.

Scarcely had he finished, when shrieks and whoops rang through the forest. A large band of

Iroquois appeared, leading Eustace. It was he, the famous Huron chief, whom they had desired above all else from this raid!

The priest hurried to the great chief's side, only to be pushed away by angry Iroquois, who threw Eustace to the ground and tied him up tightly. Without expression, the chief spoke: "My Father, as I have promised, I will remain faithful whether I live or die."

Meanwhile, William Couture had managed to escape from the Iroquois. He ran steadily down a forest trail toward the French settlement; surely he could make it within a day.

Yes, he could make it. But what about his companions? Could William return to security while they must face torture and death? No, he would die with them. William turned, and began to walk back toward the battle site.

Thus, with twenty Huron captives and three Frenchmen, the Iroquois boarded their canoes and threaded their way through a maze of channels until they reached the main river. After they felt safe from pursuit, they beached the canoes, held a council, and celebrated their victory.

That night, on a hilltop south of the St. Lawrence, Father Jogues wept. He grieved not because he and his comrades would have sufferings to offer to God, but because almost no leaders remained among the Huron Christians. These men who had been captured were soon to have been the first catechists among their people. Now they would suffer and die as Christians—but they would never preach.

The next day they made their way southward into the land of the Mohawk Iroquois. Father

Jogues felt hot tears spring to his eyes whenever he looked at Eustace, Joseph, Stephen, Charles and Paul. These men Father Jogues had described as "the sustaining columns of the Church among the Hurons." He would write later, "It is a hard thing to bear—nay, a cruel thing—when one sees the triumph of demons over whole peoples who were redeemed with so much love and paid for with such adorable Blood."

Rene Goupil, covered with wounds, treated the injuries of his fellow prisoners and the Iroquois. Father Jogues marveled at the young doctor's gentle cheerfulness, his submission to God's will, his eagerness to give up his life for the Lord Jesus.

Rene's weak health had prevented him from making the vows of a religious years before when he had been a Jesuit novice. And when he became well, he had felt unworthy to make them. Now, however, he asked Father Jogues' permission to make the vows of a Jesuit brother.

Father Jogues agreed gladly. And right there, in an Iroquois war canoe, Rene Goupil pronounced the formula of consecration he had memorized years before.

On the eighth day after the capture, the travelers met a band of two hundred Iroquois camped on an island in Lake Champlain. They greeted the raiding party with shrieks of glee, eager to begin torturing their prisoners. They sprang upon the captives, beating and pounding them without mercy.

"The gauntlet!" urged one brave.

"The gauntlet!" went up the cry.

Each warrior rushed off and returned with a

club or thorny rod. They formed two lines from the beach up a long hillside. All the prisoners were stripped naked and lined up, with the old men first, then William, more Hurons, Rene, more braves and then Father Jogues. The Iroquois hated the French even more than they hated the Hurons. And they hated the blackrobes worst of all. They wanted Father Jogues' punishment to be the worst.

The first Huron was pushed between the two lines of Iroquois, and began to run up the hill, while stinging, numbing blows came down on his head, his back, his legs. The shrieks grew savage, as one man after another ran in between the two lines; the blood lust of the frenzied Iroquois mounted and mounted.

Father Jogues watched it all. God alone knows what he thought in those moments. He knew that he would suffer the worst torture.

The last Huron was halfway up; now it was Isaac Jogues' turn. He stepped forward, tensed and began to run up the hill between the lines of savage, swinging clubs. Pain—stabbing pain, dull pain, pain that sent his head reeling and spinning.... Someone tripped him. He stumbled to his feet and ran on blindly only to feel his path blocked by another Iroquois, and another, and another.... And all the time the blows. And all the time the frenzied screams and mocking laughter. He broke away again and again and stumbled on....

Blows and kicks rained upon him, but he fell again and then knew no more.

When Father Jogues woke up, he found himself near a platform on the hilltop. William and Rene were there, too. The Iroquois tried to make him stand, but he sank to the ground. They took blazing sticks and held them against his arms and legs. One seized his hand and crunched the thumb between his teeth. Another held a burning coal against his fingers. Father Jogues lost consciousness again.

He opened his eyes to see Iroquois braves chopping William's and Rene's fingers from their hands and then, holding red-hot stones against the wounds. A cry went up as the braves saw that the blackrobe was conscious. They lunged for him, but a wiry young figure stepped before them—Paul, Eustace's nephew. "Torture me!" he urged them. "Torture me as cruelly as you like! I will take this man's place."

The Iroquois threw the Frenchmen down from the platform but instead of Paul they attacked Eustace, the Huron chief, slashing him from head to foot, holding blazing torches against the wounds to seal them so that he would not lose too much blood and die right away. True to his people's sense of honor, Eustace did not show how much pain he was in. Instead, he said all kinds of insulting things to his torturers.

Father Jogues burst into tears at the scene, and the Iroquois began to jeer and taunt him. "The blackrobe is a woman!" they shouted.

The Huron chief still had strength enough to roar: "The blackrobe is not a woman. Your cruelty, my pain and his love for me are the reason for his tears."

"Keep remembering," Father Jogues called out to his friend, "keep remembering that there is a God who sees everything and who will reward everything which we endure for his sake."

"I will remain firm even until death!" the chief replied.

Knife in hand, an Iroquois approached the priest. He reached out, grasped Father Jogues' nose with one hand, and held the knife poised in the other.

"Lord," prayed the priest silently, "take not only my nose, but also my head."

Slowly the man put down his knife. He turned and walked away. A half hour later he came back again. Again, he hesitated and turned away.

The Iroquois were done for the night. They stumbled sleepily down the hill to their campground, leaving the Frenchmen and Hurons lying bruised and bleeding in the moonlight.

Those were the first tortures. The next day the Iroquois and their prisoners resumed the journey southward. Most of this trip was overland on foot, at a dog-trot, with packs on their backs. Father Jogues and Rene, worn out from torture and lack of food, could not keep up with the party no matter how hard they tried. They dragged along behind— and talked of escape.

"I must stay with the Huron Christians," the priest told Rene. "But you could easily escape now that they've relaxed their guard. Perhaps we can persuade William to go with you."

"I shall not leave you, Father," replied Rene. "I will die with you!" And so, they remained with their Huron comrades while the Iroquois taunted them with the promise of roasting them alive and eating their white flesh.

They arrived at Ossernenon, the first Mohawk Iroquois village, located where Auriesville, New York, is today.

The date, Father Jogues calculated, was August 14—the vigil of the Assumption of Mary into heaven.

"Lord Jesus Christ," he prayed. "I thank you that on the day that the whole world rejoices in the glory of your Mother's assumption, I may share some part of your sufferings and cross."

Another gauntlet awaited them, bruised and exhausted as they were. In the middle, someone hit Rene on the face so hard that he fell, and his body was thrown out of the double line. When Father Jogues staggered up to him after his own ordeal, he found the young doctor's face smashed and swollen beyond recognition.

The tortures which followed were more horrible than those inflicted at Lake Champlain. Father Jogues' hands were mangled severely and his left thumb torn from its socket. And the Mohawk children poured hot coals on the Frenchmen's helpless bodies.

Another journey came soon. Another Mohawk village and more torture. Another journey, and still more torture. How long could this go on before they died? It seemed impossible that they would live another day.

Then the Mohawks took Father Jogues and hung him by his arms from the cross-piece of a cabin. As the weight of this body pulled on his arms more and more, he begged his tormenters to loosen the ropes a little. They tightened them instead. "They acted justly; I thank you, Lord Jesus, for letting me experience how much you suffered for me on the cross, since the whole weight of your most sacred body hung, not from ropes, but from your hands and feet pierced by nails." A young brave cut him down as he was about to lose consciousness.

The next day a council was held by the Mohawks—and at first it seemed that the Frenchmen would be killed. But many of the braves wished to end the war with the French and urged that the blackrobe and his companions be left alive. At last that group won: the Frenchmen would live as slaves among the Mohawks.

And their Huron comrades? Three would die, one in each village; the others would become slaves.

In Ossernenon that night, Father Jogues and Rene witnessed the bloody death of Eustace's nephew Paul, who had offered himself to the Iroquois as a victim in place of the priest. Shouting out his hope in a better life to come, Paul died with great courage and faith.

In the next village some miles distant, the sky glared red. There, Stephen was being burned.

And in the farthest village, William watched Eustace die, bearing his tortures with calm courage, telling Huron friends not to let his death stand in the way of a future peace between them and the Iroquois.

Father Jogues and Rene were taken as slaves by the chief who had captured them. The two Frenchmen were so weak that they could not work, and could hardly drag themselves from place to place. Pus oozed from their unhealed wounds, and clouds of flies and bugs swarmed about them. Because of their maimed hands, the prisoners could not chase away the insects. To add to their misery, they were half-starved, and since food was scarce that fall, they were given only a little ground corn and some raw squash each day.

At last the Mohawks realized how sick their prisoners were, and gave them a few little fish and some pieces of meat. As soon as they could hobble about again, they were sent into the fields with the squaws to help harvest corn and vegetables.

Father Jogues knew how to get along well with the Indians, for he had lived among the Hurons six years. He understood how superstitious they could be, and avoided doing anything which would arouse their anger. He warned Rene to do likewise. However the young doctor, accustomed to openness and sincerity, did not understand how he could irritate the Iroquois.

But he did irritate them. His face was so scarred and battered from the gauntlet that it was disgusting, and he was very clumsy. He made funny faces about their food. His gestures when he prayed made them think that he was a sorcerer weaving spells against them. His Christian virtues of gentleness and kindness seemed cowardly. The Indians desired to kill him.

If the Mohawks killed Father Jogues, the French would never agree to peace, for he was a blackrobe. But the younger man was less important it seemed. If he died, so what? A story could be made up to explain his disappearance. To make their deed easier the Iroquois separated the two Frenchmen, giving Father Jogues to another master.

Still, Rene did not guess that the Mohawks were planning to kill him.

Rene would often go out to play with the young Mohawk children. One day he picked up a boy of three or four and placed his own cap on the child's head. The little boy laughed. Rene took the tiny hand in his own mangled one, moved it from the child's forehead to his chest, to one shoulder, to the other—in the sign of the cross.

A wild scream came from the boy's grandfather, who had been sitting in the shadows watching. He thought that Rene had called down an evil spirit upon the child! The old man flew at Rene in a rage, tore the boy away from him, and began to beat and kick and pound the prisoner.

Later the same day, Father Jogues came to the cabin and called Rene to him. "Come and pray with me," he invited. They walked through the village and up a lonely hill toward their favorite prayer spot.

"I heard about what happened this morning," the priest began. "Our lives are in danger, especially yours."

"I do not fear death, Father," the younger man replied, "so long as I am in God's grace."

The priest heard Rene's confession, as he had done every other day, and absolved him of his sins. They knelt together and offered the Lord Jesus their lives and their blood, asking him to unite their sacrifice to his own for the salvation of the Iroquois.

On their way down the hill, they began the Rosary, as was their custom, with Father Jogues leading and Rene answering. Two braves met them on the trail. One of them was the uncle of the child on whom Rene had made the sign of the cross. "Go back to the village," he growled.

They walked down the slope together, the missionaries saying their Hail Marys softly, the braves stalking behind them.

"You walk ahead," one of them abruptly commanded Father Jogues. "You stay here," he ordered Rene. The priest gazed intently at the glaring man, then walked on a few steps. A rustle made him whirl—just in time to see a tomahawk crashing down on Rene's head. "Jesus, Jesus, Jesus," called the young Jesuit, as he crumbled to the earth.

The priest murmured absolution. Now it is my turn, he thought. "Just a moment," he told the Mohawks, and kneeling he said an act of contrition.

"Get up," commanded the grim-faced uncle. "I have no power over you. You belong to another family."

The priest approached his comrade. Rene still

breathed. As Father Jogues made a sign of the cross over him, the braves tore him away and finished their job.

A mob from the village swarmed to the spot, babbling excitedly. The priest was led away to his cabin, for fear that someone would kill him, too.

"How calm you are," marveled the priest's master. And indeed Father Jogues was calm. Rene had been so cheerful, so kind, so obedient, and he had just recently made the vows of religious life; his beautiful soul must have winged its way straight to heaven. It was September 29, 1642—the feast of St. Michael the Archangel.

The following morning he went in search of Rene's body, which had been dragged around the village by the children and then thrown into a ravine. The Mohawks watched him closely. Father Jogues knew that death might come any minute, but it didn't matter.

He found the body, but not having a shovel with which to dig a grave, he could only conceal it in a stream bed under a mound of stones. At the first opportunity he came back with a shovel to give the martyr's bones a fitting burial, but the Mohawks, now knowing how much those remains meant to him, had stolen them away.

Death haunted the priest continually, for only a few of the Mohawks wanted to keep him alive in case of a truce with the French. Most suspected him as being in league with evil spirits, and would have killed him the first chance they had. Yet day after day passed, and Father Jogues did not die.

"If I am to live after all," he thought, "I must try to find a way to teach them about God." He learned their language better, and found ways to slip in a word here and there about the Creator of all peoples. After all, were not these Mohawks also bought by the blood of Jesus Christ?

That fall the priest accompanied a hunting party into the Adirondack mountains. He helped the squaws carry the food and gear. During the weeks in the mountains he would go off into the forest daily to honor God in the vast solitude, where no lips had ever before spoken the name of Jesus. Peeling the bark from a tree in the form of a cross, the priest interceded for his new people.

But the Mohawks, spying on him continually, blamed the scarcity of elk and deer on his prayer and on the cross. They mocked him and beat him often. This, along with hunger, lack of clothing, the cold November snow, the memory of his past sins and the fear of torture and death, plunged the priest into the depths of despair. Then it seemed that a voice spoke to him, saying, "Serve God from love, not from fear. Do not worry about yourself." Renewed in spirit, Father Jogues returned to the village with the hunting party.

One snowy day, when crossing a swift stream on a mossy tree trunk, a Mohawk woman slipped and fell into the icy waters. The bundles and papoose cradle which were strapped to her kept pulling her under. Father Jogues plunged into the current, freed the woman from the bundles and cradle and dragged her and the baby to safety. As he lifted the baby from the stream he baptized it without letting the Mohawks see what he was doing. The child died a few weeks later.

Back in the village, the Mohawks put him to work taking care of a sick brave—one who had tortured him severely a few months before. The man was dying of a horrible disease which covered him with smelly sores. Although he could hardly stand the sight and the smell, Father Jogues nursed the sick man for two weeks.

Little by little, his master's family began to like the priest. They asked him many questions about the sun and moon and tides and accepted his answers eagerly. But as soon as he began to speak of a Creator, they lost interest.

Father Jogues was more successful among the sick. He visited them daily, as he had once done among the Hurons, and he told them about heaven and hell. A few adults consented to be baptized. He also baptized many infants who were near death.

Father Jogues went among the Huron and Algonquin prisoners in the three Mohawk villages, comforting them and hearing their confessions if they were Christian. He warned them against praying openly, because it would make their captors angry. One of them, Joseph, became accustomed to carrying on an almost continual conversation with God. He was delighted when Father Jogues taught him the Rosary, and he recited it often in secret.

In his travels, the priest often saw William, who had been adopted by a family in the third village. He was still fervent in his prayers, and well except for having frozen one of his feet.

In March, some children told the priest that they had found Rene's bones in the ravine. He hurried to the spot and searched, but found nothing. The children mocked him. Only after he had searched for a whole day did they tell him the exact spot. Tenderly, the priest gathered up those precious relics and buried them in the earth beneath a pine tree. He said the De Profundis over the remains of North America's first martyr.

On Holy Saturday, six new Algonquin prisoners were led triumphantly into the village. Having undergone the usual bloody tortures, they lay awaiting death in one of the cabins. Father Jogues tended their wounds and told them of God, the commandments and heaven. Like the catechumens in the early Church in Rome, these men received Baptism on Easter Sunday.

The sister of Father Jogues' master had grown very fond of the priest. She was a kind old woman who called Father Jogues her "nephew." In May, she took him with her when she and a band of braves went down to the Dutch settlement to trade skins and furs.

At Rensselaerswyck, also called Fort Orange, Father Jogues met and spoke with the Dutch governor, but did not try to escape. He had his new Christians to look after.

On Pentecost, back in his "own" village, he secretly baptized an Algonquin woman who was about to be burned alive by pretending to give her a drink of water.

A few days later new prisoners arrived—Huron Christians and a Frenchman. Fortunately they had not been tortured, but the priest's heart sank to see so many of his people captive and in exile. A few days later, the Mohawks butchered and burned a hundred Hurons in the neighboring villages. Father Jogues' grief knew no bounds.

That summer the Iroquois warred continuously on the French, Hurons and Algonquins along the St. Lawrence. One of the war parties took the Hurons, Joseph and Charles, with them to carry baggage, and this gave them the chance they were waiting for. The Huron warriors slipped away from their masters and hurried to tell the French about Rene, William and Father Jogues.

Meanwhile, Father Jogues was paddling his master's canoe down the rivers south of the Catskill mountains. He acted as the chief's official beast of burden. One day he met a very sick young man who called him by name. "Do you remember the man who cut your bonds in the third Mohawk village when you were at the end of your strength?"

The priest thought back to that terrible night he had been suspended from the wooden beams. "Yes, I remember very well. I owe a lot to that man. I've never been able to thank him. Do you know him?"

"It was I who did it. I took pity on you and loosened the bonds."

The priest embraced him. "I have often prayed for you," he said. "And now I have a gift for you."

He told the dying man of the reward of eternal life and what he must believe to attain it. After he had spoken, the man asked for Baptism, and he died a few hours after receiving it.

Then began the two-hundred-mile journey "home" to the Mohawk villages. Father Jogues could hardly wait to get there, for he feared that new prisoners would be tortured and killed in his absence before receiving the grace of Baptism. In his year among the Mohawks he had baptized seventy children and adults belonging to five different tribes, and he was content to remain among them as long as God should be pleased to keep him there.

"Nephew," the old chief's sister said to Father Jogues almost as soon as he had come home, "prepare to go fishing with the braves and me in the great river below the Dutch settlement."

So Father Jogues was off again. He and his companions stopped at Rensselaerswyck for about a week, during which time he wrote an account of Rene's martyrdom and his own sufferings and labors among the Iroquois. He addressed it to his superior in France. The Dutch promised to send it with the first ship.

A few weeks later the priest passed through Rensselaerswyck again on his return trip from the fishing area. To his astonishment an angry band of braves met him there.

What had happened? A Mohawk chief had delivered a message from Father Jogues to a French fort on the St. Lawrence. Since the message had contained a warning to beware of the Iroquois, the French had fired upon them immediately after reading it.

"You have betrayed us!" they screamed. "You shall die!"

The Dutch governor urged Father Jogues to escape on a ship bound for France. The priest hesitated, then said he would pray about it. Lying awake that night he thought the matter through. Now that he knew the Iroquois so well, it seemed he would be more valuable to the missions alive than dead. He could escape to France, return to Canada, and go back among the Iroquois people when the heat of their anger had cooled.

After a hair-raising escape from his Iroquois master, Father Jogues spent almost a month lying on hard planks in a hot Rensselaerswyck attic while his leg swelled with infection from a dog bite. At last he was smuggled on board a ship going down river. He was on his way to France!

It was Christmas morning, 1643, when Father Jogues set foot on French soil. His heart pounded with joy as he headed for the nearest church, and for the first time in seventeen months he made his confession and received Holy Communion.

A few days later, tattered and worn, he presented himself to his Jesuit superior in Rennes. What joy flooded the community as they gathered around their brother who had suffered so much for Christ. They gasped at the sight of his scarred and twisted hands and the thinness of his once powerful body. They shuddered when he related the tortures, and rejoiced when he told them of Rene's courageous martyrdom and the seventy baptisms. The younger Jesuits venerated Father Jogues as if he were already dead and canonized!

But Father Jogues had only three things on his mind. First, he visited his mother. Then, he wrote to the Holy Father and requested permission to celebrate Mass even though his battered fingers could no longer hold the host exactly as the rubrics required. This permission was quickly granted, and the Holy Father wrote to Father Jogues: "It would be a shame if a martyr of Christ were not allowed to drink the Blood of Christ." Then Father Jogues requested permission from his superiors to leave once again for the Canadian missions.

The ship made its way across the Atlantic, battling storms and bad weather all the way. Before they reached the St. Lawrence, every passenger on the ship had made his confession to Father Jogues.

How happy he was to see the wooded shores of his beloved Canada. Through the trees, here and there, he glimpsed the log cabins and bark huts of the Algonquins. He was home among "his people" again!

At Quebec, his fellow Jesuits greeted him with open arms. They were overjoyed to find him alive and well. Their own news was not so pleasant as his, for the Iroquois were still raiding the Hurons and Algonquins, destroying both nations little by little.

Father Jogues' superior assigned him to the island of Montreal where a fervent Christian community lived. There he spent the winter.

The following spring, council was held with the Iroquois, and some of their prisoners were released. Peace was made temporarily and renewed again the following fall. However, the French were uneasy, for they felt they could not trust the Iroquois.

"Eat a little meat," his companion urged Father Jogues often during the long winter months at Montreal.

"No, thank you," was the reply. "When I go back among the Iroquois I do not wish my thoughts to keep turning to the pleasures and comforts of this place."

His one desire was to return to the Iroquois—to the same people who had captured, tortured and enslaved him.

His chance came in midwinter, when Iroquois ambassadors returned to renew the peace. They told Father Jogues that the Mohawks would be happy to have him return among them; his "aunt's" cabin was waiting. Father Jogues asked his superior to send him among the Mohawks.

He went in May, as ambassador of the French governor, accompanied by a surveyor named John Bourdon. He went joyfully, for this was what he had hoped to do. And yet, to his superior he admitted, "My poor body trembles when I remember everything that has gone before. But our Lord, in his goodness, calmed me and will calm me still more. Father, I desire what our Lord desires. How I would regret it if I lost such a wonderful opportunity, one in which I might be responsible if some souls did not hear the Gospel preached."

Most of the Mohawks were happy to see Father Jogues again, especially when they saw that he was as kind and friendly as ever. The Turtle Clan and the Wolf Clan (to which Father Jogues' "aunt" belonged) welcomed him eagerly. However, the warlike Bear Clan listened grim-faced to the peace pledges between the Frenchmen and their tribesmen.

After the peace councils, Father Jogues found time to instruct several sick, old people and to baptize them and a few dying infants. He also reassured the Mohawks about a little black strongbox he had left in his "aunt's" cabin three years before. The Mohawks suspected that he had a demon inside the mysterious box. Father Jogues smiled at them, and showed them how to open the box with the key. He took out all the little odds and ends the box contained and let the braves examine everything. At last they seemed convinced that the box was harmless, and they agreed to keep it until the priest's return.

The two Frenchmen traveled the long route back to Montreal, where they made their report.

The following fall, Father Jogues and a young man named John de la Lande set out for the Mohawk country to spend the winter. With one

Huron as their companion, they paddled the long lonely river route through the still forests. About twenty days after leaving the St. Lawrence they left the lakes and rivers behind, and set out through the mountains on foot. It was a route which Father Jogues knew well.

There, coming up the trail to meet them, was a band of Iroquois. The priest called to them, only to see them disappear into the brush beside the trail. A moment later, furious shrieks pierced the air, and painted warriors leaped out of the forest, seized the missionaries and beat them cruelly. They dragged them down the trail to the village.

A huge mob bore down on them. Father Jogues could see that the Bear and Wolf Clans were fighting among themselves. Some of the Wolfs grabbed the Frenchmen and rushed them to the safety of the "aunt's" cabin.

Why had the Mohawks had this sudden change of heart?

Two tragedies had befallen them that summer. An epidemic had swept through their villages, killing many, and the corn crop had been destroyed by worms. They had blamed both on the "magical" black box of Father Jogues! The Bear Clan had aroused the people to take the warpath against the Algonquins, Hurons and French. It was one of the war parties which had met Father Jogues and John on the trail.

All night long the Wolves and Bears argued over the fate of the blackrobe and his young companion. The next day the warriors left to hold council in another village, leaving the Frenchmen free until an agreement should be reached. At sundown Father Jogues went with a young Wolf brave to have supper in a Bear cabin, for he had received an invitation and dared not refuse.

As Father Jogues stooped to enter through the low doorway, his young Wolf friend sensed the danger too late. A tomahawk came crashing down on the skull of the missionary, and Father Jogues crumpled to the ground, dead. With shouts of glee, the Bears cut off his head and defiantly placed it on a tall spike overlooking the forests, facing the distant St. Lawrence. The Mohawks screamed defiance against the French.

Wolf braves guarded young John de la Lande closely, warning him not to leave the cabin. However, as the hours passed by and all was silent outside, and his guards fell asleep around the fire, he felt a strong desire to see Father Jogues' body and save some relic of the martyr. He crept silently out of the cabin. He felt a stabbing pain, and then, nothing.

John's head was placed on a spike next to that of Father Jogues. The two heads were on the spikes the next day when the warriors came home to announce the council's decision to free their prisoners.

―――――――

Within a year after Father Jogues' death, the brave who had tried to save him had been baptized, and the murderer had repented and had received Baptism before being burned by Algonquin captors.

However, the Iroquois had again taken to the warpath. They massacred the Hurons and Algonquins and, in 1649, killed five more Jesuit fathers—John de Brebeuf, Anthony Daniel, Charles Garnier, Noel Chabanel and Gabriel Lalement. The blood of the eight Jesuit martyrs cried to God, who poured an abundance of graces upon the Iroquois. Many of them were soon converted, and a few years later, the Mohawks had a young saint of their own—Kateri Tekakwitha.

Father Jogues grew to love the Iroquois and he worked to spread faith in Jesus Christ among them as he had done among the Hurons. A very good way to love God and know that we are in his holy will is by doing the best we can in whatever circumstances we find ourselves, and by trying to love others as Jesus has loved us.

Bl. Kateri Tekakwitha

(1656-1680)

July 14

The fluffy white clouds appeared to be almost still, as if waiting to be admired by the young Indian girl leaning against a birch tree. Bright Star had heard her people speak of war. She shuddered. Everything about her was so peaceful, yet...

Suddenly she heard the distant sound of drums. War drums!

She must hide and pray for her dear Algonquin tribe. Only the White Manitou—God—could save them from the fierce Iroquois. Swiftly and silently, Bright Star ran into the deep forest to pray.

Soon Bright Star was alone in the cool darkness. She prayed and prayed, all night long. "O God, do not let my people be destroyed," she begged. And then, "I *know* you won't; I *know* you will take pity on them." She sighed, and gazed up at the sky.

The last star was about to go to sleep when

Bright Star heard a wild, triumphant cry behind her. An Iroquois!

With a silent prayer she began to run—but it was too late. Another Iroquois rose from the bushes in her path and grabbed her by the wrists. "Now we will burn the squaw at the stake!" he cried in savage glee.

"Wait!" ordered the first Indian. "I, chief of the Turtle Clan, will speak!"

The brave relaxed his grip a little and listened.

The chief looked at the young maiden. Never had he seen a more beautiful squaw. "The squaw has found favor in Great Turtle's eyes. She will be *my* squaw. I have spoken."

"That is good," answered the brave.

Bright Star followed Great Turtle. "Jesus," she whispered, "be with me and protect me."

Great Turtle took Bright Star to live with him in the valley of the Mohawks.

Although she was an Algonquin, her captors did not treat her harshly. She was a kind person, and everyone came to love her. Great Turtle took her as his wife and soon they were blessed with a beautiful baby girl.

For the moment, Great Turtle forgot all about his many worries, his war councils and his tribal meetings. He proudly held the infant in his arms and asked, "Bright Star, what shall we name our little one?"

Bright Star wanted to give her child a Christian name, but she did not dare ask Great Turtle. He was not a Christian and he did not understand the prayers of Bright Star.

"Let us call her Tekakwitha," she said.

"Good!" agreed Great Turtle. "Tekakwitha will do just what her name means: she will *move—all—that—is—before—her.*"

He then gently placed the sleeping child in her mother's arms and left.

Bright Star's eyes filled with tears. "Someday," she said softly, "Someday I will have the blackrobes pour the water of life on you, my little one. Then you, too, will be a child of God."

"Hush! You must be careful what you say," warned Anastasia, an old Christian squaw who was a friend of Bright Star. "If you are not careful, our great chief will have all of us Christians punished."

"You are right, Anastasia," said Bright Star. "But I will try to make Great Turtle love the White Manitou. He must become a Christian, too!"

The young squaw kissed her child and placed her on a mat. "The blackrobes are far away," she said to Anastasia, "but I will do my best to tell her about Jesus and his Blessed Mother Mary."

"You do well, but be careful, for her aunts are not Christians either. In fact, they hate the Christians."

"I know. Will you promise me to take care of my Tekakwitha if something should happen to me?"

"Yes, I promise."

Almost every night, when the stars were twin-
kling brightly in the sky, Bright Star would creep
out of her cabin and kneel in prayer. She had never
given up hope that Great Turtle and Tekakwitha
would be baptized. Soon she was praying also for
the baptism of a new little son!

One morning Anastasia said to Tekakwitha's
mother, "Your prayers have been heard by the
Great White Manitou. The blackrobes have come
to stay nearby."

"I shall go at once and ask them to baptize my
children!" cried Bright Star joyfully.

"Wait! You must remember that if you make
Great Turtle angry, he will have all of us Christians killed!"

"You are right, Anastasia; I must be patient,"
sighed Bright Star.

Wherever Bright Star went Tekakwitha followed her, full of curiosity and always asking
questions. She loved to hear stories, especially
about Jesus, his mother and the saints.

"Mamma, where do the birds come from?"
asked Tekakwitha. She had heard the answer
many times, but she liked to hear her mother
repeat it again and again.

"God made them, my little one. God made all
the beautiful things of this world: he made the
trees, the flowers, the birds and the lakes; he
made everything. Then he made Adam and Eve.

They were our first parents. Because God loved Adam and Eve, he gave them each a soul which would live forever."

"I wish I could see the soul. It must be beautiful," said Tekakwitha.

"Yes, it is beautiful because it is made in the very image of God. But—we must keep it beautiful by never committing any sins."

"Adam and Eve did."

"Yes, they disobeyed God and he punished them just as I punish you and your little brother when you are naughty. God sent them out of their beautiful garden, because by sinning they had broken their special friendship with God. That friendship is called grace. It was God's special gift to them. But to show his love for our first parents and for us, God promised them a Redeemer, a Savior, who would come on earth and take away the sin from man and regain for him God's friendship. He would reopen the gates of heaven."

"Jesus opened heaven for us. And the beautiful Mary is his mother and ours too!" cried Tekakwitha.

"Yes, my little one, and she loves us very much. Love her, and never offend her by sinning," said Bright Star.

One morning, while Tekakwitha was playing in the forest, she heard a heavy rolling of drums.

"What does that mean?" she asked out loud.

After a while she heard the drums again. It was a strange new way of beating the drums. Tekakwitha was frightened.

"Mother, Mother," she cried as she ran toward the lodge.

Bright Star came out and the child threw herself into her mother's protecting arms.

"Why are they beating the drums?" asked Tekakwitha.

Bright Star shook her head sadly. "My little one, the *Purple Devil* has visited our tribe. Many of our people have died already."

"What is the Purple Devil, Mother?"

"It is a sickness. The white man calls it small-pox. When it strikes, it usually kills," answered Bright Star.

"But Father is a great chief. He will kill the Purple Devil," said Tekakwitha.

"My little one, it is not in his power. Only the White Manitou can help us."

While she was talking, Bright Star's arms let go her child. Her eyes began to stare and she fell to the ground.

"Mother! Mother!" cried Tekakwitha. "Don't let the Purple Devil get you!"

But Bright Star did not hear. She was hot and feverish.

Anastasia came running as soon as she heard Tekakwitha scream. She tried to help Bright Star, but she could do nothing for her. The good squaw ran to see Tekakwitha's little brother. He lay so still on his mat....

———————

"My little one, don't cry. You are the daughter of a great chief. You must be strong."

"Yes, Anastasia, I will try to be brave. But I miss my mother, my father and my little brother."

"I miss them, too, Tekakwitha. But they are in heaven, with Jesus. And someday we will join them again!"

"Anastasia," begged Tekakwitha, "why can't I live with you?"

"My little one, your uncle has the right to take you as his daughter. He loves you. You will be treated well," answered Anastasia. "He is now the chief of the Turtle Clan and you must obey him."

"But his squaw doesn't smile. She doesn't like me," said Tekakwitha sadly.

"You are a good child. You will obey old Anastasia, won't you?"

"Yes, Anastasia, I will try. But I wish I didn't have to go," insisted Tekakwitha. "I will never become a Christian now."

Anastasia wrapped her arms around the small girl. "Don't worry," she said. "Someday you will become a Christian, and you will help many others become Christians too."

Tekakwitha's eyes opened wide. "Will I really? Then I will go to my uncle. I am not afraid."

Her uncle treated her well, but her aunt, Light Feet, disliked her and was jealous of the attention which Thunder Cloud gave her. Yet Light Feet did not dare hurt the child, for fear of the great chief.

Three years passed and Tekakwitha was now eleven-years-old. All of the Indian girls worked hard, but Light Feet made her frail niece work harder than all the rest. Tekakwitha never complained, but she was often exhausted. Because of the smallpox she had as a child she was small and her face was scarred. But Tekakwitha had a strong will.

Her eyesight was also poor because of the smallpox. The sunlight hurt her eyes a lot and she tried to stay inside the lodge or out in the dark forest.

One day, while she was weaving a new mat, Anastasia came to visit her. She was excited. What news could she have, to make her so happy?

"Tekakwitha," she cried excitedly, "the blackrobes are coming! I heard them speaking with your uncle. They are to stay at *your uncle's lodge* for three days!"

"Anastasia!" exclaimed Tekakwitha happily.

"Your good mother's prayers are finally answered. Perhaps you will receive Baptism now."

"I hope so, Anastasia, I do want to become a child of God."

"Tekakwitha, Tekakwitha, where are you?" called Light Feet. "Oh, there you are! Quickly! Prepare the meal. We have guests. But don't you speak to them!"

Tekakwitha prepared food for the guests. Then she went out to fetch some water. On her return she saw three blackrobes—Jesuit missionaries who had come to speak to the Mohawk chiefs about a peace treaty with the French.

After the meal, Tekakwitha was busy cleaning the lodge as usual. One of the missionaries came up to her and asked, "Are you Tekakwitha?"

One day, while Kateri was weaving a new mat, a very excited Anastasia came to visit her. What news could Anastasia have which made her so happy?

"Yes, I am," she answered.

"I am Father Pirron. Tell me, do you love the White Manitou as much as Anastasia said you do?"

"O, yes. I love him and his mother, Mary. I would be so happy if I could hear more about them."

"Well, pray to them and try to always be good and patient with all. You will be happy soon."

But Tekakwitha had to wait many years to be baptized.

———————

"Tekakwitha," screamed Light Feet one day, "come here at once! We must gather all our belongings. We are moving!"

With heavy packs on their backs, the Turtle Clan walked many miles through the forest. They stopped on the north bank of the Mohawk River. This was to be their new home.

"Tekakwitha," called Light Feet. "Hurry! Don't be lazy! We must build our cabin quickly, because it might rain tonight."

Tekakwitha was very tired, but it was the women's duty to build their houses.

"Anastasia," confided Tekakwitha that night, "I wish I could do something to show my love for God."

"You can, my child."

"How?"

"Instead of suffering everything in silence because you are the daughter of a chief, suffer it in union with Jesus on the cross. Pray that all our people will come to know and love Jesus."

"Oh, yes, that I will do willingly. What else can I do?"

"Be as kind as you can to those who hurt you."

"Thank you, dear Anastasia, I will try my best to do so."

"Try to be like Mary, the mother of Jesus, in her humility, modesty and charity, and you will live as a Christian."

———————

"Tekakwitha," called Light Feet, "come quickly. We must dress well. We are having guests tonight."

Soon all was ready and the guests arrived. The men sat in a group and talked and smoked. The women were sitting nearby. They, too, were busy talking.

When the men stopped smoking, Thunder Cloud gave Light Feet a signal.

Light Feet understood. She gave a bowl of porridge to Tekakwitha. The brave next to her put out his hands to accept the bowl from her. By this action they would be married. Tekakwitha understood that she was being tricked into marriage.

Poor Tekakwitha! She wanted to belong only to the White Manitou, so she threw down the bowl of porridge and ran out of the lodge! Her uncle and the brave ran after her, but could not find her.

"I will punish her for this," said Light Feet. "She has brought dishonor upon our family."

From then on, Tekakwitha was given the hardest work. She was sent to gather firewood in the winter cold. Tekakwitha's fingers froze, and the sunlight made the snow sparkle so that its brightness hurt her eyes.

But she never complained; she was happy to have something to offer to God.

Whenever someone hurt her, she repaid them by being very kind to them.

One day, while she was home alone, she was surprised by a visitor. It was a blackrobe!

"Father de Lamberville is my name," he said smiling. "Anastasia told me you would like to see a blackrobe."

"Oh, yes! Please, O blackrobe, may I be baptized? I want to belong wholly to the White Manitou."

"But first you must know something of the Catholic faith."

"O blackrobe, my mother was a Christian. She taught me many things and so did Anastasia."

Father de Lamberville asked Tekakwitha many questions. He was very surprised when she answered all of them quickly and correctly.

"You know a great deal about the Catholic faith, but before I can baptize you, you must have your uncle's consent. Then I will prepare you for Baptism."

Tekakwitha asked her uncle that very night. "Dear uncle, you know how much I desire to be baptized. May I?"

Thunder Cloud looked at her for a long time. He loved his niece. Finally he gave his consent.

Tekakwitha flew to Anastasia. "Anastasia!" she

called. "Tell the blackrobe I have permission to become a Christian!"

Of course Light Feet was angry. She did not want Tekakwitha to be baptized. But Thunder Cloud had spoken....

On Easter Sunday, April 18, 1676—Tekakwitha's twentieth birthday—she heard the beautiful words: "Kateri, I baptize you in the Name of the Father, and of the Son, and of the Holy Ghost." Kateri was the happiest girl in the whole Turtle Clan.

But her joy was soon turned to sorrow.

"I have come to say good-bye," said Anastasia. "I am going north to the Christian village. There I will worship God in peace."

"Take me with you," pleaded Kateri. "I will ask my uncle to let me come with you."

But Thunder Cloud would not let Kateri go. "Never will I let you leave our clan," he said. So Kateri remained with her uncle and aunt. After the girl's baptism, Light Feet tried to find new ways of hurting her to make her suffer as much as possible. She did not understand her niece and thought Kateri was making fun of her by being so kind all the time.

Not only did Kateri's aunt make her suffer, but also many of the neighbors hurt her, scolding her when she refused to work in the fields on Sunday. And they laughed at her when she prayed. In their tribe only the men took time to pray to the great Spirit.

Kateri did not listen to them. She always did her work, but she often recited the Rosary while working and did so twice before the holy days.

One day there was great excitement in the village. An Oneida chief, who had become a Christian, had come to the village. His Christian name was Louis. He and a companion were now preaching about Jesus among the tribes of the Mohawk Valley.

Kateri was filled with joy. She drank in all the words of those Indian missionaries!

In the evening, Kateri ran to the missionaries' cabin. "Please," she pleaded, "please take me to Canada where you and all the other Indian Christians live. I want to be free to live as a true Christian."

"We will gladly take you, but do you have permission to come?" asked Louis.

"No, I don't. I know my uncle will never grant it, but my aunt would be happy to see me go. Please take me!"

So early one morning Kateri slipped out of the cabin while her uncle was not at home and sped into the forest where the missionaries were waiting to take the trail north. When at last they arrived at the Christian settlement, Kateri was overjoyed to see her old friend, Anastasia.

"Kateri! How happy I am to see you!" exclaimed Anastasia. "Did your uncle give his consent?"

"No, he didn't. I know that my uncle misses me. In fact, he followed us for quite a distance. But God is good to me and did not let him find me," answered Kateri.

"You will live with me," said Anastasia. "Come, I

will show you our cabin. Then we will go to meet our good neighbors."

How happy Kateri was! She immediately began living as she had always desired. Even when it was bitter cold, she went to church every morning at four o'clock to begin her prayers. Then she would participate at the Mass which the whole village attended each day.

Anastasia enjoyed Kateri's company. She told her many things about God and his saints.

Kateri listened attentively. She tried to remember God's presence all the time. As often as possible, she recited the Rosary, because she loved the Blessed Mother very much.

She could always be found helping someone in need. But her greatest joy was taking care of the children.

Because of her goodness and her deep understanding of her new religion, she was granted permission to receive Holy Communion. This was a great honor for Kateri because in those days the newly baptized Indians usually had to wait several years for this privilege. Kateri received her First Communion on Christmas morning. From that day on, she went to receive our Lord frequently.

One day Kateri could not get up. She was too ill to even go to Mass.

"What is the trouble?" asked Anastasia.

"I—I can't move. I feel pain all over," said Kateri.

Anastasia went to speak to the priest.

"I will come at once," said Father Cholonec.

Kateri smiled when she saw him. "Don't worry," she said, "I won't die until tomorrow. You may rest tonight."

The following day she received Holy Communion and the Sacrament of the Anointing of the Sick. Then she died peacefully. She was twenty-four-years-old.

A few minutes after Kateri's death something strange and wonderful happened.

Her face, scarred from smallpox which she had suffered when a child, became smooth and lovely! She was beautiful! Everyone who witnessed this miracle knew that Kateri was a saint. She is the first native North American to be declared Blessed by the Church.

Sometimes we have to wait many years for something we want very much, just as Kateri Tekakwitha waited years for her baptism. The important thing is never to stop praying and trusting that God will give us what we wish, if it is for our good.

St. Margaret Mary Alacoque

(1647-1690)

October 16

Margaret was the fifth of seven children born to Mr. and Mrs. Alacoque, of Janots, Burgundy (now France). Her father was a public official and the family lived in a large house, surrounded by the villagers who farmed their land. Mrs. Alacoque was a good mother who made sure that prayers and Bible stories were the first things her children learned. Tragedy struck the family, though, when Mr. Alacoque died suddenly in an accident. Mrs. Alacoque became so sick from her grief that she was unable to care for her children. Eight-year-old Margaret was sent away to a boarding school run by Poor Clare nuns.

At the boarding school, Margaret loved to get up early and go into the chapel to hear the sisters chanting the psalms. And she was often found there at night praying the Rosary. In fact, Margaret was so well known for her prayers and love for Jesus that she was able to make her First Holy Communion when she was only nine years old.

At that time, most children were not allowed to receive Communion until they were at least thirteen.

Margaret loved to watch the nuns, and in her heart she often promised Jesus that as soon as she was old enough, she would enter the convent and consecrate her whole life to God. But when she was eleven, Margaret became ill with a form of rheumatism and had to leave the boarding school. One of her relatives came to take her back to Janots.

She was shocked to find that one of her uncles had moved into their house and taken control of all her father's money and property. Her mother and brothers and sisters (who were still too young to protest) were being treated as servants in their own home! But for several months, Margaret was too sick to think too much about it. As she began to feel stronger Margaret missed the long hours she had spent praying in the chapel at her school. She asked her uncle for permission to go out to the village church and pray each day. At first, he refused to let her go.

Margaret went every day to ask his permission. Sometimes he said yes; most of the time he said no. For the sake of her mother, Margaret tried to make the best of their situation. She even began to make friends with some of the young men and women who frequently came to the parties her uncle held. Soon, both Margaret's mother and uncle were encouraging her to decide which of the young men she would like to marry. Margaret was so well liked that she could have her pick! Yet something made her hesitate.

She remembered the promise she had so often made to Jesus, to join the convent and consecrate her whole being to God

"It is your duty to marry," her mother told her. Margaret did not know what to say, for she knew that she did not want to marry. But her mother kept urging, "Choose one young man, or another, but choose *someone*."

Margaret was praying after Holy Communion one day, asking God to help her know what to do, when Jesus appeared right in front of her. He was so powerful and handsome! But he looked sad, too. "I have chosen you to be my own," said Jesus. "We were happily promised to each other when you were still very young...before the world looked so attractive to you."

Margaret realized that she was crying. She had been thinking of forsaking God's special call for an earthly husband! She saw how foolish she had been. "My Lord," she promised, "even if it should cost me a million lives, I will never be anything but a religious."

Her mind was made up now, and she was firm when she told her family that she wished to become a religious sister. "Please send away all the young men who wish to marry me," she said. She entered the community of Visitation nuns at Paray-le-Monial and took the name Sister Margaret Mary.

Sister Margaret Mary's love for God grew deeper all the time. She spent hours adoring him in the Blessed Sacrament. "Oh, my God," she would say, "I love you so much that I want to be consumed by love, just as a candle is consumed by the flame!"

One day, on the Feast of St. John the Evangelist, Jesus appeared to Margaret and invited her to rest her head on his heart, just as St. John had done at the Last Supper. This was the first of many times that Jesus came and spoke to her about his heart. Jesus told Margaret that she had been chosen to tell all people about his love for them and to explain the devotion they must have to his Sacred Heart. He told her about the pain he suffered because people hardly seemed to know that he was waiting for them in every tabernacle all over the world, longing to be their closest friend. They hardly talked to him at all; they hardly ever told him they loved him; they hardly ever gave their whole hearts to him who had given his whole heart to them!

Jesus told Sister Margaret Mary, "My Divine Heart is so on fire with love for people that It cannot hold the flames of love inside any longer. It must spread to them by means of you!"

Jesus told her, too, that many people were in danger of going to hell because of their sins. He asked her to have a special feast day established to honor his Sacred Heart so that those who loved him could pray for those who did not love him. He asked that on the first Thursday evening of each month, people make a holy hour, meditating on him in the Garden of Gethsemane, just before his passion. Then, they were to receive Holy Communion at Mass on the first Friday of the month.

This message of Jesus was a reminder that he had become a human being to show us how to live as children of God, and that he had suffered and died for the love of *all* people. This message was important because in the days of Margaret

Jesus told Margaret to tell all people about his love for them and explain the love they must have for his Sacred Heart.

Mary many people had forgotten how much Jesus loved them. Many people thought of God as a harsh judge, and they were afraid to receive Holy Communion. They thought that God only loved a small portion of humanity, and certainly not the common person.

Sister Margaret Mary found it very hard to tell the sisters in her community about her visions of Jesus. They were an extraordinary gift of God, and many of the sisters thought that she was making it all up. It was only after many years, and with the help of a good priest, Father Claude de la Columbiere, that they came to believe her. In June of 1686, the sisters at Paray-le-Monial celebrated the Feast of the Sacred Heart for the first time. By then, Sister Margaret Mary had been appointed the directress of novices and she was able to explain to them how Jesus wanted all people to pray on the first Friday of the month.

Eventually, news of the visions and the request of Jesus to make known the love of his Heart for all people spread throughout France. Sister Margaret Mary's name would eventually become known all over the world as the Apostle of the Sacred Heart. But she would not live to see the devotion spread far. In 1690, she became ill and died suddenly, but peacefully. Before she died, she said, "My only need is God, and to lose myself in the Heart of Jesus."

Whenever we see a picture of the Sacred Heart of Jesus, we can remember that the message given to St. Margaret Mary was that he loves each and every one of us. We must never give up hope, but always trust in the mercy of Jesus.

St. Benedict Joseph Labre

(1748-1783)

April 16

Twelve-year-old Benedict Joseph Labre looked hopefully at his uncle. "Do you really think I can come and live with you, Father Francis?"

"It's entirely your choice," the priest answered. "You might have a vocation to the priesthood. If you come to be my assistant, I will teach you some theology and Latin. You will need to know these subjects if you want to be a priest someday."

Benedict thought about what his uncle had said. A twelve-year-old, in the mid-1700s, was practically an adult. Benedict's future was in his own hands. Benedict thought and prayed. Before long, he said good-bye to his family and went to join his uncle, the priest.

Years passed. Benedict learned more than theology. He learned how to pray and how to serve others. Then one day a traveler came by. Benedict listened as the visitor told of a group of monks called "Trappists." "These men give their lives to

God as no others do!" the visitor said with conviction.

The story impressed Benedict. More than anything, he wanted to live with and for Jesus alone. After some time, Benedict confided to his uncle, "I have been praying and thinking. And I believe God is calling me to be a monk."

When he was twenty-two, Benedict was accepted as a Trappist novice. For a while everything was fine. Benedict was very happy working and praying with the others. But he began to worry that he was not keeping the rule well enough. (He really was, but he could not stop worrying.) Then he got a terrible fever. Sadly, the abbot told Benedict, "My son, you are a very good and holy young man. But I think God is not directing you to our community. Go back to your family. God will guide you."

Benedict returned home, full of doubt. Eleven more times he tried to live as a Trappist, but each time he was sent home with the same words: "God is not calling you to this life."

"What do you want of me, Lord?" he prayed. "I am ready to give you everything. But why am I not able to be a monk?"

Benedict decided to make a pilgrimage to Rome. Along the way he stopped at every shrine, praying to know how he could best love God. This pilgrimage was the first of many for Benedict.

Like all eighteenth century pilgrims, Benedict traveled on foot and begged for food. At convents or monasteries he slept in shelters set up for travelers. When he wasn't near a shelter he slept outdoors.

Once Benedict wrote to his mother: "I would like to hear news of you and of my brothers and sisters, but that is not possible because I have no address."

Benedict soon discovered that thieves and criminals often pretended to be pilgrims. This made things difficult. Sometimes children made fun of the pilgrims, throwing rocks at them. At first Benedict did not know how to react. He was not a criminal! He had never hurt anyone, and he was certainly not lazy! Then Benedict realized that Jesus had been treated in the same way.

The other travelers, and the many people who were homeless beggars, were suspicious of Benedict. They thought he was a fake because he was good to everyone, he never gambled or got drunk and he never used bad language. Instead, Benedict would say, "These things offend God— and they are not good for you, either. Try to work if you can. If you can't work, be good to the people who care for you."

Benedict gradually came to understand that God was calling him to live among the street people of Rome, accepting insults, hunger, dirt and bad smells. Benedict spent whole days praying for the other street people. Once he wrote to his mother: "I would like to hear news of you and of my brothers and sisters, but that is not possible, because I have no address."

One day a priest saw Benedict sitting by the road. He was only thirty-one, but he was as weak as an old man. The young beggar's legs were swollen and cut. "Benedict, what's wrong?" the priest exclaimed. Benedict could not even walk. Father helped the young man to the church shelter and had him registered as a permanent guest. (Usually men could stay only three nights in a row.) When he felt better, Benedict helped at the shelter. He knew, though, that soon he would reach the day he was waiting for: the day he would join Jesus in heaven.

Holy Week was Benedict's favorite time of year. He looked forward to the beautiful Mass of the Lord's Supper on Holy Thursday, and to the special Good Friday services. But his friends at church noticed that Benedict was paler than usual during the Holy Week of 1783. At the end of one of the services, Benedict fell to the floor.

Gently, people carried the holy beggar to a nearby home. A priest hurried to give him the Anointing of the Sick. When Benedict died, the whole city of Rome mourned. At his funeral, so many people came to pray that the army had to direct traffic!

Many people who had not known Benedict were surprised. They had heard of holy priests, holy nuns and holy kings or queens. But a holy *beggar?*

The life of Benedict Joseph Labre is proof that God's grace can be present in a person no matter what their material circumstances are. St. Benedict Joseph Labre, the holy beggar, is a model for all those who are searching to know God's will, and for all those who, for whatever reason, are traveling the streets, with no place to call home.

St. Bartholomea

(1807-1833)

July 26

"Let's see which of us will become a saint first!"

Sister Frances, who had spoken, smiled as the young students crowded about her shouting, "I will!"

"No, I"

"No, me!"

Bartholomea who was new at the school, stared at the sister wide-eyed. A saint? Become a saint?

"Well, let's draw straws."

Sister Frances began to search for straws of various lengths. Meanwhile, eleven-year-old Bartholomea ran across the courtyard to the chapel, rushed inside, and fell to her knees before the Blessed Virgin's altar.

"Oh, Heavenly Mother," she begged, "let me draw the long straw! I promise you I *will* become a saint, no matter what the cost!"

She quickly said three Hail Marys, and hurried back to the courtyard, already confident that her desire would be granted.

The drawing began. With trembling hand, Bartholomea pulled, and looked.

"Bartholomea has drawn the long straw!"

In a second she was running back to the chapel, kneeling before the Blessed Virgin's Statue to say a prayer of thanks. Bartholomea knew that picking the straw was not the *reason* she would become a saint, but she looked upon the event as an encouragement to the fulfilling of her great desire.

Bartholomea's love for prayer and strong desire to become a saint did not prevent her from being a popluar person at school. In fact, she became a leader in games, usually playing the part of the mother or the teacher. And she would make up stories to entertain her companions. Often she would take smaller neighborhood children to church and teach them their prayers in front of the Blessed Virgin's altar.

After hearing a sermon about how much Jesus suffered because of our sins, Bartholomea promised, "Oh, Jesus, I shall never offend you again!"

But Bartholomea's childhood was far from being all sweetness!

Her father was an alcoholic, and had a violent temper. Often he came home angry and suspicious, ready to quarrel at the slightest excuse. Sometimes he beat Bartholomea's mother; he often drove her out of the house. But he was fond of

Bartholomea's father was an alcoholic and had a violent temper. But he was fond of Bartholomea and listened to her when she tried to calm him down.

Bartholomea and listened at least a little when she tried to calm him down.

Her mother feared for her daughter's safety, and sent her to live at the school of the Sisters of St. Clare—where Bartholomea made her resolution to become a saint.

No sooner had the girl made her decision than she set about finding a way to accomplish it. She wrote:

"I resolve to become a saint. That is the goal to which you, my God, invite me.

"It is an ambitious saying, which would be proud if I did not place all my confidence in you, my God.

"I propose to make myself a saint by the practice of three virtues: humility, self-denial and prayer.

"Mary, my dear Mother, please, help me to become a saint."

———————

When Bartholomea was fourteen, her nine-year-old sister, Camilla, came to stay at the school. She was a lot like their father, and used to having her own way. Camilla was often in trouble with her teachers, and this made Bartholomea feel terrible, even though she wanted the sisters to correct Camilla for her own good. Often Bartholomea was blamed for Camilla's difficulties, but she did not mind. She knew how difficult it had been at home with their father. She tried her best to convince Camilla to be good and to take her classes seriously. But Camilla was jealous of her older sister and was often rude to her.

In her final two years of school Bartholomea helped the sisters teach the younger children. She was a good teacher and the children loved and trusted her. They knew she was their friend.

When Bartholomea completed her studies, her parents called her home. They wanted her with them, and much as she wanted to become a sister, Bartholomea went home to her family. Her father's drinking was worse than ever, and Bartholomea knew that her mother needed help caring for the family.

Back at home, Bartholomea would look for her father when he was out drinking, and bring him home before trouble started.

One time she stopped at a friend's house.

"Yes, your father was here but he has gone to the bar. If you want, I'll go call him."

"No, I'll go," Bartholomea replied.

"Into a bar? Aren't you afraid?"

"Oh, no. I'm not afraid." And off she went.

She found her father playing cards. Seating herself nearby, she said, "Daddy, as soon as you finish this hand, I need to speak with you."

She led him out—and home! No one in the bar had said a rude word to her, because of her courage, modesty and devotedness.

On another occasion, a neighbor insulted Bartholomea's father. He tried to control his anger at first, but as insult followed insult, rage welled up in his heart and he lunged at the other man.

Bartholomea ran up to him and urged, "It's not worth it, Daddy. It's not worth it. Come on, let's go home!" Father and daughter turned and left quietly.

Bartholomea acquired such strength and courage because of the daily schedule she made for herself shortly after she returned home. This schedule included daily Mass, an hour of meditation each morning and another half hour of prayer at night.

Bartholomea never forgot that her whole life belonged to Jesus. Every day she would often recall that Jesus was with her—that he was calling her to her household duties, urging her to be kind, assuring her that he would never abandon her and asking her to perform every action only for him.

Bartholomea loved God so much that she wanted to convince as many people as she could to love him, too. Soon after she went home to her parents, she opened a private school right in the house, where the young village children could come to be taught. Soon there was not enough space, and they moved the school to a larger house.

Bartholomea was a wonderful teacher, and her students learned quickly. From Bartholomea, they learned other things along with reading, writing and arithmetic! They learned humility, kindness and patience! At the end of each year, the parents were amazed to see how much better behaved even their most rebellious children had become.

Bartholomea's teaching method was to love her students and to sacrifice herself for them. Seeing how truly she loved them, the children responded with all their best efforts. Every day she would propose a virtue for them to practice and told them *how* they could practice it. Often she rewarded those who tried the hardest.

She knew that some students learn faster than others, and helped each one without showing any partiality. She never hesitated to point out their mistakes, but did it so kindly that they immediately tried to improve.

Pastors of parishes in the nearby towns began to send teenage girls to Bartholomea so that they, too, would learn to teach as she did. Within a few years, Bartholomea's influence spread throughout the whole region—about eighty-four villages!

Bartholomea was not just a teacher. When two older women, Catherine and Rose Gerosa, opened a hospital for the poor, they begged Bartholomea to take charge of the hospital's finances, and she accepted the duty. She often visited the sick in the wards, stopping to say a comforting word and encourage each patient to prepare for confession and Communion. Upon her arrival, word would pass joyously from person to person: "Bartholomea is here!"

Once two soldiers were admitted to the hospital, more sick in soul than they were in body. They cared little or nothing for God and religion. Yet Bartholomea's holiness, together with her prayers for their conversion, turned them into God-fearing men.

Another man, who had led a wicked life, refused at first to listen to Bartholomea's gentle urgings. After a time, however, her prayers won out. He made a good confession and firm resolutions and, upon leaving the hospital, became a religious brother. Whenever he heard anyone speak of Lovere, where Bartholomea lived, he would say, "There is a saint in that town!"

Bartholomea never gave up her concern for her father. One summer he became very sick. As he grew worse and worse, she prayed with him, urging him to say with her the acts of love and contrition and acts of resignation to God's will. Like a lamb, he did everything she told him to do.

When her father made his last confession he confided to the priest that it was his daughter who had helped him prepare it. He knew that Bartholomea was the means of his conversion, and he kept her near him till the end. When he died, toward the end of October of 1831, Bartholomea wept, but she had the consolation of knowing that he had died a changed man. She assisted at many Masses for the repose of his soul.

After her father's death, Bartholomea continued to teach children, and to care for the poor and the sick. But more and more clearly she saw the need for a new religious congregation to do these works.

Her friend Catherine Gerosa joined her in the project. At first they encountered many obstacles which seemed to block their plans. But one by one these were overcome, thanks to the firm faith and unfailing prayers of the two holy women.

The Institute of the Sisters of Charity of Lovere was founded on the Feast of the Presentation of Mary, 1832. As it began, Bartholomea's own work on earth was ending. In April of 1833, she came down with a fever which rose higher and higher. Her mother and sister (and indeed the whole village) were very sad, for she was only twenty-six-years-old.

"Mother, listen," Bartholomea soothed. "You know that everyone has to die. If I were to live forty more years, I would still have to die. This is the moment when God in his mercy wills to receive me into Paradise. Do not be saddened by my death, but instead thank God!"

To die meant to abandon the Institute at its very birth and to leave it in other hands. It was a great sacrifice, but to Catherine Gerosa, Bartholomea said, "In heaven I will be more useful to the Institute than I would have been on earth."

On July 26, she went into her death agony. From time to time she kissed the crucifix and a small statue of the Blessed Virgin. Then, murmuring prayers, smiling as if dropping into a deep sleep, she died.

"What shall I do now?" Catherine Gerosa kept repeating to herself. "I am good for nothing; it is better for me to return to my home. Without Bartholomea I can do nothing; she was an eagle; I am an ox."

But Bartholomea's confessor told Catherine to have courage. The Institute was necessary, he declared. She must pray and have faith.

"Let us go ahead then," Catherine agreed. "God obviously wants to do this work all by himself."

Soon young women, former pupils of Bartholomea, came to join Catherine. Camilla came, too. On the Feast of Our Lady's Presentation, 1835, they received the religious habit.

The Institute grew quickly and spread throughout northern Italy, even sending missionaries to India and Brazil. A hundred years after its founding the Congregation numbered 8,150 sisters working in 1,723 institutions, in more than 600 localities. The sisters cared for abandoned children, old people, lepers, the mentally ill, the plague-stricken and homeless teenagers. They worked in hospitals, orphanages, public and private schools. All this because an eleven-year-old girl once made a decision to become a saint—and did something about it!

Obtaining strength through daily prayer, Bartholomea was able to overcome the difficulties of living with an alcoholic parent. We can pray to her, asking for strength and courage in facing the difficulties in our lives with faith and confidence in God's loving care. Like her, we can strongly desire to become a saint.

St. Elizabeth Ann Seton

(1774-1821)

January 4

Four-year-old Elizabeth sat on the porch steps, watching big, puffy clouds go floating by. She didn't seem to care that inside the house, only a few feet away, rested a tiny coffin containing the body of a small child.

"Elizabeth," a voice asked. "What are you doing? Your dear sister Kitty is dead, and you are not even crying?"

"No," replied the little girl. "I am not crying because Kitty has gone to heaven. And I wish I could go to heaven to be with my mother, too!"

Elizabeth Bayley had been taught by her mother that God is a loving Father, and that he has prepared a beautiful reward in heaven for all who love him. Now that her mother and little sister had gone to their heavenly home, she wished only to follow them. However, it would be many, many years before that blessed reunion.

In a few years, Elizabeth was helping her new

stepmother around the house and caring for new baby sisters. She enjoyed teaching the little ones their prayers and playing "school" with them.

Elizabeth's father, Dr. Richard Bayley, was a wealthy and generous man. He helped the many poor people in New York City as much as he could, treating them just as well as those who could afford to pay for his services.

One day another doctor asked him, "Could you come help me perform a difficult and dangerous operation?"

"I have a very full schedule," Dr. Bayley replied, "and I'm tired besides. Surely another doctor can come."

"I doubt if another would be willing," the friend replied. "I'll be sorry to tell the family of your refusal. They are poor people—penniless."

Dr. Bayley jumped to his feet. "Poor?" he asked. "Why didn't you say so before? Let's go at once! They shouldn't be left without care because they are poor."

At eighteen, Elizabeth was an intelligent and prayerful young woman. She had delicate features and beautiful, dark eyes. William Seton, a young businessman, fell in love with her and asked her to marry him. Since they were Episcopalians, they were married in an Episcopal Church in New York City in 1794.

William and Elizabeth were very happy, but a heavy burden soon fell on them. After his father's death, William, the oldest son, had to take over the family business and support his twelve brothers and sisters. Elizabeth, sad to see him becoming worried and tense, helped with the bookkeeping and tried to find ways to keep William's courage up. Now and then, she would speak of the great reward God prepares for those who are resigned to his will. She knew the Bible and often consoled her husband with thoughts and prayers from Scripture.

Soon Elizabeth and William had five young children: Anna Mary, William, Richard, Catherine and Rebecca. Elizabeth regarded each child as a gift from God, and was careful to see that the children grew up obedient and kind. When they needed discipline, she would discipline them, gently but firmly, knowing that this was for their good.

In 1803, William became very sick. The doctors suggested that a voyage would do him good.

"Leave the younger children with us, Elizabeth," urged kind relatives. "You will be able to take better care of William that way." Sad as she was to part from her little ones, Elizabeth agreed. She, William and Anna Mary set sail for Italy, where William had spent some time as a young man. They were to stay with some old friends of his, the Filicchi family.

But when the ship reached port, William was placed under quarantine, because the officials were afraid he might have "yellow fever." They did not know that he was dying of tuberculosis.

The quarantine shack was dirty and cold. William's condition grew worse and worse in spite of the good food and medicines that the Filicchis sent to him. Helpless, Elizabeth watched as her husband started having violent coughing spells. Soon he was coughing up blood.

At last William's quarantine was ended, and he was brought to the Filicchi home. But it was too late. Elizabeth watched by his bedside for three days and nights while he suffered intensely. And then it was over. Elizabeth was heartbroken, but she knew she had done everything she could.

William was buried the next morning.

The Filicchi family was very kind, and asked Elizabeth and Anna Mary to stay with them for a few weeks. One day Elizabeth went to church with them. The services amazed her, for she had never before attended the liturgy of the Roman Catholic Church. She went to church with her new friends again and again.

One morning, at the elevation of the Sacred Host, Elizabeth thought of the words of St. Paul—"discerning the Body of the Lord"—and tears began to flow down her cheeks. Was Jesus truly present here, as St. Paul had said he was? Oh, if only he were!

Often at that time in Italy, the Blessed Sacrament was carried through the streets in procession. Whenever she saw a procession pass her window, Elizabeth had a deep sense of loneliness. If only she could believe that God was truly present in the Eucharist! One day she fell to her knees and prayed silently, "My God, bless me if you are truly present. My soul desires you!"

One of Mrs. Filicchi's prayerbooks was on a table nearby. Elizabeth opened it, and there was a prayer to the Blessed Mother. Elizabeth said the prayer slowly. She was sure that God would not refuse his Mother anything, and that Mary would have only love and mercy for the souls for whom her Son had suffered. Elizabeth prayed, and she felt that the Blessed Mother was *her* mother, a tender, compassionate mother. She began to cry in relief, and finally fell asleep.

The return ocean voyage to New York had been long, but Elizabeth forgot the length of it and all her worries when she saw that her younger children were all well. Even though William was gone, God would take care of them.

"I have good reason to place my trust in you, my God," Elizabeth wrote in her diary. "Whom do I have in heaven except you? And whom on earth besides you?"

She had been thinking long and carefully, and had decided to become a Roman Catholic. She knew, now, that Jesus was truly present in the Blessed Sacrament, and she longed to participate in Holy Mass and to receive Holy Communion.

Her husband's family strongly objected. They did not like the Roman Catholic Church and threatened to have nothing to do with her if she should take this step. Elizabeth then went to her friend, Father Cheverus, and poured out her story. He told her that she, indeed, was making the right choice—the only one that would bring her happiness. And so, in the only Catholic church in New York City, on March 14, 1805, Elizabeth became a Catholic. She was thirty- years - old.

After receiving the Sacrament of Reconciliation for the first time, Elizabeth began to prepare for her First Holy Communion, which she received on the Feast of the Annunciation. "At last," she wrote, "God is mine, and I am his!"

Elizabeth's relatives did abandon her, leaving her and her children without income. But she did not care. She had peace, and no price was too great to pay for that. She opened a school and began to teach. At night she would play the piano while her five children sang and danced. After they had gone to bed she would wash and mend their clothes. At midnight she would go to bed, only to rise early and walk several blocks to Mass. It was a hard schedule, but she did not mind. When William had been alive, he had scolded her for working too hard, and she had replied, "Love makes all effort easy." Now it was both love for her children and for her faith that made such a difficult time "easy."

One day Elizabeth was introduced to a young priest from Baltimore, who told her of the great need of that city for a religious community to teach young girls. Could Elizabeth found such a community? After all, she was an excellent teacher, and a fervent Catholic, and she clearly did not intend to remarry.

Elizabeth felt quite incapable of such a task, but she prayed about it and consulted her spiritual director. Then she agreed to try.

Soon, several young women who wished to become teaching sisters joined Elizabeth. By 1812, twenty sisters were sharing a common way of life. Elizabeth and the new community experienced many difficulties. Several of its members died because of hardships suffered during the War of 1812. Then Anna Mary, who had become a novice, became ill and died. About the same time Elizabeth's youngest daughter, Rebecca, injured her leg. A tumor began to grow in the leg. Rebecca, who was only ten, suffered for months. Elizabeth stayed at her bedside day and night, telling her about the beauties of heaven that would soon be hers. She marveled at Rebecca's patience, for the girl was in great pain. After Rebecca's death Elizabeth wrote to young William, "If you had been given the opportunity of seeing our Rebecca fly to heaven as a little angel, you could not be more certain that she is with God."

Just as Elizabeth had been a good wife and mother, she was also a wonderful superior. She gave her sisters a marvelous example of prayerfulness, calmness, generosity and self-sacrifice. She looked after each sister and each young pupil as

Soon, several young women who wished to become teaching sisters joined Elizabeth. By 1812 twenty women were sharing a common way of life.

diligently as she had looked after her own children.

Her thoughts were fixed on heaven, as they had been when she was a child. As she grew weaker day by day, Elizabeth knew that her own death was coming. "Eternity seems so near," she would exclaim. "Think of it when you feel oppressed or annoyed. It will be a beautiful endless day!"

After receiving the Anointing of the Sick, Elizabeth said, "Thank you! Oh, how grateful I am!" Then she said to her sisters. "Pray for me!" The next day, saying the name of "Jesus" over and over, she died peacefully, to rejoin her loved ones forever in the land of eternal joy.

Elizabeth Seton once wrote to a friend: "My dear, think of me, battering the waves of my changeable life. Yet, if I were to change one shade or trial of it, that would be madness and working in the dark. No, the adored will of God be done through every moment of life!" Like her, let us accept the circumstances of life with courage, knowing that God is with us in every joy and every difficulty.

St. Joseph Cottolengo

(1786-1842)

April 29

One day, in the year 1827, a young family from France was traveling near the city of Turin, Italy. Unexpectedly, the mother of the family became very sick. The father hurried to take her to the city's hospital, but the hospital would not admit her because they had no money to pay for her care. The father and the three children were very upset because she was obviously dying. Someone who had seen their desperate situation had called a priest, hoping that he could help them. But when he arrived it was too late—he gave the woman the Sacrament of the Anointing of the Sick before she died.

Father Cottolengo was the priest the poor man called. As he stood by, helpless to do any more, the woman's husband and her three little children sobbed desperately.

Father Cottolengo thought of how that woman might have been saved if that hospital had only taken her in and cared for her. As he thought about it, he made a resolution: that sort of thing would never happen again in Turin!

It didn't take the determined priest very long to put his plan into action. He found a small building near the center of the city which could be turned into a hospital. He opened it up and brought in the most desperately sick people he could find. But then troubles came, and he had to close the little hospital.

Father Cottolengo did not give up his idea. He waited, looked around and soon found a large meadow with a little house in the center of it. This would be his next hospital! Two sisters and a kind lady joined Father.

On April 27, 1832, a little cart pulled by a donkey came bumping along the road to the house. In the cart was their first patient—a gentleman with a diseased leg. And that was when the "Little House of Divine Providence" started. It was a poor beginning, but full of joy and faith.

More and more patients came. Soon another house had to be built, then another and another. Streets were built between the houses, and before long there was no meadow left at all—just buildings filled with all kinds of sick people. He started a group of religious women to live at the hospital and help care for the patients.

Father Cottolengo was working hard all the time making sure that all the needs of the sick, of the sisters and other nurses were provided for. He worked hard, but he prayed even harder, because only help from God could keep his great project going. More food, more medicine, more doctors, sisters, priests.... People began to wonder what would happen when Father Cottolengo would die. Would God still provide, without the faith and prayers of the holy priest?

That question bothered the king of Italy, too. One day he sent for Father Cottolengo and asked him if he had made any plans for the future. For a minute the priest didn't say anything. He walked over to the window and looked down into the big square below. "If you please, Your Majesty, come look at this," he said. There below them the palace guard was changing. One group of soldiers was dismounting from their horses; other soldiers took their place. It all happened very calmly and without excitement.

"That's just the way that someone will take my place when God calls me. Don't you think so, Your Majesty?"

The king was impressed. From that time on, he had great respect and admiration for Father Cottolengo. He always spoke of him as "my friend Cottolengo."

To Father Cottolengo, patients in his Little House were the most important people in the world. When he was with them, nothing could take him away. One day an archbishop came to visit. He found Father Cottolengo playing ball with a mentally ill man named Doro.

"I would like to speak with you, Father," said the archbishop.

"I'm delighted to see you, Your Excellency," replied the priest. "I'm playing with this man right

The patients in the Little House were the most important people in the world to Father Cottolengo. When he was with them, nothing could take him away.

now, and he might feel offended if I stop. I hope you don't mind waiting."

So the archbishop waited, and even kept score for the players! He didn't mind, because he realized that every person is very special in the eyes of God no matter who they are.

Saints can be described in many ways, depending on what virtues they practice the most. Love and hope both describe St. Joseph Cottolengo very well, but another virtue stood out even more clearly in him, and that was his faith in Divine Providence. "Every time someone new enters the Little House," he said, "more bread comes down from heaven— and the best thing about it is that *I'm* not the one who makes it come; it is Divine Providence which takes joy in raining down the loaves one by one."

Father Cottolengo was never worried, never discouraged. When things seemed the worst, he was the happiest. Then he felt that the Providence of God was very close. Sometimes, he could predict the arrival of something they needed almost to the exact minute. One day, for instance, they ran out of flour, rice and noodles; it was almost mealtime, and there were thousands of sick people to feed!

The cook was worried. She hurried to Father Cottolengo. "Oh, Father, there's nothing to prepare!"

"Really? Well, put the kettles on and start the water boiling. Let's not waste any time."

As soon as the water was boiling in the big kettles, the doorbell rang. There was a big wagon full of bread and rice which someone had donated!"

"The Little House will grow as long as it does not have a steady source of income," Father Cottolengo often said. "It will grow only as long as it has nothing."

One day Father Cottolengo had to leave on a trip. His brother, Father Louis Cottolengo, came to take his place. "Here is the money bag, Louis," said the saint. "Spend whatever you need to spend, but never look inside the bag to see what is left. If you do as I say, the money will last."

Many, many expenses came up in the days that followed. Father Louis had to pay a great deal of money. He was amazed that the little bag always provided whatever he needed and more! It didn't seem possible that it could have held so much!

Another time the superior of the sisters came to him looking quite upset. "What's the trouble, Sister?" he asked kindly.

"I have so many things to buy, Father, and this is all the money I have!"

"That's all? Let me see it."

She handed it to him. It was a very small sum indeed. "Quite right," said Father Cottolengo. He walked over to the window and tossed the money outside!

"That's all right," said Father Cottolengo. "It's been planted now. Wait a few hours, and it will bear fruit."

That evening a woman came to see Father Cottolengo. She gave him a large sum of money.

Another time a sister came and said, "Father,

what are we going to do? There's no bread, no flour, no potatoes—there's nothing! And it's almost dinnertime!" She held up a nickel. "This is all we have!"

"Give it to me," replied the priest. He flung the nickel out the window. "There! Now we really have nothing, and Providence *has* to provide!"

"Go to the church and pray," he told the sister. "I'll go and pray, too. When noon comes, *send everyone to the dining hall as usual.*"

Noon came and everyone came to the dining hall as usual. There was a knock at the gate. Someone hurried to open it. And what came rolling in through the gate but wagon after wagon, loaded with already cooked meals! Those meals had been for a regiment of soldiers who were in the field on battle maneuvers. But the soldiers had been delayed, and their officers had decided to send the food to the Little House so as not to waste it.

One day the sister who did all the buying told Father Cottolengo that she didn't want to do it any longer.

"And why not?" asked the priest.

"The storekeepers want us to pay our bills before they sell us anything else!"

"You have no faith," replied the saint. "As a penance, say Psalm 52, the 'Miserere,' and then go out as usual."

The sister didn't say a word. She just prayed, and left.

First, the storekeeper came up and handed her a receipt for what had been owed: "A lady came and paid me for you, Sister!"

It happened again and again, all along the street. One woman even handed the sister some extra money. "The lady left it for you," she said.

Father Cottolengo listened to the story without surprise. *He* knew who the mysterious Lady was!

One time a very angry man came to the Little House and demanded that his bill be paid. "I won't leave until you pay every single cent!" he roared.

"I haven't even one cent," replied Father Cottolengo.

The man said something nasty.

"Please don't swear," said Father Cottolengo. "Come back tomorrow, and we'll pay it all."

"Nothing doing! I'm not moving from here until you pay up!"

"All right," agreed the saint. "Wait just a moment, please."

It was very quiet for a minute. Father Cottolengo reached into his pocket very slowly. When he pulled his hand out, it held two large rolls of money.

The man went away amazed.

There are many stories like these about the faith of St. Joseph Cottolengo. His life was full of miracles. In fact, the miracles have continued since his death, almost as if he were guiding the Little House from heaven. Even to this day, the Little House runs smoothly, operating only on the gifts of God!

Even when everything seems to go wrong, let us trust that God will bring good from it in the end.

St. Dominic Savio

(1842-1857)

March 9

Dominic Savio was the son of a blacksmith who lived in the small town of Rira, in northern Italy. Even when he was very small he liked to pray. Each morning Dominic would get up at five o'clock with his father and go to the church to serve Mass. When he was seven-years-old, Dominic was allowed to receive his First Holy Communion. This was a big exception at that time, because most children could not receive Communion until they were at least thirteen. On that wonderful day, Dominic told Jesus all the secret hopes of his young, loving heart. He made a promise to Jesus and adopted this motto which he afterwards told to his pastor: "Death, but not sin!" This was the sort of motto which a hero would have, and Dominic would prove to be a hero in living up to it.

———————

By the time Dominic was twelve-years-old, he knew that he wanted to be a priest more than anything else. And he was eager to begin the studies which would prepare him for that great goal. Father John Bosco (who was later canonized also), encouraged Dominic and admitted him to the Salesian Oratory he had founded. This was a special school for boys who wanted to better their lives. There Dominic joyfully began his studies.

When not studying, Dominic often visited the Blessed Sacrament by himself or with friends whom he invited along. An eager little group often gathered around him, and they would tell each other stories about great saints and the wonderful things they did. On Fridays, Dominic gave up the usual games and went to chapel to honor the sorrows of the Blessed Virgin in a special way; often he asked his companions to join in these prayers. On Sundays, he taught catechism to younger children.

Dominic never looked at any bad pictures or pornographic magazines, even though these were popular with some of the students. If he did see something by accident he ignored it and said a prayer to the Blessed Virgin. In fact, sometimes he would not look at things which were harmless, just so he could offer the sacrifice to our Lord and strengthen his own will so that he would not give in to temptations which would come later on.

Each week Dominic went to confession and he

God willing, Dominic decided, I will become a priest. He was now twelve, and eager to begin the studies which would prepare him for that great goal.

received Communion every day. He urged his friends to go to confession often and he founded a club called the Sodality of the Immaculate Conception, to encourage frequent reception of Holy Communion. The members of the Sodality strove to be good Catholic students in every way and to have a great devotion to Mary.

Dominic once said to Don Bosco ("Don" means "Father" in Italian), "I have to become a saint, Father!" He never lost sight of that goal. Dominic was always urging his friends to do good deeds and to avoid everything which could lead them to sin. Of course, he did not pretend to be wearing a halo, either! He was a lively, high-spirited teenager and he was always involved in the students' ball games and plays.

But Dominic became very ill when he was fourteen and was sent home to his parents in the hope that the change of climate would make him feel healthy again. How hard it was for Dominic to leave his dear teacher and friend, Don Bosco! He had a feeling that they would not meet again except in heaven.

At home, Dominic grew worse instead of better. The parish priest came and administered the Sacrament of the Anointing of the Sick and gave him Communion. The boy felt all the strength draining out of his body and in his last moments he kept praying, "Jesus, Mary, Joseph, assist me in my last agony!" Suddenly a change came over him. He sat up straight and held out his arms eagerly. His eyes shone. "Oh, what a beautiful sight!" he exclaimed.

Then, with a smile on his lips, St. Dominic Savio died.

Dominic Savio's life was very short and very ordinary! He was a good friend and a good student, but he was not "the best" at anything. He didn't live long enough to attain his goal of priestly ordination. But Dominic is a saint because he let his love for Jesus guide him in everything he did. We, too, can let the life and love of Jesus be the guiding light in our daily work and fun.

St. Bernadette Soubirous

(1844-1879)

April 16

On February 11, 1858, the city of Lourdes in southern France was enveloped in a blanket of fog. In the poor little room of the Soubirous family there was not even a bit of wood to light a fire.

"We'll go get some, Mamma," volunteered the girls, Bernadette and Mary. Their friend Joan was eager to go, too.

Thinking of her older girl's asthma, Mamma Soubirous protested, "Bernadette, don't go out. Your cough might come back again."

"Mamma, don't worry," replied Bernadette quickly. "I'll put on my coat and I won't be cold." Her mother nodded consent and the three girls went out.

Bernadette was the oldest child in her family, but she was not as strong as her sister Mary because of her asthma, and she was very slow in schoolwork. At fourteen, she had not yet memorized her catechism, and so had not been permitted to make

471

her First Communion. But Bernadette loved God very much.

Bernadette, Mary and their friend ran off toward the wooded area of Massabielle, where they would find dry branches. On their way, they had to wade across a shallow, cold stream. Mary and Joan waded across quickly. Bernadette, who was not able to go into such cold water, threw stones into the stream trying to make a way across, but the water was too high and covered them.

While her sister and Joan moved away to gather wood, a light breeze touched Bernadette, although the air all around was still and the branches of the trees were not moving at all. Then, in a small grotto near the stream, a beautiful young Lady appeared. Bernadette gasped, dropped to her knees and reached for her worn-out rosary beads. The Vision smiled and invited Bernadette to recite the Rosary. At the end of each decade, the Lady joined with the girl in saying the "Glory be to the Father."

After the Lady had disappeared, Bernadette rejoined Mary and Joan. She told them about the Vision and the other girls excitedly made her tell what she had seen. Unable to keep it a secret, the girls told her parents and some friends. Bernadette's parents thought it nonsense but her friends were curious.

The next Sunday, Bernadette took a bottle of holy water and, with several friends, went to the grotto. There, she knelt and began to say the Rosary and the others followed her example, waiting expectantly. She gazed upward, watching intently. Her companions saw nothing, but they knew that the Lady had come.

"Quick, Quick!" urged one of the girls. "Throw the holy water!"

Bernadette threw some of the holy water. "If you come from God, come forward!" she said to the Vision.

Obediently the Lady advanced, bowed her head and smiled. Bernadette's face lit up with a divine light. Her eyes were fixed on the spot, on a sight that filled her soul with a heavenly joy.

After this apparition, the news reached the city officials. They did not believe the story, but were eager to find out more about it, thinking it to be some sort of trick of Bernadette's to make money for her parents. Bernadette's father was known to be an alcoholic and the family was often without money.

On Thursday, February 18, the Lady again appeared. The girl begged her, "My Lady, please write your name and tell me what you desire of me."

As soon as Bernadette had made the request, she grew worried. Had she been too bold with the Lady? She held her breath, but the Vision smiled.

"There is no need to write what I want," she said. "Will you be kind enough to come back here fifteen times?"

"Yes, my Lady!"

The Lady continued, "I promise to make you happy, but not in this world. I desire to have many people come here."

Soon after this, Bernadette was taken to the office of Police Commissioner Jacomet, who asked her many confusing questions and then accused her of lying.

The next Sunday, Bernadette went again to the grotto. There, she knelt and began to say the Rosary and the other girls followed her example, waiting expectantly.

"Now, listen," stormed Jacomet. "First you say one thing, then you say another. You're trying to fool me! I tell you, girl, if you don't promise not to return to the grotto, I'll call in the police!" He was shouting in uncontrollable anger when Francis Soubirous entered.

"I am her father, Commissioner," Francis introduced himself. "Give me back my child."

Immediately Jacomet turned his anger upon him. "When are you going to end this lie you started in order to get money? If you don't end it, I will!"

"Believe me, sir, my wife and I are tired of the whole thing," Francis declared. "And I promise you that Bernadette will not go to the grotto at Massabielle again."

"All right," snapped Jacomet. "But if she does, I have my police...and you know them! Now go!"

But Bernadette's father *did* let her go to the grotto again.

One morning, Bernadette made her way to the grotto through an especially large crowd and knelt in prayer as usual. As the girl began to say the Rosary, the Lady said, "Go to drink and wash yourself in the spring. Then eat some of the grass you will find there."

Bernadette was puzzled; there was no spring! Perhaps it doesn't matter where I take the water from, Bernadette thought, as she rose and began to walk toward the river.

The Lady was calling her softly. "Not in the river," she said, and motioned to the earth near the grotto. Bernadette hastened to the spot, and began to dig in the sand. Soon she had a small hole filled with muddy water. As soon as the mud had settled, she scooped up some of the water and drank it. Then she washed her face, and began to eat some of the bitter grass which was growing beside her.

The onlookers gasped. They did not understand what Bernadette was doing.

During the following days, the little trickle of water swelled into a stream. (Today it flows into nine great tanks where the sick are bathed and often cured.)

Another day, the Lady asked Bernadette, "Would it make you upset to kiss the ground for sinners?"

"No, my Lady," the girl replied. She kissed the ground several times, then stood up with her face wet with tears. Turning to the crowd, she ordered, "Kiss the ground."

The people did not understand. Bernadette told them again, and a murmur went through the crowd; all bent to kiss the ground.

On the following day, Bernadette went to see the pastor. He had heard of the events at the grotto, but had shown no interest in them. However, now he would have to take some sort of position regarding them, for the Lady had given Bernadette a message.

"Who are you?" asked the pastor.

"I am Bernadette Soubirous," the girl replied.

"Oh, I've heard about you. What do you want?"

"The Lady asked me to tell the priests that she wishes to have a chapel built at Massabielle. She wants people to go there to pray and to be sorry for their sins."

"The Lady! What's her name?"

"I don't know, Father," Bernadette replied. "She is a very beautiful young woman who appears to me at the grotto."

"Neither you nor I know who she is. So tell her that the pastor doesn't deal with people he doesn't know and that she must tell you her name."

On March 25, Bernadette hurried to Massabielle with the first rays of dawn. The Vision was already smiling at her from the rocks. Bernadette gathered courage and pleaded, "My Lady, won't you be kind enough to tell me who you are?"

Three times the young girl dared to question her. Finally, the Lady opened her arms and extended them toward the earth; she lifted her gaze to heaven, then joined her hands over her heart, and said, "I am the Immaculate Conception."

After that, the Lady disappeared in a great cloud of light.

Eagerly the crowd questioned Bernadette: "Did she tell you her name?"

"Is it really the Blessed Virgin?"

Bernadette hesitated, for the name the Lady had told her was one which she had never heard before. "I don't know," she murmured, and then ran off to tell the pastor.

"Is she the Blessed Virgin?" he asked.

Bernadette replied, "She said, 'I am the Immaculate Conception.'"

The pastor gasped. "The Immaculate Conception!... Maybe you don't remember, Bernadette?"

But the girl was sure. "Oh, I do, Reverend

Father, because I repeated the name all the way from Massabielle until now."

When the girl had left, the priest thought long and hard about what she had said. Only four years before, Pope Pius IX had proclaimed the Immaculate Conception a dogma of the Church. Was heaven itself now voicing its approval of that declaration? If the lady had said, "I am the Immaculate Conception," it would mean that she was the Blessed Virgin Mary! Soon, the priest and other Church authorities believed that Bernadette was being visited by Our Lady.

On June 3, Bernadette received her First Holy Communion. In the silence of her heart she spoke to her God: O Jesus, I love you. Forgive all sinners and save them. For them I offer you my life. Accept it, O Jesus."

The joy of her First Holy Communion prepared her for the parting with her beautiful Lady. It was the evening of July 16, when Bernadette asked her aunt, "Aunt Lucille, come with me! The Blessed Virgin is waiting for me."

Willingly her aunt accompanied her to the grotto. A barricade had been placed about it to keep the crowds of people away. Bernadette and her aunt stopped and gazed up at the grotto.

Suddenly Bernadette exclaimed: "She is there! She is looking at us and smiling at us across the barricade."

Fifteen minutes of wonderful happiness passed by. This was the farewell visit, and Bernadette knew it. She fixed her gaze on the splendor of her Lady, who appeared more beautiful than ever before. As the figure of the Virgin slowly disappeared, Bernadette was left with a sweet peace of heart.

"I shall not see her again on this earth...but I *will* see her again!"

———————

Thousands of people had heard of Bernadette's vision and many were traveling to Lourdes, wanting to talk to her. Soon she was seeking shelter from the crowds. First she stayed at the convent of the Sisters of Lourdes. One day the bishop asked her, "What do you intend to do, Bernadette, in return for what the Blessed Virgin has done for you?"

"I would like to live with the sisters as their maid, Your Excellency," Bernadette replied. "Would that be possible?"

"And have you ever thought of entering their Congregation?" the bishop continued.

"Your Excellency," Bernadette protested. "I am poor and ignorant."

But poverty and ignorance matter little when a person wants to serve God. Thus, Bernadette soon left Lourdes for Nevers, where the Mother General of the Sisters of Charity was happy to receive her.

"Bernadette," said the Mother General, "I hope you will be happy among us. What do you know how to do?"

"Very little, Reverend Mother. I know how to peel potatoes and scrub pots."

"In the house of the Lord," replied the Mother General, "one action is just as noble and good as another. Now, then, you will help the sister in the kitchen."

Bernadette smiled, "I am very grateful to you for accepting me, Reverend Mother."

On July 29, 1866, the bishop, came to give Bernadette the habit of the Congregation.

"From now on," said the bishop, "you will be called Sister Mary Bernard."

One day a sister asked Sister Mary Bernard, "Have you ever felt that you were better than the rest of us because you were so favored by the Blessed Virgin?"

Sister Mary Bernard was amazed. "But don't you know that the Blessed Virgin chose me because I am the most ignorant? If she had found anyone more ignorant, she would have chosen that person."

Another time she said, "I served as a broom for the Blessed Virgin. And when she no longer had any use for me she put me in my place, behind the door. There I am and there I shall remain."

———

The Virgin had told Bernadette, "I shall not make you happy on this earth," and Sister Mary Bernard knew that suffering was her mission. Before long, she was very sick with tuberculosis.

As Sister Mary Bernard lay dying, the Blessed Mother came again to visit her; her smile lightened the pain. The dying sister begged, "Mary Most Holy, Mother of God, pray for me, a poor sinner."

Then Sister Mary Bernard's large eyes shone

with happiness; her lips curved into a smile. Slowly she bowed her head. She had taken flight with her Lady—toward the gates of heaven.

Although Sister Mary Bernard has gone from this earth, the spring which she dug continues to bubble up and calls people to Mary's shrine. Trains bring the sick to Lourdes from all over the world. For although doctors cannot cure all their afflictions, God can.

In the shrine at Lourdes, people find Jesus. In the Most Blessed Sacrament, he passes among the rows of sick waiting in the square in front of the basilica. While he blesses them, they pray:

"Jesus, have pity on us."

"Lord, that I may see!"

"Lord, make me walk!"

In the grotto where our Lady appeared are the crutches of the sick who have been cured through her intercession. Long processions make their way along the square in front of the basilica toward the grotto. Just as Bernadette used to do, the faithful recite the Rosary together and ask God's forgiveness for their sins.

St. Bernadette never became proud of the special favor God gave her. She knew the vision of Mary was God's gift, and not something she had deserved. Let us never look down on others who are not as smart, as strong or as well-dressed as we are, because everything we have is God's gift to us.

St. John Bosco

(1815-1888)

January 31

The great wars of Napoleon caused much suffering and misery in Europe. Many schools had been destroyed, and young children worked instead. They were forced to spend long hours at their jobs, even on Sundays, for many people had forgotten about God. The wars and the foolish ideas of a few proud men had taken him out of their hearts.

Some boys could not find work. Many of them were homeless and became thieves, who were picked up by the police and thrown into prisons. There they learned from hardened criminals about worse crimes and evils.

But not everyone had forgotten about God. Many people were trying their best to raise their children as good Christians. John Bosco was born into such a family.

John's mother was a good, hard-working widow who taught her son to be kind and good.

John used every chance he could to study the Bible and to read and write. He could often be seen out in the fields with a book in his hands. "Come play with us!" his friends would call, because they enjoyed playing with him. But John would reply, "I want to become a priest! I must study!"

One night, John had a marvelous dream. He was standing in a group of children who were fighting and swearing. He tried to make them stop, but they wouldn't listen. Then he tried with his fists, as he had done before. But that didn't work either.

Suddenly, he saw a man in white coming toward him. He was smiling. "You will make them your friends with love, not with blows," the man said. "You will show them how to become good."

"Me? How can I?"

"By being obedient and studying hard you will be able to do it."

"Who are you?" asked the boy.

"I am the Son of the Lady your mother has taught you to pray to so often. Ask My Mother for help!"

And there she was! The Blessed Mother, whom he honored daily in the beautiful prayer, the Angelus. She said sweetly, "Look!" Suddenly, the raging children around John were changed into wild beasts. "As I do with these wild beasts, so will you do with the children." And the beasts became meek little lambs, ready to be led away to pasture!

From then on, John knew that his special purpose in life was to help children.

One day, his mother took him to a country fair where he watched the stunts of the acrobats. An idea came into his mind. Back home again, he stretched a rope between two trees and tried to walk it.

Of course, he fell many times. His brother Anthony laughed. But John was not discouraged; he just tried again and again. Soon he was walking the rope quite easily.

Then he learned other acrobatic stunts. At last, one Sunday night, he called some men and boys to see his "show." They enjoyed it and clapped enthusiastically. Then John, who had another motive, began to sing a hymn to Mary. Everyone joined in, and the beautiful notes soared toward heaven. Then the boy said, "Now unless you say the Rosary while I perform, I'll fall and break my head!" The people began to pray. At the close of his performance, John sat down and repeated the sermon the priest had given that morning at Mass.

John never stopped wanting to be a priest. But he knew that his mother would have to save a lot of money if he was going to study. He didn't want to ask her to make such a sacrifice. His mother told him not to worry about her, but to do what God wanted him to do. "I was born poor," she said. "I am poor, and I wish to die poor." So at the age of sixteen, John Bosco entered the seminary.

Whenever he could spare a moment from his

studies, the youth would gather together all the ragged and lonely boys he could find. He would take them on outings and instruct them in the catechism.

When John was ordained to the priesthood, the whole village assisted at his first Mass. Tears of joy streamed down his mother's cheeks. Now her boy was no longer Johnny, but Father, or Don Bosco.

A few months later, Don Bosco was in the sacristy, preparing to say Mass, when he heard a commotion. Turning around, he saw the sacristan mistreating a boy because he did not know how to serve Mass.

The young priest hurried over. He sent the sacristan away. "Would you like me to teach you how to serve?" he asked the boy. Gratefully the youngster nodded his head. After Don Bosco had finished the lesson, he asked the boy to bring his friends with him the next day.

Soon Don Bosco had many pupils. Every feast day morning they came to assist at Mass and go to confession; in the evening they would come to study catechism and sing hymns. So many of the boys were homeless that the priest soon found himself looking for places for them to live, and his own mother came to join him to help him care for them.

One evening as Don Bosco was out walking, a strange thing happened. Four men approached him. They looked like they wanted to beat him, even kill him. But a huge dog came out of the

After a few years, Don Bosco realized that a community of religious was needed to take care of the homeless boys, both in his own city and in other parts of the world.

shadows and leaped at one of the robbers. The rest turned and fled, and Don Bosco called the dog away from the man he was about to kill. The dog walked home with the priest, and then disappeared into the night shadows again. Many other times in Don Bosco's life, that big dog came to help him when he was in danger.

Whenever one of "his boys" looked troubled, Don Bosco would take him aside and quietly ask him about it. Often it was a matter for confession. How peaceful and happy each boy looked when he had made a good confession.

After a few years, Don Bosco saw that a religious order was needed to take care of the boys—and not only boys in his own city, but all over the world. So he founded the Salesians, whom he named after St. Francis de Sales. Don Bosco watched his Salesian Order grow and spread to South America, France and Spain. It was a consolation to him in his old age to see how much was being done for young people all over the world.

In the winter of 1888, Don Bosco died. He was canonized by one of his greatest admirers, Pope Pius XI, in 1934.

From his early childhood, St. John Bosco wanted to help others get closer to God. One way we can do this is by being good ourselves. Our example will help our friends.

St. Therese of Lisieux

(1873-1897)

October 1

Therese Martin, born in Alençon, France, on January 2, 1873, was the youngest in a family of five girls. Zelie Martin, her mother, died when Therese was just four, so the child was reared by her older sisters, Pauline and Marie. They were very devout Catholics and all the girls learned their prayers before anything else.

One day, Pauline showed Therese how all the people in heaven are completely happy even though some have more glory than others. She did this by taking a cup and a thimble and filling each with water. "Now," she asked, "which is the fullest?" Therese was puzzled, for neither of them could have held another drop. "That's how it will be in heaven," Pauline said. "Every soul will be completely filled with happiness, but some will have more room for it, because they had a greater love of God while on earth." At once, Therese decided to become a soul with great love of God.

Pauline also taught her little sister all about the religious feasts. Therese's favorite was Corpus Christi, when the Blessed Sacrament was carried in procession and the children spread flowers along the road in front of It. Therese thought that each flower was like a kiss to Jesus hidden in the Host.

Therese's life also had its funny moments. Therese and her cousin, Marie Guerin, were walking down the street one day playing "hermit." They pretended they were in the desert, and as they walked they closed their eyes at the same time. They soon walked straight into a stack of boxes piled in front of a grocery store. The desert forgotten, the "hermits" turned and fled as the boxes fell all over the street!

On the beautiful day of her First Holy Communion, Therese told Jesus that she was entirely his. She was crying for joy. Being united to the Model of all virtue, she listed her resolutions for progress: "I will never let myself become discouraged. I will say the Memorare daily. I will try to be humble."

When the Holy Spirit came to her in Confirmation, Therese felt great joy, for she knew she had been given strength for the spiritual battles which would come in her life.

Therese could not bear the thought of anyone going to hell. She knew that Jesus wanted everyone to be happy with him forever in heaven. She prayed often for the conversion of those people

who refuse to love God and obey the commandments.

Once, when Therese was fifteen, the newspapers were filled with reports about a murderer
who was going to be executed but would not
repent of his crime. This was her chance to pray
for a *particular* sinner! "Dear God," she prayed,
"send that poor sinner the grace of repentance,
because of the merits of the passion of Jesus!"
She prayed long and hard for that man, and
offered sacrifices for his conversion. At the same
time, she confided to Jesus: "He's my *first* sinner,
so please give me a sign—any little sign."

The day of the execution came . And what did
the newspapers say about the criminal's death?
Just before he died, the murderer asked for the
chaplain whom he had ignored until then. The
priest held up a crucifix, and the man kissed it
three times. He had repented! Therese had her
sign, and knew that her "first sinner" had been
converted.

By this time, Marie and Pauline had entered
the Carmelite Order of sisters. Therese, wanted
to enter Carmel, too. But she was not sure how
she should tell her father, because he loved her
in a special way. Now that he was growing old he
would feel lonely without her. But Jesus came
first, so on a spring night when she and her
father were walking together in the garden,
Therese forced herself to speak.

At first her father didn't know what to say.
This was a real blow to him, and he did not want

On a spring night while she and her father were walking together in the garden, Therese forced herself to speak.

his youngest daughter to leave. But after Therese told him how much she really wished to go to Carmel, he agreed to let her go.

But that was just the first problem. Therese's legal guardian was her uncle, and he said that she was too young to enter such a strict order. Therese cried, but then she prayed and waited.

Three painful days passed. Then Therese's uncle changed his mind completely and consented.

Therese applied for admission to the convent. "You are too young," she was told. "We cannot admit a girl as young as you!" Not defeated, Therese appealed to the bishop, but he told her the same thing.

Her father suggested that they make a pilgrimage to Rome to appeal to the Holy Father himself. Therese, her father, and her sister Celine set out for the Eternal City. On the way, they visited many beautiful and holy places, including the Holy House of Loreto where, according to legend, the Holy Family had lived, and which had been carried from Nazareth by the angels hundreds of years before.

When the pilgrims went in to see the Pope, Therese was told not to speak to the Holy Father. But she had to! So when she went up to kiss his ring, she knelt there at his feet and begged the Holy Father to let her enter Carmel at fifteen. He replied firmly, "You will enter if it is God's will."

Poor Therese! It seemed that the journey had been in vain! She, Celine and their father were very sad as they began their return journey to France. But Therese kept on praying. About a month after she returned home, the bishop unexpectedly agreed to let her enter Carmel!

Therese began her religious life by offering her prayers, works and sacrifices for the priests in the missions. She had a strong desire to become a saint, and she asked God's help to do each duty in the best way possible out of love for him.

Her famous "little way" to holiness consisted in daily prayer, humility and love. She was convinced that *anyone* could become holy who truly loved God and did each small thing well. Whether it was time to sweep the hall, or pray or help care for a sick sister, Therese did it as if it were the most important thing in the world. She was very devoted to St. Joseph, and often thought about how he lived his whole life as a carpenter—but in the company of Mary and Jesus!

Thinking of this "little way to holiness" helped Therese to give an extra bright smile to the sister who annoyed her the most. Or when someone didn't approve of her way of doing something, she would do it all over again as the other person suggested. She accepted the cold in the winter and the heat in the summer without complaining. Sometimes it was difficult because it was terribly cold in wintertime and often she hardly slept at all. But she never let the others know about it, and she tried to be as cheerful and full of energy in the daytime as she would have been after a full night of rest.

After Therese made her vows, she was put in charge of the novices. She taught them her "little way" of doing each thing well, for the love of God. Little by little, though, her health became weaker and weaker. By the time the doctor was called in, there was nothing he could do to save her. She had a very painful form of tuberculosis.

Therese's final days were filled with almost unbearable pain. Therese knew she was not suffering by herself. She felt herself united to Jesus on the cross. Like Jesus, she offered all her pain to God in reparation for sin and so that sinners would repent and return to God's love. She also prayed in a special way for priests, that they would always know how much love God has for them.

To St. Therese "little things" were what mattered. Let us never be annoyed by little problems and sufferings, but let us offer them to God as acts of love. Let us especially remember to pray for priests working in the missions.

St. Maria Goretti

(1890-1902)

July 6

St. Maria Goretti, the first twentieth-century martyr, is often called "The New Agnes"—for like that heroic young saint of the early Church, she gave up her life to preserve her virginity.

Maria was born in Italy, near the city of Corinaldo, on October 16, 1890, the oldest girl in a family of seven children. Her parents were pious, honest and hard-working. But like many people in that area, they were very poor and everyone in the family worked. Maria's job was to clean the house and cook while her parents worked for a neighboring farmer.

Tragedy struck the family when Louis Goretti, Maria's father, died. Now they were poorer than ever before. Sometimes Maria's mother would become discouraged, as she wondered how they would manage to get enough food and clothing. At such times, ten-year-old Maria would say, "Be brave, Mother. After all, we're growing up. Soon we'll all be able to work and support the whole family. And until then, God will provide for us."

In many little ways, Maria tried to help her mother. For instance, whenever she and her mother had to cross a field, Maria would walk in front to scare away the snakes, because her mother was afraid of snakes. She also helped care for her younger brothers and sisters at night so that her mother could rest.

What made Maria so good? Well, she wasn't really "born" that way. At times, it was a struggle for her to do the best thing. But she did it because she knew that God would be pleased. Her whole life was centered around God.

To go to Mass meant a two-hour walk, but Maria was usually the first to enter the church and the last to leave. As often as she could, she went to confession. After Mass, on the day Maria received her First Holy Communion, the priest gave a special sermon for the young boys and girls. He urged them to preserve their purity always. And Maria's young heart renewed its determination to remain pure.

By this time, the Gorettis lived with a family named Serenelli—a man named John and his son Alexander, who was about twenty. Alexander was a troubled young man who read the pornographic magazines which his father bought and left around the house. Often during the day, while all the other men were out working, Alexander was home with these magazines

The Gorettis lived with a family named Serenelli—a man named John and his son, Alexander, who was about twenty.

or out with his friends, drinking.

This must have bothered Maria who stayed home with the children during the day, while her mother worked. One day, Alexander came up to her and demanded that she have sex with him. Maria refused him and kept away from him. Ten days later, Alexander tried again. Horrified, Maria told him that what he wanted was detestable in the eyes of God. He grabbed her—but she used all her strength, broke away and ran.

By now Maria was terrified. Should she tell her mother? Oh, how she wanted to! But she didn't dare. Already Alexander had told her he'd kill her if she told her mother what he was up to. She didn't dare tell. So she became silent and tearful, but she never said what was bothering her.

"Mamma, don't go out to work! Please stay home!" There were tears in her eyes and tears in her voice, as Maria made the plea.

"But, why, Maria?" her mother asked in surprise.

"Don't go, Mamma," Maria begged again, but she wouldn't say why.

She must be going through a stage, the mother thought. Even good children have strange ideas sometimes, she guessed. She put the notion out of her head and went to work.

Later in the same day, Maria's mother scolded her daughter for forgetting one of her duties. "I won't forget again, Mamma," Maria promised meekly.

The next day, the Gorettis and Serenellis were busy threshing beans. Under a blazing July sun, Alexander drove the oxen around and around the village threshing-floor, while Maria's young brothers and sisters rode in the wagon behind, and their mother did the winnowing. Around three o'clock, Alexander made an excuse to leave, and asked Maria's mother to take his place. He headed for the house.

John Serenelli was resting in the shade outside, for he had a fever. Maria was sitting on the outside stairway, in plain sight of the threshing floor mending Alexander's shirt, which her mother had asked her to do.

Alexander came up the steps and passed Maria without a word. He went into the house and walked over to a box that held old pieces of iron, and took out a piece that was about a foot long. One end had been sharpened to a point, like a dagger.

"Maria!" called Alexander. "Come here a minute!"

Maria's heart froze. She did not answer. She didn't even move.

Quick as lightning, Alexander stepped out onto the landing and seized Maria. She struggled wildly as he dragged her into the house and barred the door. She tried to scream but Alexander stuffed a handkerchief into her mouth. Yet she managed to say, and to keep saying, "No, no, God doesn't want it; if you do it you'll commit a mortal sin; you'll go to hell!" She fought him off time and again. At last he seized the dagger.

Furiously, Alexander thrust the dagger into Maria again and again. She crumpled to the floor unconscious.

She's dead, Alexander thought. He turned away and went into his bedroom.

Slowly Maria came to. She was in horrible pain, but managed to dragged herself to the door. She reached up and unbarred it. "John," she called, "Come! Alexander has killed me!"

But as soon as he heard her voice, Alexander rushed back into the room. He seized her by the throat and stabbed her six more times. "My God! My God!" cried Maria. "I'm dying! Mamma!"

Alexander ran back into his room and barred the door as his father came in with Maria's brother Mariano. When the little boy saw what had happened, he turned and ran in horror.

When Maria's mother and the neighbors reached the scene, Maria was still conscious, but her mother fainted from the shock. After she revived, she asked Maria what had happened.

"Alexander did it."

"But why?"

"Because he wanted me to have sex with him and I wouldn't."

While the police came and took Alexander to jail, friends tried to bandage the fourteen horrid wounds in Maria's body. They placed her in a Red Cross ambulance, and took her over rough roads—each jolt adding to the martyr's misery—

to the clinic in a neighboring city. Maria tried not to show her mother how much she was suffering.

It was evening when they reached the clinic. A priest was called to hear Maria's confession, and as soon as he had finished, the doctors came in to stitch up her wounds. They knew that they couldn't save her, but it was all that they could do.

A picture of the Blessed Virgin greeted Maria from the wall of the little room into which she was taken. Maria looked at it lovingly. She prayed to Mary during those long, tortured hours when she was waiting to die. She prayed, too, to the Sacred Heart and to St. Joseph, patron of the dying.

"Do you forgive your murderer?" she was asked.

"I do forgive him," she replied, "and I believe that God will forgive him too!"

Now cruel thirst joined itself to the torment of Maria's wounds. But she was unable to take even a drop of water. Think of Jesus on the cross, Maria told herself. Think of Jesus, tormented. Do it for him."

Toward the end, they brought Jesus to her in Holy Communion. When she had received him, her face glowed with a supernatural light. She kissed a picture of him repeatedly, and another of the Blessed Mother. Then delirium came over her, and she no longer knew what she was doing.

In her last moments, the unconscious girl relived the nightmare of a few hours before. "What are you doing, Alexander?" she cried.

"You'll go to hell!" She made a quick motion as if she were driving him back, then with a mighty effort she tried to leap from the bed. The strain was too great, and she fell back lifeless, while her pure and beautiful soul sped to heaven.

The year was 1902, and the martyr was eleven-and-a-half-years-old. But it was not the martyrdom which had made her a saint. Her love of God, obedience and charity had already been heroic; her purity had been complete. It was her daily practice of virtue in little ways, which had obtained for her the grace to keep her purity unspotted in the hour of greatest trial. Martyrdom was the crown to an already holy life. Forgiving Alexander was her last act of charity.

Maria has answered many prayers with miracles and obtained countless graces. One of them was the repentance of Alexander after Maria appeared to him while he was serving his long prison sentence. After he was released from jail, Alexander became a Capuchin monk and spent the rest of his life doing penance for his horrible crime. Both Alexander and Maria's mother, were present in Rome when Maria was canonized in 1950.

The virtue of purity is safeguarded by the virtue of modesty. Modesty means dressing, walking, standing and sitting with dignity, remembering that we are temples of the Holy Spirit. Modesty also means watching over our eyes and all our senses, refusing to look at pornographic pictures, movies or videos.

St. Gemma Galgani

(1878-1903)

April 11

"But, Reverend Father," said the young mother, "I don't think we should call the child Gemma as my brother-in-law wishes. I have never heard of a saint in heaven by that name— and I certainly want my little one in heaven one day!"

"Certainly gems are to be found in heaven," consoled the priest. "Let's hope this child will be a heavenly gem."

And so the day-old infant was baptized Gemma Umberta Pia Galgani on March 13, 1878.

Mrs. Galgani was a very good mother. She went to Communion every day. When her children were still small, she taught them the ugliness of sin and the importance of pleasing God in every way. Often she would show Gemma the crucifix and say, "See, Gemma, this dear Jesus died on the cross for us." Taking the child's hand she would place it on the crown of thorns, the nails, the wound in the side. Gemma would take the crucifix from her mother's hands, clasp it to her and kiss the wounds.

Every Saturday, Mrs. Galgani would prepare Gemma's three older brothers for confession and she took them to church herself whenever she could. When Gemma turned seven and prepared for her first confession, her mother was very happy to see how serious the child was.

She said something that must have puzzled Gemma at first. "Oh, I wish I could take you with me! Would you come?"

"Where are you going?"

"To Paradise, where Jesus lives with his angels."

"Yes! Yes!" exclaimed Gemma, her eyes shining at the thought.

Young as she was, Gemma knew that her mother was very ill. Every day she became weaker, and soon she could not get out of bed.

"This disease is highly contagious," the doctor declared. "The children must be sent away."

But Gemma cried and refused to go. Finally, her father sent the boys away and kept Gemma home.

She became her mother's nurse and took care of her every need. Many times she would kneel beside her mother's pillow and together they would pray the Rosary.

When Gemma received the Sacrament of Confirmation, her first thought after thanking

God was to pray for her mother. It seemed to her she heard a voice asking, "Will you give me your mother?"

"Yes," she answered silently, "but only if you will take me, too."

"No," was the reply. "You must stay with your father. I will take your mother to heaven, but will you give her up willingly?" Gemma felt that she had to say yes.

When she reached home and saw her poor mother suffering so patiently, Gemma began to cry but she did not say why.

Mrs. Galgani seemed to get better for a little while, then she began to be tormented by severe pains. Gemma knelt by her bed. Gemma felt as if the whole world had fallen to pieces. She wanted so much to stay with her mother, until her mother went to Paradise where she would have no more suffering and pain. But her father could not bear to see the little girl kneeling there silently so he sent her away to stay with her aunt in another village.

———————

Months later, Gemma came back to an empty house—even though it was full of children and her father was there as always. Gemma hid her own sorrow and became the comfort of the whole family, for whenever she saw one of the boys crying over their mother, she would say, "Why are you crying? Mother is in heaven. She is not suffering any longer—and she suffered so much!"

Every day the little girl went to a school taught by the Sisters of St. Zita. She paid careful attention in class, and joined in the games during recess. The sisters noticed that she always had a smile for everyone.

First Communion day was one of the most wonderful days of Gemma's life. She prepared herself carefully, with sincere sorrow for all her sins, for she knew that soon Jesus himself would be coming to her in the Eucharist. Because of her good preparation and her deep longing for Communion, she felt Jesus' presence in her soul as soon as she had received the Sacred Host.

But one day all her joy was gone. Until now Gemma had felt a strong love of God, an attraction for prayer, a longing for heaven. Suddenly, she felt nothing at all. Life seemed empty, aimless, without purpose or meaning.

She knew in her mind that God loved her and that heaven awaited her—but she *felt* nothing. It became difficult to pray, difficult to work, to play, to laugh.

But in spite of how she felt, Gemma kept on praying every day. She continued to smile, although she felt sad inside. She worked as energetically as ever, although she felt like doing nothing at all. She gave generously to the poor, as she had always done.

In that time of darkness, Gemma's faith and love grew strong, because she had to *force* herself to have faith; she had to *force* herself to love. When at last a feeling of happiness returned to her, she had become much more convinced of God's special love for her.

Not long after the darkness lifted from Gemma's soul, another sorrow came into her life. Her brother Gino, who had entered the seminary, contracted a dangerous disease. He returned home and Gemma nursed him for many long, anxious months. Over and over the youth offered himself to God. Then he died.

Within three years, Gemma's father also died, and the children were left orphans and utterly poor.

Gemma was nineteen. An aunt took her in and urged her to marry a nice young man, a doctor's son, who had fallen in love with the quiet, attractive young woman. He had already asked the aunt if he could marry Gemma. The aunt thought this was wonderful—but Gemma did not. Gemma wanted her heart to belong only to Jesus, and desired to enter a convent.

The young man persisted. So did the aunt.

"My Jesus," Gemma prayed, "deliver me from this distressing situation."

The deliverance was immediate and painful. Gemma developed a terrible pain in her spine, followed by deafness and almost complete paralysis. She suffered intensely, with the crucifix as her only consolation. Almost continuously she meditated on Jesus in his passion. She prayed constantly to St. Gabriel Possenti for help, and began reading a book on his life which someone had lent to her. The pain became less violent.

Gemma soon felt drawn to St. Gabriel, for she learned that he had had a great devotion to the passion of Jesus and to Our Lady, as she did. One night, St. Gabriel appeared to Gemma and invited her to make a vow of virginity. Overjoyed, Gemma made her vow the very next morning, after the priest had brought her Holy Communion.

She was growing weaker and weaker. The doctor could see no hope. Quite willing to die if it were God's will, Gemma waited patiently.

One night she heard St. Gabriel praying the Our Father. He paused in the middle, and Gemma tried to finish the prayer, although she was in such great pain she could hardly speak. Together she and her guest said the Hail Mary and Glory Be—and repeated the prayers eight more times. It was a novena!

"Do you wish to be cured?" asked the saint.

"It doesn't matter to me," replied the suffering girl. She only wanted to do God's will.

"Yes, you will be cured. At this hour every night I will come and we will pray together to the Sacred Heart of Jesus."

Several nights passed in that way. The novena was almost over when the priest came to hear Gemma's confession and bring her first Friday Communion. After Communion, Gemma could feel Jesus asking her, "Gemma, do you wish to be cured?"

Overwhelmed by his tenderness, the girl could not reply, but suddenly she knew that she had been cured.

"My daughter," said Jesus, "I give myself all to you, and you must belong entirely to me. I am your Father, and my mother will be your mother. My fatherly help can never fail those who abandon themselves in my hands. You will be all right even though I have taken away those who loved and helped you the most."

Gemma was cured! Everyone in the house cried for joy.

What a consolation it was to the orphan Gemma to have the Blessed Mother as her own mother! She had always loved our Lady, but now she turned to her with all the trust of a small child. In every need she sought her heavenly Mother's help. "Keep my heart with you in heaven," she prayed.

Often she would picture to herself that tender mother standing at the foot of the cross, suffering silently with her Son. Seeing those two most gentle persons in such agony, she felt an intense desire to suffer with them.

"How deeply I feel your sorrow, my Mother, seeing you at the foot of the cross, but do you know my greatest sorrow? It is that I cannot comfort you; on the contrary, I feel worse, because I myself have been a cause of so much of your suffering."

And so Gemma began asking Mary for the cross. Every day which passed without some suffering, she regarded as wasted.

"My Jesus," she prayed one day, after having been refused entrance to a convent because of her poor health, "I want to love you—oh, so much—but I do not know how."

"Do you wish to love Jesus now and forever?" a voice asked. "Then never cease suffering for him. The cross is the throne of those who really love Jesus; the cross is the heritage of the elect in this life."

Gemma found the cross in many ways. She

Gemma would imagine Mary, the mother of Jesus, standing at the foot of the cross, suffering silently with her Son. Seeing those two most gentle persons in such agony, she felt an intense desire to suffer with them.

found it when she went to live with a kind family, whose servants immediately became jealous of her. To one old servant who was especially mean, Gemma was very gentle. The woman had a horrible ulcer on her leg. Gemma would change the bandages for her, and would run all sorts of errands for her. Once she even leaned over and kissed the horrid wound.

She found the cross in the sufferings of Jesus' passion, which he began to let her feel every Thursday night and Friday morning—in the hours when he had suffered so terribly. During those hours, Gemma bore the stigmata—the gaping wounds of Jesus—in hands, feet and heart. She felt the whips tearing at her back; she felt the thorns piercing her head. The pain was intense—and in addition to it she felt weighed down by the burden of the sins of the world.

She sought the cross in her own penances, too. And yet Gemma feared pain! "I shrink every time I look at the cross," she wrote, "because I feel I could die thinking of the pain of it, yet in spite of this, my heart welcomes the sufferings." Why? Because Jesus had suffered, and Gemma loved Jesus very much.

After Communion one day, Jesus said to Gemma, "My daughter, I need strong, courageous souls who do not shrink from being victims of my Father's Divine Justice.... Oh, if I could only make you understand the anger of my Father with this world which has deliberately renounced him.... He is preparing a severe punishment for the entire earth."

Gemma knew Jesus was asking her to suffer still more. "Of course I will sacrifice myself, dear

Lord. There is no torment, however painful, that I would not endure for you; I would shed every drop of my blood to please your Sacred Heart and to prevent sinners from offending you."

So Gemma continued to suffer, drawing strength and consolation from the Holy Eucharist. Her Communions were so fervent that she began to feel the joy of heaven whenever she consumed the Sacred Host.

"Come, Jesus. Can there be any of your creatures who do not love you? I feel you in my heart. What a mystery! I feel as if I am in heaven. I forget all the troubles of the world, and taste and love only you."

Gemma's last months on earth were filled with the intense pains of a mysterious illness. The darkness of spirit she had felt years before returned to her. The devil tempted her to despair. Life was empty of all joy.

Gemma turned to her Heavenly Mother, and asked her to intercede for her. She continued to talk to Jesus even though she could not feel his presence.

One day a nurse asked her, "What would you do if Our Lord let you choose between going to heaven at once and staying on earth to suffer more and add to his glory?"

"It would be better to stay and suffer," Gemma replied. "Jesus' glory always comes first."

On Wednesday and again on Thursday of Holy Week, 1903, Gemma received Holy Communion. Then on Good Friday, at about ten o'clock, she exclaimed, "I have to be crucified with Jesus."

Lying on her sickbed, she extended her arms as if she were on the cross. She said nothing, and on her face was an expression of desolation and suffering, but also of love and calm. She remained that way three and a half hours. She continued to suffer the rest of that day and most of the next. Holy Saturday evening she received the Sacrament of Anointing and the Eucharist for the last time. Then, bowing her head as Jesus had on the cross, Gemma Galgani commended her soul to God.

She was twenty-five-years-old.

Gemma was buried in the Passionist Convent of her city, Lucca, where she had longed to be during life. This is the inscription on her tomb:

"Gemma Galgani from Lucca, most pure virgin, being in her twenty-fifth year, died of tuberculosis but was more consumed by the fires of divine love than by her wasting disease. On the eleventh of April, 1903, the vigil of Easter, her soul took its flight to the bosom of her celestial Spouse. Beautiful soul—in peace with the Angels."

In every sorrow, including her parents' death, St. Gemma turned for help to Jesus in the Eucharist and the Blessed Mother. We, too, will find sorrow easier to bear if we "talk it over" with Jesus and Mary.

St. Frances Xavier Cabrini

(1850-1917)

November 13

Little Mary Frances liked to listen to the stories of missionaries, which her father read aloud to the family every evening.

"I'm going to be a missionary, too!" she told her big sister, Rose, one day.

"You? You're too small. Missionaries must be strong!"

"I'll grow," Frances promised. She thought of St. Francis Xavier with his great love for Jesus crucified and how he had traveled up and down the Orient and was headed for China when he died.

"Do Chinese children know about Jesus?" she asked.

"Some do, but many have never heard of him," answered Rose patiently.

"Oh, how much I would like to tell them about him!" the little girl exclaimed.

As Frances grew to be a young woman, her desire to be a missionary grew also. Yet her health was poor and every time she tried to enter religious life, she was told, "This is not for you; you are too weak for such a life!"

Each time, Frances said to herself, "God's will be done," but she still wanted to serve him as completely as possible. She finished high school and became a teacher, but she wanted to do much more than that.

When she was twenty-four, Frances received a message from a priest she knew. He wanted her to take charge of an orphanage which had been managed poorly. Could she put it in order in two weeks time? Frances said she would try. She went to work with an energetic will and fervent prayers—and succeeded.

The priest then asked Frances to remain at the orphanage and keep things running smoothly. This was difficult, since she was not really in charge, and had to work with people who always wanted their own way and argued among themselves. It was hard for Frances to keep the peace and still get things done. But again she succeeded. And in the meantime, she achieved her desire to become a religious!

With seven young women who had been her students, Frances made her first religious vows—six years after arriving at the orphanage. Soon afterward, the local bishop directed her to form a new missionary community and be its superior. Frances didn't hesitate. "I'll look for a house," she said.

"The Missionary Sisters of the Sacred Heart!" Frances exclaimed. How beautiful it sounded.

She and her sisters would go throughout the world telling everyone of the great love of Jesus for humankind. Perhaps they would go to China. Her childhood dream had not been forgotten.

Orphanages, schools, catechism classes and more sisters to staff them! The little community grew rapidly. Soon it had several houses in Italy, and an invitation to go to America.

Why America? Wondered Mother Cabrini. She had her heart set on the Orient.

"The Italian immigrants there need you." explained Bishop Scalabrini, who had founded an order of priests to work among the immigrants. "They have no one to teach catechism to the children. There is no one to take care of the sick, for they are too poor to be admitted into the regular hospitals. People are taking advantage of them materially and they are starving spiritually as well."

Frances was not sure what she should do. Finally, she asked the Holy Father himself whether she should send missionaries to America or to China. After a moment of reflection, Pope Leo XIII told her, "You must not go to the East but to the West." America it would be.

Frances and some of her sisters arrived in New York on March 31, 1889. The first institution they opened was a day school. Next came an orphanage. In four months' time there were four hundred orphans!

Then came a wonderful offer of a beautiful piece of property which could be used for another orphanage and a novitiate house. The price was low, but there was one problem: no water. Mother Cabrini smiled, and bought the property. "God will provide," she said.

And provide he did! The sisters began a novena to our Lady, and on the fifth day of it they marched out onto the grounds with hoes and shovels.

"Dig here," Mother Cabrini said, pointing at a certain spot.

Soon the shovels were turning up rich, brown soil instead of dry sand. And then—water, clear, running water!

In the depths of her heart, Mother Cabrini thanked God. "We shall build a shrine to our Lady near the spring," she promised.

All of Mother Cabrini's undertakings were full of the same kind of faith that she showed when searching for the spring. She traveled from the United States to Italy to Central and South America, founding orphanages, hospitals and schools in an amazingly short period of time in spite of all kinds of obstacles. She succeeded only through prayer, courage and faith.

Her faith was great when confronted with natural dangers, too. Many times in her frequent sea journeys violent storms arose, forcing her companions to take to their berths but leaving her calm and prayerful—giving courage to all who saw her. When traveling from Chile to Argentina, she undertook a perilous journey over the Andes mountains on a mule. Her motto was a line from St. Paul: *I can do all things in him who strengthens me.*

Life was hard for Mother Cabrini's sisters, especially in New Orleans and in Central America. Mother Cabrini realized this, and knew, too, that the sisters must strive to become always more fervent. Once she wrote: "Our great Patron, St. Frances Xavier, said, 'He who goes holy to the missions will find many occasions to sanctify himself more, but he who goes poorly provided with holiness, runs the risk of losing what he has and of falling away.' I become more convinced of this truth every day, and as experience is a great master, let us take advantage of the lessons it teaches and never let a day pass without examining our conscience and making serious resolutions to acquire the virtues we need."

The sisters in New York went often to visit the prisons, encouraging the prisoners, speaking to them of heaven. One day at Sing Sing prison, they visited a bitter young man who had been condemned to death. He declared that he was innocent and in his bitterness refused to listen to the sisters.

"We must do something to help him," the sisters decided. They appealed to the governor to delay the execution.

The young man was grateful for what they had done and listened as they told him about God's mercy. They visited him two days a week, praying with him and reading from spiritual books.

But no new evidence came forth to change his sentence, and the execution was rescheduled.

The sisters in New York often went to visit the city prisons, encouraging the prisoners and speaking to them of heaven.

The prisoner was plunged into despair. Praying harder than ever, the sisters begged that he might receive the grace of resignation.

Two days before the execution, the prisoner became calm. "I forgive all," he said, "and though I am innocent, I accept my death as Jesus Christ accepted his." As he got into the electric chair, he clutched a crucifix in his hands.

Another spectacular conversion took place in Nicaragua in 1893. A revolution had put in power an antireligious government which ordered Mother Cabrini's sisters to leave the country at once. Carrying a few little bundles, the sisters filed out of the convent between a double line of soldiers, amid the sobs of their students. From all sides people flocked to say good-bye.

In the middle of the crowd was an antireligious man, Don Jose Paos, who had come out of curiosity. As he stood there, a young student went up to one of the sisters and asked, "How can you leave like this without even crying?"

"Why should we cry?" the sister replied. She lifted a crucifix she was carrying. "We had this with us when we came, and we have it with us now!"

Don Jose felt something stirring in the depths of his soul. He returned to his home, locked himself in his room and refused to see anyone until the next morning. Then he went to the bishop and asked to be readmitted into the Church. Soon he was one of the most active defenders of the faith. Years later he said,

"A religion which inspires young sisters with such serenity, resignation and peace in times of hardship and strife must be the true religion."

When Pope Leo XIII celebrated his golden jubilee as a priest, Mother Cabrini paid him a visit to ask his blessing. "Let us work, let us work," the Holy Father urged her, "for after this there is a beautiful Paradise." The words struck home. No matter how much she had done there was still more to be accomplished. She must never stop; never rest; never say she had done enough.

On another occasion Pope Leo told her, "You know how much I am devoted to the Sacred Heart. I have consecrated the world to It, and you must help spread this devotion, since he has elected you for this purpose."

One of the new fields where the devotion—and even knowledge of religion—was sadly lacking was Denver, Colorado, in 1902. Many Italian immigrants had settled there as miners and factory workers but not enough Italian priests had followed them, nor were there any Catholic schools. Very few of the people went to Mass on Sundays; many children had not been baptized; some men and women thirty-years-old had not yet made their First Communion.

Mother Cabrini opened a school for the children in Denver, and assigned two of her sisters to visit the homes, mines and factories with words of gentle encouragement. Soon many families returned to Mass and the sacraments—so many that new churches were needed.

In New Orleans, many people were unkind to the sisters, but their opinion changed during the yellow fever epidemic of 1905. The sisters sent the orphans to a home outside the city and used the orphanage in the city as a hospital for the sick women and children, whom they cared for lovingly until the epidemic had passed. How grateful those people were!

That year marked the twenty-fifth anniversary of the Missionary Sisters of the Sacred Heart. They now numbered one thousand sisters on three different continents. Five thousand orphans were under their care, and they had cared for over one hundred thousand sick.

Mother Cabrini died peacefully in one of her own hospitals in Chicago on December 22, 1917. It was fitting indeed that she should die in the land to which she had come out of obedience to the Holy Father and in which she had done such great good. She was the first American citizen to be canonized a saint.

Even though young Frances' desire to be a sister seemed impossible, she continued to pray and to do the work she was able to do. In spite of herself, she was the foundress of a new community of sisters! Even when we can't understand where our life is going, we can trust that God knows and is with us on our way.

Bl. Miguel Augustin Pro, SJ

(1891-1927)

November 23

The young man leaned on the railing of the *Cuba* as the ship's captain yelled, "Land ahead! Veracruz ahead!" Within a few hours they had docked and the passengers were herded into the customs hall. Miguel tipped his hat jauntily and lit a cigarette as he walked confidently past the armed officers. No one suspected that this well-dressed young man was not the play-boy that he appeared to be. And it was a good thing, because in 1926, it was against the law for Catholic priests to enter Mexico. Miguel breathed a sigh of relief and said a prayer of gratitude as his baggage came through unopened. The chalice and vestments that he had received at his recent ordination in Belgium would certainly have cost him his life.

Still wearing his disguise, Father Miguel Pro made his way through the crowded streets. It had been twelve years since he and his fellow seminarians had been forced to flee from their homeland. But he remembered the way to the Jesuit provincial house. Arriving in time for the evening meal, he was greeted warmly by his provincial superior.

"Miguel, you are looking well! How did you survive such a long voyage so soon after your operation?" The young priest sat down in a chair across from his superior at the table, and the two men said their meal blessing together.

"God is good, Father. And with the Virgin Mary of Guadalupe watching over me, I had nothing to fear! Besides, since the operation in Belgium, my stomach has given me no trouble at all!" Father Miguel took a bite of the freshly baked buñuelo before asking, with a grin, "How do you like my costume?"

Father provincial laughed. "Well, you certainly don't look like a newly ordained Jesuit priest! What guardian angel warned you to come so well disguised?"

"There were Mexican travelers visiting our house in Belgium shortly before I left. They filled us in on the thirty-three articles regarding religious practices in our new constitutions. Is it true that President Calles has closed the schools?"

"Not only the schools, but the hospitals and orphanages as well. All Catholic institutions had to either close or turn themselves over to the state." Father Provincial pushed his bowl of soup to one side. "What will happen to the poor people? The sisters had gradually been establishing schools in even the remotest villages. Calles says he is for the poor working people, but without education there will be no future for our country— and the Church was the only hope of the poor for education!"

"And what about the churches?" asked Miguel. "I have heard that he intends to close them as well."

"Yes. On July 31, the feast of our patron, St. Ignatius, the churches will be officially closed." The older man looked intently at Father Miguel. The young man's reputation for intelligence and prayer had impressed him. "Father Miguel, are you prepared to go underground? To risk your very life to bring the sacraments and the Gospel to our people?"

Miguel thought for a moment before he replied. "Yes, Father. I have offered my life to God through my vows as a religious. And through my priestly ordination, I have committed all my energy to preaching the Gospel and to celebrating the sacraments with my fellow Mexicans. I am prepared to do whatever is necessary."

"I thought you would say that! *¡Que bien!* Tomorrow, you will go to visit your family in Mexico City. We will send word to you there as to where we shall meet again. In the meantime, Miguel, don't let anyone know your true identity. The people are flocking to confession by the hundreds, trying to receive the sacrament one last time before July 31. Try to go in and out of the church at night. Your identity is not known to the police yet; let's keep it that way."

Late that night, still dressed as a rich play-boy, Father Miguel set out for Mexico City. When he arrived, he exchanged his fine clothes for the dress of the poorest Mexican. His once wealthy family was now impoverished, and Miguel did not want to attract attention to himself while visiting them. During the day, he talked and laughed with his elderly father and teenage brothers and sisters. They had missed their oldest brother while he had been away studying for his ordination. And he missed his mother now; she had died only a few weeks before his return. At night, Father Miguel celebrated Mass and heard confessions.

As July 31 approached, the city was tense. Violence often erupted between those loyal to the Catholic Church and those who supported the atheistic government of President Calles. But most faithful Catholics chose to oppose the antireligious government in nonviolent ways. They boycotted stores and industries known to be Calles' supporters. They refused to attend prayer services at the "national churches" established by the government. And they formed underground networks enabling priests to say Mass and celebrate the sacraments in secret.

One way the Catholics kept up their courage was by distributing leaflets with parts of the Gospel, the catechism and prayers printed on them. These leaflets were illegal. Anyone caught distributing them could be shot—with no trial.

One afternoon a police officer spotted Father Miguel, who was disguised as a street cleaner, and picked him up for questioning. Miguel's

One afternoon a police officer spotted Father Miguel, who was disguised as a street cleaner, and picked him up for questioning.

pockets were filled with Catholic leaflets. Maintaining his disguise, he began to tell the officer stories of the crazy things he had done as a youngster. Lucky for Miguel that he was a good storyteller! As the officer was laughing uncontrollably, Father Miguel tossed the leaflets out the car window. By the time they reached the police station, the officer decided to let his delightful young prisoner go without questioning.

But Father Miguel knew it had been a close call. There were government spies everywhere. Almost all the priests in the city had either fled for their lives, or had been caught and killed—often while celebrating the Mass. The city officials knew of Father Miguel's clever disguises, but so far he had always managed to slip by the security officers posted throughout the city. In the meantime, Catholics in the city had never been so devoted to their prayers. Because so many of the Catholic hospitals and orphanages had been closed, the women formed groups to help care for the sick and the homeless children.

On the Feast of Christ the King, 1926, the people organized a peaceful procession to the shrine of Our Lady of Guadalupe. Thousands of men, women and children took part. Armed police were everywhere, looking for any excuse to begin shooting at the crowd of pilgrims. But there was no trouble. The people sang hymns and prayed the Rosary. Father Miguel, disguised as a worker, marched proudly with his people. *"Vivo Cristo Rey!"* The familiar cry—"Long live Christ the King!"— had become the rallying motto of the persecuted Church of Mexico.

President Calles became more corrupt. He ran the country as a military state with his side-kick, General Obregon. The people who opposed him had to think of creative ways to spread the truth to the people of Mexico. Only by doing so could the people hope to band together and vote him out of office. Among the most active opponents of Calles were Hubert and Roberto Pro, Miguel's younger brothers. On December 4, 1926, they carried out a daring act. Stuffing six hundred balloons with anti-Calles leaflets, they filled the balloons with helium and released them over Mexico City. When the balloons reached a certain height, they burst. The antigovernment propaganda rained down on the busy streets.

Furious, President Calles demanded that somebody be arrested. Since the Pro brothers were known for their anti-Calles activities, the police went to their home first. But they found only Miguel. He was arrested and spent that night and the next day in jail. Fortunately, no one discovered his identity as a priest and he was let go.

As it became clear that his attempts to crush the Catholic faith in Mexico were not meeting with success, President Calles stepped up the violent persecution. Over ten thousand government soldiers were sent out to arrest and shoot anyone suspected of promoting the Catholic faith—or of opposing the government of Calles. Hundreds of priests and religious sisters were martyred for the faith; many laypeople and children were killed as well. Father Miguel Pro was at the top of the "most wanted" list.

One afternoon, the tension in the city reached its peak when three young men tried to throw a bomb into the car of President Calles and General Obregon. The two leaders were not hurt, but their body-guards opened fire and two of the young men were killed. The third escaped, but was later picked up. Infuriated by this bold attack, a sweep was made of the city and all the men ever suspected of opposing Calles were arrested, including Miguel and his two brothers. It was November 13, 1927.

For six days Miguel led the prisoners in prayer and song. No longer able to hide his identity, he acted openly as a priest, hearing the confessions of prisoners and guards. At first, they hoped for a release as there was no evidence to convict them. But on the sixth day, Miguel announced seriously, "Today, I think, will be our last."

This stunned his fellow prisoners. Father Miguel had always encouraged them to hope for an acquittal! Concerned, they gathered around him in the dirty cell.

"Do not be afraid," he told them. "We go to the Lord with clear consciences!" Then, he lifted up his hand and yelled, *"Vivo Cristo Rey!"* Together, the men repeated his cry and began to laugh and sing again. They play-wrestled to pass the time until a guard's harsh voice called out: "Miguel Pro! Come with me!"

The men were silent as Miguel picked up his jacket. The serious, sad eyes of the guard told him all he needed to know. Clasping his brothers' hands in a final farewell, Miguel marched down the hall in front of the guard. As he was pushed out into the bright courtyard, Father Miguel gasped. A large crowd had gathered. He recognized many important dignitaries, newspaper photographers and some of his faithful Catholic friends. They had all come to witness the death of a Jesuit priest who had eluded the police for over a year. His only crime was preaching the Gospel, forming catechists and celebrating the sacraments in the homes of faithful Catholics.

Clutching his rosary in one hand and his crucifix in the other, Father Miguel raised his head. Begging the Virgin of Guadalupe to give him courage, he forced his trembling legs to walk toward the wall of execution. Along the way, one of the police officers fell to his knees and grabbed Miguel's legs. With tears pouring down his face, he begged, "Father, forgive me!"

"I have nothing to forgive, my friend," replied Miguel. Then he embraced the man and said, "I will pray for you all."

In a few minutes, it was all over. Father Miguel Pro had offered his life for the sake of his Catholic faith and his activities as a priest of the Church. Intending to scare the Catholic population into submission, President Calles ordered several of the young men who had been imprisoned with Father Miguel to be shot that day as well. Among them was twenty-three-year-old Hubert Pro.

But there was probably nothing that could have

been done to strengthen the faith of the Catholics more than the murder of their favorite priest. As news of the deaths was broadcast, hundreds of thousands of people took to the streets, shouting, "*Vivo Cristo Rey!*" "Long live the Pope! Long live the Catholic Church!" Leading the crowds was seventy-five-year-old Señor Pro. At the graves of his two sons the next day, he led the huge crowd in singing the *Te Deum*, a hymn of praise sung only on the most solemn and joyful of feast days.

The Church in Mexico still had a long struggle ahead before achieving freedom. But recognizing the holiness of their new, young martyr, the people used his memory as a source of inspiration and courage. In many nations of the world today, the Church is still persecuted and people are oppressed by unjust rulers. We can pray to Father Miguel Augustin Pro for the grace to be proud of our Catholic faith and to use all our talents and energies to spread the Gospel of Jesus without fear.

Bl. Edith Stein

(1891-1942)

August 9

As the train pulled into the busy Breslau station (in what was then Germany), Sister Teresa Benedicta's heart reached its breaking point. How many other summers in her fifty-one years had she arrived at this station and been greeted by loving family and friends? Now, she longed for even a glimpse of the platform, but there were no windows in this train car, filled with dirty, sick and dying Jews. Edith Stein (Sister Theresa's name before she took vows as a Carmelite) kept her sleeve held to her nose so she wouldn't have to smell the terrible odors.

Unexpectedly, the door of the freight car swung open. The people gasped for air, groaning in pain as the bright sunlight hit their eyes. Edith clung to the doorway and leaned out, scanning the crowded platform for a familiar face. But there were none. And if anyone *had* recognized this brilliant philosopher, it would have been foolish indeed to speak to her. This was a freight car full of Jews, the condemned victims of Nazi Germany.

Yet a young postal worker couldn't help but stare at the spectacle. Covering his nose, he moved closer. Was that a Carmelite nun packed in with the rest of the Jews? "Hello," he called. "Where are you going? Can I get you anything?"

Edith stared at him, almost forgetting that not *all* of Germany was aware of the horrors of the concentration camps. "No, thank you," she replied. "We accept nothing. We are going to our death."

Stunned, the young man was helpless as his friends pulled him away, angry at him for talking to the Jews. As the door of the freight car slammed shut and the darkness again covered them, Edith hugged her sister, Rosa, as tears flowed silently down their faces. As she had done so often in the past weeks, Edith Stein renewed her offering of herself to God in atonement for the horrors of this war and for her beloved Jewish people.

———

Edith remembered the summer she had told her mother that she was going to join the Carmelite sisters in Cologne, Germany. It was the summer of 1933. Augusta Stein was overjoyed to have her youngest daughter—the scholar of the family—home for the summer. A devout Jew, Frau Stein had not understood at all when Edith had announced her decision to enter the Catholic Church. But she had gotten used to the idea. And now that Jews in Nazi Germany were not allowed to teach in universities or hold government jobs, she had been relieved when Edith found a position at a Catholic girls' school. Her brilliant Edith, who had received a doctorate in philosophy with highest honors, who had been among the first recognized female scholars of Germany, was now a Catholic. Frau Stein could accept that. But now, on Edith's birthday, Frau Stein sensed that Edith was holding back a secret.

"So, Edith, you are not returning to the school in Speyer. Who will teach the girls if you leave?"

"No, Mama, I am not going back to Speyer," replied Edith. She knew the moment of truth had come. "The school will survive without me."

"So, why don't you stay here in Breslau with me? Surely you can find a position here?" Frau Stein bit her lip. It would be humiliating to have her daughter living openly as a Catholic in their hometown. But she would gladly endure that in order to have her Edith back at home.

"Mama, you know I have already arranged to go to Cologne."

"To Cologne? Yes, I know, to the *Carmelites* in Cologne." Frau Stein let her knitting fall to her lap as she asked, her voice trembling, "And what will you be doing with the Carmelites in Cologne?"

Edith could not look at her mother. Turning toward the window, she said firmly, "I'm going to live with them, Mama. I'm going to be a Carmelite nun." Her mother's desperate cry echoed through the house. Edith rushed to her side. As the older woman sobbed violently, Edith stooped and held her mother's head close to her heart. When at last her crying quieted, Edith led her eighty-two-year-old mother upstairs and helped her into bed. The next day, they had embraced for the last time before Edith stepped onto the train for Cologne.

The train lurched, bouncing the tired, frightened people against one another. In one corner, the bucket they had been using as a toilet spilled, increasing the stench in the hot air as a man cursed loudly. "Edith," gasped Rosa, "I'm glad that Mama did not live to see this evil day."

"So am I, Rosa. I am sure that Mama is in heaven even now."

The idea of heaven had been one of the beliefs that had led Edith to the Christian faith. As a child, she and all her brothers and sisters had said the traditional Jewish prayers with their mother. Since their father had died when Edith was only two, it was Frau Stein who took her seven children to synagogue every Sabbath and taught Edith's brothers the traditional prayers and blessings. But one by one, the Stein children had abandoned their Jewish traditions. In her autobiography, Edith noted that she consciously and deliberately quit praying as a young teenager. She had filled her mind and soul with the study of psychology first, then philosophy.

As one of the first women to study philosophy at a German university, Edith had felt challenged to prove herself. But within a few short years, her reputation as scholar was well established. Her teacher was the famous Edmund Husserl, whom the students called "the master." At twenty-one, Edith had found herself surrounded by a group of peers who totally accepted her place among them. On holidays they would take hiking trips through the German countryside. At exam time, they would encourage one another. Edith had gradually become aware that her most respected friends and teachers had all struggled with their belief in God—and that most were now Christians. This puzzled Edith. For her, the answers to life's mysteries were to be found in her books and studies.

In 1915, Edith's happy life as a scholar ended as World War I swept across Europe. Most of her male friends were soon in the army. Edith volunteered as a Red Cross nurse to help care for the sick and wounded. She kept in close contact with her friends, often sending them packages of food and clothing. She was saddened as many of them were killed in the fighting at the front. It was especially sad news when one of her teachers, Adolph Reinach, was killed. Edith had become close to Adolph and his wife, Frau Anna Reinach. She had felt obliged to go and try to comfort Anna in her time of grief.

Edith had expected Anna to be devastated by the death of her husband. She was surprised to find

Edith gradually became aware that all of her most respected friends and teachers had struggled with their belief in God. Now, most of them were Christians.

her sad, but peaceful. Anna and Adolph, she learned, had recently been baptized. Now Anna was comforting Edith with her firm belief in the reality of heaven and of the resurrection of the dead. The seeds of faith were planted, and Edith began to seek the God whom she longed so much to believe in.

Edith fell asleep leaning on Rosa's shoulder, dreaming of the day of her baptism. Just as she recalled the glorious moment when she first received the Eucharist, the train screeched to a halt. Voices screamed in the cool summer night as the doors again swung open. Half-starved and cramped from the long ride, the women, men and children half fell and half jumped to the ground. The strongest among the few hundred Jews in this transport were herded off to one side. They would be sent to one of the work camps. The rest, they were told, would remain here at Birkenau, just outside of Auschwitz. First they were all to have showers.

Edith and Rosa clung to one another in the night. Having been forced to remove their clothing, the prisoners were lined up in the woods, outside of the "shower houses." No one spoke, but they all knew by now—what awaited them was not a hot shower, but death by poisonous gas.

It was August 9, 1942. Sister Teresa Benedicta's offering of herself for her people was complete. Those who survived and had been in the camps with her, remembered her serenity and calm. Overcoming her own fears, she had gathered the children around her, cleaning them and finding them food. She had prayed constantly, both with her fellow Jews and her fellow Christians. Edith Stein prayed that their sufferings not be in vain. She knew that the innocent Jesus on the cross was with her innocent people suffering in the concentration camps.

Edith Stein's legacy as a scholar remains in the books and essays that she wrote. Most of these were scholarly works of philosophy. But she also wrote meditations and explanations of the writings of St. Thomas Aquinas and St. John of the Cross. But it was for her faithfulness to the vocation God had called her to, for her tremendous love for her people and for her example of faith at the moment of death that the Church remembers Blessed Edith Stein.

Many times we are tempted to quit praying and going to church. We may still feel the need for God, but it seems that God is absent from our lives. We can pray to Blessed Edith Stein, asking her to send us good friends who will lead us back to Jesus and help us believe in His great love for us.

INDEX

Although we can pray to any saint to intercede for any need or intention, some saints have become especially popular for particular needs. The following is an alphabetical listing of the saints in this book, their feast date, and what they are known for or what they are the patron of.

Agnes *January 21*
    Chastity; Girl Scouts 90
Aloysius Gonzaga *June 21*
    Youth 306
Anne *July 26*
    Grandmothers; Homemakers 10
Anthony of Padua *June 13*
    Lost Articles; Cemetery Workers 200
Augustine of Hippo (Doctor of the Church) *August 28*
    Theologians 109
Bartholomea *July 26*
    Children of Alcoholics; Teachers 439
Benedict *July 11*
    Monastics; Victims of Poisoning 132
Benedict Joseph Labre *April 16*
    Homeless People 434
Benedict the Moor *April 4*
    Renewal in Religious Life 297
Bernadette Soubirous *April 16*
    Asthma; Children of Alcoholics 471
Bernardine of Siena *May 20*
    Advertising; Addicts to Gambling 237
Brigid *July 23*
    Dairy Workers; Newborn Babies 124
Camillus de Lellis *July 14*
    Nurses; the Sick 337
Catherine of Siena (Doctor of the Church) *April 29*
    Fire Prevention 228
Cecilia *November 22*
    Musicians 57
Clare (Foundress of the Poor Clares) *August 11*
    Television 191
Columban *November 23*
    Irish Monasticism 145
Dominic Savio *March 9*
    Choir Boys 466

Dymphna *May 15*
  Mental Illness; Family Stability 158
Edith Stein *August 9*
  Martyr at Auschwitz 533
Elizabeth Ann Seton *January 4*
  First American Saint 449
Elizabeth of Hungary *November 17*
  Soup Kitchens and Shelters 208
Francis of Assisi *October 4*
  Animals and the Environment 176
Frances Xavier Cabrini *November 13*
  Immigrants 514
Frances Xavier *December 3*
  Missionaries; Apostleship of Prayer 260
Gabriel the Archangel *September 29*
  Communications Media; Mail Carriers 7
Gemma Galgani *April 11*
  Eucharistic Devotion; Consecrated Virgins 503
Germaine *June 15*
  Sheep Herders 327
Guardian Angels *October 2* 7
Helen *August 18*
  Archaeologists 98
Isaac Jogues *October 19*
  North American Martyr 382
Jane Frances de Chantal (Foundress of the Visitation Sisters)
  August 21 Hunters 373
Joachim *July 26*
  Grandfathers 10
Joan of Arc *May 30*
  Service Women; Virgins 250
John Berchmans *November 26*
  Altar Boys; Students 347
John Bosco *January 31*
  Editors; Youth 482
Joseph *May 1; March 19*
  Families; Carpenters; the Dying; the Church 15
Joseph Cottolengo *April 29*
  Hospital Administrators; the Physically Disabled 458
Kateri Tekakwitha *July 14*
  Native Americans 412
Kevin *June 13*
  Catechists 139

Lucy *December 13*
   Eyes 83
Margaret Mary Alacoque *October 16*
   Apostle of the Sacred Heart 428
Margaret of Scotland *November 16*
   Learning 169
Maria Goretti *July 6*
   Virgins; Chastity 495
Martin de Porres *November 3*
   Black Americans 357
Martin of Tours *November 11*
   Soldiers 103
Michael the Archangel *September 29*
   Helper in Temptation; Persons in Battle 7
Miguel Pro *November 23*
   Martyr for the Church in Mexico 523
Monica *August 27*
   Mothers; Converts 109
Patrick *March 17*
   Ireland 116
Paul *January 25; June 29*
   Journalists; Converts 35
Peregrine Laziosi *May 1*
   Victims of Cancer 217
Peter (First Pope) *June 29*
   Fishermen 21
Philip Neri *May 26*
   Teenagers 316
Raphael the Archangel *September 29*
   Physicians; Lovers 7
Rene Goupil *October 19*
   North American Martyr 382
Sebastian *January 20*
   Archers; Gardeners 77
Stanislaus Kostka *April 11*
   Sacrament of the Sick 284
Tarcisius *August 15*
   First Communicants 66
Thecla *August 19*
   Catechists 49
Therese of Lisieux *October 1*
   Missionaries; Persons with Tuberculosis 488

St. Paul Book & Media Centers

ALASKA
750 West 5th Ave., Anchorage, AK 99501; 907-272-8183

CALIFORNIA
3908 Sepulveda Blvd., Culver City, CA 90230; 310-397-8676
5945 Balboa Ave., San Diego, CA 92111; 619-565-9181
46 Geary Street, San Francisco, CA 94108; 415-781-5180

FLORIDA
145 S.W. 107th Ave., Miami, FL 33174; 305-559-6715

HAWAII
1143 Bishop Street, Honolulu, HI 96813; 808-521-2731

ILLINOIS
172 North Michigan Ave., Chicago, IL 60601; 312-346-4228

LOUISIANA
4403 Veterans Memorial Blvd., Metairie, LA 70006; 504-887-7631

MASSACHUSETTS
50 St. Paul's Ave., Jamaica Plain, Boston, MA 02130; 617-522-8911
Rte. 1, 885 Providence Hwy., Dedham, MA 02026; 617-326-5385

MISSOURI
9804 Watson Rd., St. Louis, MO 63126; 314-965-3512

NEW JERSEY
561 U.S. Route 1, Wick Plaza, Edison, NJ 08817; 908-572-1200

NEW YORK
150 East 52nd Street, New York, NY 10022; 212-754-1110
78 Fort Place, Staten Island, NY 10301; 718-447-5071

OHIO
2105 Ontario Street, Cleveland, OH 44115; 216-621-9427

PENNSYLVANIA
214 W. DeKalb Pike, King of Prussia, PA 19406; 610-337-1882

SOUTH CAROLINA
243 King Street, Charleston, SC 29401; 803-577-0175

TENNESSEE
4811 Poplar Ave., Memphis, TN 38117; 901-761-0874

TEXAS
114 Main Plaza, San Antonio, TX 78205; 210-224-8101

VIRGINIA
1025 King Street, Alexandria, VA 22314; 703-549-3806

GUAM
285 Farenholt Avenue, Suite 308, Tamuning, Guam 96911; 671-646-7745

CANADA
3022 Dufferin Street, Toronto, Ontario, Canada M6B 3T5; 416-781-9131